NOTE: *A donation from every sale of each publication will be donated to the Registered Charity 'Scope'*

Scope is a Registered Charity Number. 208231

LEE DUFFY

'THE WHOLE OF THE MOON'

By Jamie Boyle

www.warcrypress.co.uk
Jamie Boyle (c)

NOTE:

The views and opinions expressed in this book are those of the interviewees obtained during recorded interview and do not necessarily reflect the opinions of the author.

LEE DUFFY 'THE WHOLE OF THE MOON'

ISBN: 978-1-912543-07-6

All rights reserved. No part of this publication may be reproduced or transmitted in any form or by any means, including photocopying and recording, without the written permission of the copyright holder, application for which should be addressed to the publisher via the dealing agent at warcrypress@roobix.co.uk. Such written permission must also be obtained before any part of this publication is stored in a retrieval system of any nature. This book is sold subject to the Standard Terms and Conditions of Sale of New Books and may not be re-sold in the UK below the net price fixed by the Publisher/Agent LEE DUFFY 'THE WHOLE OF THE MOON' Produced by Warcry Press (part of Roobix Ltd) on behalf of Jamie Boyle, Northallerton (c) 2018.

Cover Design: James R Foreman - cargocollective.com/jamesryanforeman

Printed and bound in Great Britain by Clays, Elcograf S.p.A

Find out more at: facebook.com/leeduffybook

I dedicate this book to my stepdaughter Katie Megan. I've been in her life since she was four and watched her grow into a beautiful young woman, with a determination not many could match, she is now attending University and we are all very proud of her. Keep reaching for the stars Katie God bless you, love Jamie xx

I will be forever grateful to the people who have supported me whilst writing this book, massive thanks goes to:

Boris, Floyd and the guys at Warcry Press, Michael Costello, Simon Ambler (for the temp front cover), Terry Dicko (for his connections), Dan King, everyone who contributed towards the chapters herein, also to the people who wanted to remain anonymous, you know who you are. The Evening Gazette Archives and the Northern Echo Archives and last but not least my beautiful Wife Shirley without whom these books would not be possible.

"Now then, Now then".

Lee Duffy

Chapters

Foreword – Bronson	1
The Crescent	3
Rod Jones	24
Yvonne Cox	41
Alan McKittrick	47
Mary	64
Buster Atkinson	71
Robbie	82
Darren Collins	93
Gina	103
John Butchworth	107
Harry	121
Stephen Lenagham	131
Reuben	140
Terence Nivens	165
Jack	174

John Dryden	185
Donald Wright	188
Peter Appleby	193
Terry Dicko	204
'B'	220
Gram Seed	226
Den Hunt	239
Barry Faulkner	250
Richie Davison	258
Dean Lewtes	264
Anth Walls	267
Peter Wilson	277
Terry Downes	287
Michael	296
Dominic Negus	302
Lorna Lancaster	308

The Day the End Came	314
The Last Month's of Lee's Life	328
The Full Moon	330
The Whole of the Moon – Lyrics	338

FOREWORD

Charles Salvador (Bronson)
Fellow Lag

I did time with Lee the once, in Armley Jail, Leeds, late 1980's 'Top Geezer'. Lots of respect for him.

We served up a right nonce in the Bath House, funny it was (screamed like a pig).

What I liked about Lee, he was what he was, no act, staunch, fearless, a great guy with old school morals.

Strong as a bull. like a bulldozer, fast, in and out! One geezer you would not want to cross, believe me.

Sadly, a violent life, always ends violently and that was Lee Duffy's ending.

You live by the sword, you die by it. But he lives on in many folk's memories.

There was more good in him than bad and I was privileged to have spent a little time with him.

When he got out he never forgot me, he sent me in the odd parcel. That's how you find out a good man. Their word is their bond. He was a true prison legend.

Charles Salvador

"See, people with power understand exactly one thing: violence.

Noam Chomsky

The Crescent

It was a bank holiday weekend and a gloriously warm Sunday morning, that morning of August 25th 1991 in Middlesbrough, I'll never forget it. I was 11 years old and only a week or two from going to St Anthony's in Town Farm, Middlesbrough, which was my local secondary school. The reason I'll never forget that day, 27 years ago, was because of a conversation I had with an older lad at the bottom of my street, Keasdon Close in Berwick Hills. He must have been around 17 or 18 at the time, and I only knew him as "Hamo", although I believe Craig Hamilton was his real name. I was just setting off from home to play football on the Old Vic field and as I walked past his house, he told me the devastating news, "Lee Duffy was killed last night". Craig looked like he was in sheer disbelief and it seemed like he was telling me this not because he was gossiping but because he had to say it out loud for it to be true, he had a look of devastation and amazement in equal measures on his face! I couldn't believe it either! The news was like I imagined it would be if the Queen had been pronounced dead. Well the truth is I didn't know Lee Duffy, I'd never met him in my life and I'm almost sure that "Hamo" hadn't met him either but everybody and I mean everybody, and their dog had heard of "The Duff".

In reality I was an 11 year old boy, the only things I was interested in at the time was Celtic FC and WWF Wrestling, so why did I feel so shocked and saddened that some guy I'd only ever seen in the Gazette

(Middlesbrough paper) for doing naughty things was dead? I think the reason was, that although I'd never met Lee Duffy, I'd been hearing his name since I was around 8 years old. I believed in Father Christmas until I was 9 so to be frank I'd known of "The Duff" before I knew that fairy tales weren't true like a lot of kids in Middlesbrough. Kids used to talk about him in my primary school like he was some kind of hero, so I imagined him to be about 8ft tall and looking a bit like batman!

Like I said I had known of Lee Paul Duffy for a good few years before that strange summer's morning in August. The reason I'd heard so much of the man, who everybody in my town spoke of in awe, was because I hung around with a lot of lads who were older than me. When I was growing up I was football mad and would play daily on the Old Vic field. Quite often, just to get a kick about I would join in playing with lads 5, 6 even 7 years older than me. Of course, there was no internet in them days, it was either a game of "Knocky Knocky Hido", a game of footy or you twiddled your thumbs. There were so many times when I'd hear the older boys' second hand gossip about this man who, in my mind, was almost super hero like. I would often crick my neck to listen to these tales which would spread across the town of Middlesbrough like the great fire of London. Of course, boys will be boys and often many of the lads telling the stories would say they knew Lee really well or had met him at some point. I heard so many tales of Lee which are now embedded in Teesside folklore forevermore.

I can clearly remember the tale of when he was shot in the foot at a late night blues party on Princess Road. The story I would hear as a 10 year old boy was that Lee was shot in the foot and chased the culprits down Newport Road in Middlesbrough town centre which was a full mile long, when in fact, Lee was found in the old Rooney's bar doorway (now The Oak) by two police officers. So, in reality it was a case of Chinese whispers, but I had him down as some kind of fucking Terminator, like out of the second film that was out at the time. Another film out at the time was Steven Seagal's 'Out for Justice' which is about a man on a one man mission who goes searching to payback the people who wronged him just like Lee Duffy did. I can really remember when Lee was the man about town and the stories I would hear about him. On one hand I would think this man is the hardest man in Middlesbrough with special powers, but I can also recall clearly feeling sorry for this poor man who everybody was out to kill!

I'll never forget the strange feeling that there was in the town on that day and for days after for as long as I live, it didn't matter who I spoke to or where I went, Middlesbrough was in a state of shock and a black cloud hung around over it for a while. Nothing has ever come close to that feeling in Middlesbrough since then.

Over the years, I myself don't mind admitting, that I've became greatly fascinated with the life of Lee Paul Duffy, as have a lot of people whether they like to admit it or not. Who was he? What was he really about? Was he as bad as the tabloids have made him out to be for over a quarter of a century? Surely, he was still just a kid at 26, wasn't he?

I must admit, it took me around 5 or 6 months of haggling with my senses to do this book! As much as Lee's life intrigued me, I had my doubts that maybe this one was a little too close to home, I mean I grew up under the smog of Middlesbrough and the last thing I wanted to do was kick a hornet's nest as I'd had experience of doing just that when I wrote the two books about Paul Sykes from Wakefield. They were written in a similar style to this one, I like the reader to be presented with a balanced view of the good and bad and leave them to make their own minds up. To several people in Wakefield, well I'm not their favourite person to say the least! Think of when Salman Rushdie wrote 'The Satanic Verses' in 1988 which provoked protests and he had contracts put out on his life, well I had a similar experience. Although I've been called a few unpleasantries and had the odd death threat or two over it I was told by his Sister that he'd have loved books being written about him. Similarly, I've been told that Lee predicted a book about himself saying "they'll write books about me one day", I can't say he'd be pleased about it or not, who knows what he would be thinking at 53 years old, would he have turned his life around, we'll never know. Anyway, it was all very well causing such a stir in a place sixty odd miles away, but for me to do it in my hometown, a place some members of my family still live in to this day took some real consideration.

The reality of it was that it wasn't really until I'd spent a bit of time with one of Lee's closest friends and he said to me he actually thought it was a good idea to do the Duff's story that I decided to write it. I only half-heartedly put it to him as more than half of me wanted him to tell me it really wasn't a great idea and then I could have forgotten about it, but he replied saying "If you do it you need to make sure you do this one properly Jamie"! He was referring to the previous books which had been written about Lee which, on having read them twice I can see his point as to why he was annoyed by a few things in them.

I'd like to clarify that, whatever people in this book have said about Lee I've had no control over. Like I've said and will always say, I didn't know him and had never met him, I have just tried to get a balanced view, I can't make him look like Mother Teresa and I haven't influenced anyone in any way, whether they loved Lee or said he epitomised everything evil.

I certainly have no axe to grind with any of the Duffy family in bringing this book to Teesside and I understand their mistrust as there's been so many inaccuracies printed about him and things said that have been taken out of context. I don't think there's anything clever about being a bully or how Lee Duffy went about his business, but also, I don't think there's anything clever about a man who'd just turned 26 by two months losing his life.

I will speak from the heart and say the biggest thing that jumps out at me when I look over the life of Lee Duffy is that it was an absolute tragedy! I have heard the monster stories of Lee, the vicious brute who revelled in his acts of violence, the fear he would instil into the people of Teesside, but in truth we're talking about a 26 year old young kid here. I'll speak from my own experience and I'm sure you'll relate that each and every one of us have all been through bad periods but have come through our troubled fazes to regain normality. When I make my point here I'd like to use my friend Gram Seed as an example if I may for a moment. What I mean is that Gram lived the life of a thug, football hooligan, thief, bully, alcoholic and did more porridge than Goldilocks and the three bears, and that was just his good points! He served thirteen different prison sentences because he liked it that much! By his own admission he was the biggest scumbag to ever walk the town of Middlesbrough and many of you, if you can remember Gram in the early 90s, will be nodding your head in agreement when reading this. Grams struggle has been well documented in Teesside and he had got to the point where he even lived on the streets for a couple of years and he had to drink twenty one litres of White Lightening a day to even function. Well in 1996 Gram slipped into a coma due to the life he was leading and even a priest came and read him his last rites. His own mother Pat was advised to give the hospital permission to turn his life support machine off. At that time big Gram, who is around 6ft 5, had been a thorn in Middlesbrough town centre's side for a few years! You name it, if there was an element of anti-social behaviour about it then Gram Seed was at the centre of it. Normally it would be for thieving or beating somebody up, but his modus operandi varied.

There's a story Gram told me himself about one of the priests in Middlesbrough who said that the only miracle he has ever witnessed was when Gram went to his church to ask for money with his arm in pot saying it was broken, the priest took pity on Gram and handed over the cash only to see him again that day without so much as a broken finger! Gram had spent the money on another two litres of Cider and his attitude was "another one bites the dust" and off he would go to con the next poor gullible soul who would buy his crap. But going back to Gram's lifeless body in a coma, believe me when I say that the whole of the town of Middlesbrough's opinion on Grams near death state was to say, "Good, good riddance to bad rubbish, why has it taken so long"! Now I'm not saying Lee Duffy was as big as a scumbag as Gram Seed was, nor am I trying to say Gram was anywhere in the same league as Lee Duffy. What I am saying is Gram Seed didn't turn his life around until he was 32. That's 6 years older than Lee Duffy ever was. Gram has turned his life around and has spent the last 22 years of his life dedicating it to helping people through his church Sowing Seeds in Stockton. I'm not saying Lee Duffy would have found Jesus and lived happily ever after, but even Lee's close friend, who I won't name, told me that Lee had told him many times that he wanted out of the seedy brutal Teesside underworld of which he was the undisputed top dog. Even Lee's girlfriend at the time has said before that she saw Lee break down uncontrollably many times because everywhere he went people were out to try and kill him. Lee was saying he wanted to get away from the life he'd built up for himself over the previous 8 years, live the quiet life and bring his baby daughter up with his girlfriend and be around for his other children.

I'm not making excuses for Lee's behaviour by any means, but when the only thing you've known all your life is extreme violence at the drop of a hat, or having to fight out of the roughest area in one of the most working class towns around it would make it that bit harder for him to say "do you know what, I don't want to do this anymore please, I'd rather not fight tonight" and walk away, but there were certain individuals who wouldn't have allowed him to do that.

I haven't become a top psychologist since researching Lee's life, but when you led the life that Lee did and considering his upbringing, I don't think he would have had the tools socially to adapt to a new life without something catastrophic happening. Maybe if Lee had survived the fatal attempt on his life that night maybe things might have fallen into place for him and allowed him to change. Remember it took my friend until he was read the last rites to change!

Only Lee's closest family will have the answers as to whether he would have had it in him to change had he survived in the early hours of that fateful morning.

The opinion of many people that were in his circle was that if Lee hadn't passed that day then he wouldn't have survived long after it. People have laughed at the mere mention of Lee changing as they have said he loved the way he was and what his life was about and that the only thing that would end his reign of terror would be his death, but I have to wonder how much of that was the real Lee and how much of it was a macho front that he felt he had to play out every day of his life unless he was in the safety of his home.

In the summer of 2006 I would be put on labouring job for a good few months. I would end up working on Gillbrook school in Eston, which incidentally is next door to the final resting place of Lee Duffy. At the time I would have an hour for my lunch and as it took me 10 minutes to eat the pack up that the Wife would do me, it left me a lot of time to sit in a bait cabin talking about football to hairy arsed builders. I mentioned that I was reading the Tax Mans, aka Brian Cockerill's, book at the time and one of the lads said, "his mate Lee Duffy is buried right in the corner of Eston cemetery at the back, it's under a camera as it's been vandalised so many times, you can't miss it". He also went on to tell me that before Lee was buried, there were rumours he was to be concreted in as there were serious threats made that he was going to be dug up! How abhorrent that Lee's family had to deal with situations like that after they had lost him, it's beyond words how sick some people are.

Me being my inquisitive self and growing up hearing all the stories of Lee, I went along one dinner time to visit Lee's grave. Walking in the cemetery I noticed Middlesbrough footballing legend and fellow South Bank boy Wilf Mannion's grave, who'd passed 6 years earlier in 2000.

When I got to Lee's grave, I was struck with a real sense of sadness, his grave was surrounded by all these graves of people who had passed away in old age and Lee was only 26! One of the most bizarre things on that day which was uncanny, was when I looked at his tombstone which said the words of his favourite song by Little Caesar but written by The Water Boys in 1985, "They saw the crescent, he saw the whole of the moon". It suddenly dawned on me that Lee was exactly 26 years, two months and 2 weeks to the day when he passed. That day I was at his grave I was a couple of days off from being 26 years old two months and 2 weeks myself. As I looked at the grave of this man who I'd never met, it hit me just how young this fella was he'd already been passed 15 years by then. I started thinking of all the stupid shit I was doing at that very point in my life!

So, you see, you can agree with the hordes of stories of his wickedness that are linked to Lee Duffy forever. Even the ones he may never have done, what did it matter because he's dead and we'll believe it anyway. Or you can think a bit deeper and think of the word "empathy". It's a word which doesn't really come to anybody in life until you're a little more well balanced and grown up. I must admit, sometimes I don't even look at situations in life that come my way with "empathy". Empathy is a tool which lets you look at the full picture, but then understands and looks at it from both points of view and asks questions of us like "Why he behaved the way he did later in life?!" They do say that in every action there's a reaction. So, for everybody who's taken the stance of "well he was a fucking bully who got what he deserved" even though they may not have known him personally, remember that there's only one person who can judge us all and that will be when our day of judgement comes!

What I will say for the record and let me just put my shrink hat on for a minute, Lee had a troublesome childhood, there's no denying that, but in my opinion, what really stayed with him until his dying day was the horrific extent of the bullying he suffered in his younger days and the sheer determination that no one and I mean no one would ever bully him again.

I'm sure there's people far more qualified than me to go on record and say, the bullied become the bullies! Lee was even asking friends to pull over in his adult life, so he could go fill someone in the middle of the street as he'd seen a person who used to bully him maybe 12-15 years earlier, he just never recovered, mentally. It wasn't only other older children who bullied the younger Lee on the tough streets of South Bank. I've heard Lee's brother speaking on YouTube of the times, in their early years, when Lee's father Lawrie was abusive in the home under the influence of alcohol. In one of my other books, I can recall East End hardman Dominic Negus saying to me, "I grew up looking up to Lenny Mclean and Roy Shaw, so was I ever going to turn out different"? and I can understand where he's coming from on that. Of course, someone Lee looked up to was his Uncle Rod who was a professional criminal, Lee idolised him and wanted to be just like him.

Maybe because of the start Lee Paul Duffy had, he was never going to end up any different. I've no doubt in my mind Lee Duffy could have been a decent fighter had he stuck to boxing if only he had chosen that path instead.

I've spoken to people around the Middlesbrough boxing scene who've told me Lee Duffy was blessed and was the perfect cruiserweight, but Lee lacked the patience required to be a champion fighter because he was over eager to go all out and "gung ho" to quote Joe Walton's boxing coach Eddie O'Donoghue. Lee was just a knock out machine and not Ed's type of fighter, but he did acknowledge his boxing quality.

Another funny thing that happened to me was, when I was still in two minds as to whether to do the book or not, and I was waiting to hear back from some of Lee's close friends to put me at ease with their backing, I must have heard The Whole of The Moon on the radio a good five or six times in a matter of a couple of weeks. I took that as a sign that I was being given the green light. Lee used to say the reason he loved that song so much was because it reminded him of his life. When you hear the lyrics of 'you climbed on that ladder' and 'you came like a comet, blazing your trail, too high, too far, too soon' you can relate to what Lee was saying because he climbed on that ladder and got to a place in life when it was too far and too soon for him.

One of the most surreal things that I heard was when I met up with Lee's biological Son, he told me that he had married recently, and that song came on the radio right before he left for the church, it was the last song he heard before becoming a married man. It was almost as if Lee was sending a message to his boy to let him know that he was with him on the most important day of his life.

I'd say at least 70% of the people in Middlesbrough think only of one man when they hear of the title of this book. Many years ago when I myself was growing up and started going out drinking in 96, 97, I'd put that song on the duke box in my old haunts like The Eagle or Newcastle House in Berwick Hills all the locals would say that it was Lee Duffy's song.

Remember Lee was 26 when he died but he'd been doing things that he probably shouldn't have since he was just a skinny kid of 18 years old, putting it on the toes of 35 year old mature men with big names in the town.

Lee Paul Duffy paid the ultimate price and he's been dead now longer than he was alive.

When I finally decided to do this book and spoke with Lee's friend in his home around Christmas 2017, I gave him my word that it would be done right. I wanted to go and find people who knew Lee or were around him through the various stages of his life. No disrespect to any of the other books from any Newcastle contingent, but I wanted this book to be something that hadn't already been done. That was to write a book purely on how the good folk of Teesside saw their most infamous son.

This book is the voice of the Middlesbrough people for the very first time regarding Lee Paul Duffy. Forget what you've heard in the past and judge him by the people who really knew Lee for good or bad. I've been told so many things regarding Lee Duffy these last couple of months. You will read in here stories of his violence but there are ones of the other side of Lee Duffy the Lee Duffy who had a generous heart, so much so that when complimented on his new black leather Jacket by Frankie 'Bam' Pointon, in the Kensington Road Blues, he took it off his back and gave it to Frankie, a £700 jacket!

He was just this crazy one-off and I've been in awe at many of things that he used to get up to. Sometimes in a good way but at times in shock.

I've heard tales of Lee playing a game with Brian Cockerill on who could smash the most car windows in one go with your fist, Brian did 17 and Lee managed to go one better and do 18! Then because Brian had been beaten, Brian then picked up the last car and moved it on to the pavement, so you could say that their relationship was a competitive one.

There's also the stories of when three of Lee's friends went to visit him in Durham prison. When they turned up they were told Lee wasn't allowed in the usual visitor's hall with the other prisoners and that he had to have his visit in the block, basically the prison inside of the prison where the worst of the worst are kept like Paul Sykes and Fred "the head" Mills etc... All the way through that visit Lee had a joint behind his ear whilst smoking another. That just doesn't happen in British prisons usually.

The only time I was told that Lee met his prison rival for the alpha male title, was in the Havana a few months before he died. Paul Sykes who will have been 45 then, was brought to Middlesbrough by Tony Spensley for a night out, and Paul went to shake the Duff's hand, Lee put his back to Sykes and continued dancing and said "Who does he think he is, me"? whilst laughing. Lee was very childlike like that a few of his friends have told me.

Lee once looked after Brian Charrington, the international drug dealer whilst they were inside prison. When Lee got out Brian gave Lee a seven grand Rolex as a thank you.

It is true Lee stopped a lot of people in Middlesbrough selling drugs and people were then having to go to places like Manchester just to get them. Lee didn't really capitalise on the void by selling the stuff himself as I'm told that Lee couldn't run a bath. When Lee did have big bags of ecstasy he would eat most of them himself, sometimes being on them for days on end in Newcastle and other places he would flee to live the party lifestyle he so loved.

Sometimes Lee would get by on two hours sleep a night because he was partying that much. One of Lee's close friends told me that a book could have been written about each day in Lee's life as he was up to that much. In fact, one of Lee's favourite sayings was "you can put this in a book when I'm gone".

Lee spoke all the time about his death and he had an instinct that he wouldn't make old bones, anyone close to Lee will know that. He predicted also that one day someone would write a book on him. There have been several books touching on his life whilst writing about other people so I suppose this is the only one that is solely about Lee, but I hope this one will be the most balanced one!

Another time Lee offered his best friend a huge amount of money just so he would stay out with him another night after they'd been out two days already smoking dope up Eston Hills.

I asked one of his closest friends what Lee was like as a kid? To which his reply was "Lee Duffy was never a kid, even at 15 he was like a man". On one side of Lee you've got this big monster of a man who looked the part and was capable of battering people, then on the other hand you've got this big cumbersome kid who was still childlike and still very damaged from the abuse he suffered years before.

It is true that when Lee was in prison he would seek out the hardest in the place and want to take over. In Walton prison Lee went on the exercise yard and demanded to know who the top man was. I have it on good authority that the Scousers were petrified of him and Lee was even more violent inside prison because there were no weapons inside or any risk of him being shot. Even men in their gangs didn't want to tackle the Duff and I'll quote my source "he knocked them all dead as a nit".

Lee was an extra bad lad in jail. Not many people realise that Lee and Davie Allo did time together in Walton prison and after Davie got out he even ran Lee's girlfriend back on a visit. Yes, Lee and Allo had been friends, as much as you could be friends with Lee, as I have been told that even if he classed you as a friend you still had to be on your guard with him. Allo got on with Lee at times that is true, but I've been told that the bad blood started because he wouldn't bow to Lee and Lee wasn't having that. It's well known in Middlesbrough that Allo was a staunch man who would have a do with anyone.

The fact was Lee and Allo came to blows on three separate occasions. Once in the Blaises foyer whilst scuffling it is said that Allo was seen to be getting the better of him as they had fallen and Allo had landed on top of Lee. Then at the Law Courts Lee had been in a car with a friend and saw Allo and told his mate to pull over and asked him to watch his back as Allo was with a couple of mates drinking, Lee approached Allo and said, "I hear you've been looking for me" and from there it quickly escalated into them trading blows, Lee getting the better of Allo that time. Then the last time, well everyone knows how that ended.

The real bad feeling between them two really started at John Graham's wedding just a couple of months before their last confrontation outside the Western & Afro Caribbean Centre on Marton Road. I've been told one of Lee's party tricks was to let the people whose company he was in drink fast while Lee poured his drinks out. Brian Jaffray caught Lee doing that a few times, spitting his drinks out on the pub carpet.

People close to Lee have told me that Lee never used to relax. He never sat down and watched the T.V and switched off from the outside world and that he lived his life at 100 miles per hour every single day.

Another thing Lee wouldn't do is sleep in the same house for more than one consecutive night, he would regularly sleep at different houses all over Middlesbrough.

One guy, who was close to Lee, said that he often said his ambition in life was to kill a man with his bare hands by the time he was 30 years old. The same source told me that Lee used to say by the time they were 30 Joe Livingstone, David Allison or himself would be dead.

The prisons couldn't contain him and that's why he ended up in twenty two different prisons during the twenty six months of the four year sentence he served because they'd move him along to try and break his spirit. That would only normally happen to double A CAT's, but they put Lee on what they called the circuit just to basically wind him in, even though he was only ever CAT B at worst. That's what got him his notoriety in the British prison system.

I would have loved to have included Neil Booth, John Fail, Mark Hartley, John Black, Kevin Duckling and Joe Livingstone for this book but a lot from Lee's generation politely declined. I know Lee and Neil were particularly close and Neil has never forgotten Lee and named his Son Samuel Lee Booth and his Grandson is Frankie Lee Booth.

I only knew of the other men mentioned but being from Berwick Hills myself I was very familiar with Joe, having worked for him several times. From my experience Berwick Hills / Parkend was a safer cleaner place when Joe kept order there, he wouldn't allow those streets to become saturated with the drugs that unfortunately they are now. I know that when Lee's youngest Daughter was shot in the eye with an air pellet gun, she was only 15 at the time, the Gazette reported that an anonymous business man paid for her and her Mother to have a season ticket each for Middlesbrough FC, that was Joe too.

They all have new lives now etc... They are no longer jack the lads, but now respectable family men/business men and some of them even have grand-children, so their lives are completely opposite to what they were nearly 30 years ago when they hung around with Middlesbrough's ultimate bad boy and I've had to respect that and although those people declined I still think that I have managed to speak to some of the right people to answer my questions.

One thing I didn't want to do was put billy bullshitters in this book, I've met many people that say he was their mate when actually they maybe where just in the same pub at the same time back in 1988! When you read the chapters I hope you conclude that I have got the right balance.

I was told that if Lee Duffy was still here today that he'd be the exact same person he was back in 1991. He didn't want to change, that he was happy being a gangster, he'd have only become bigger, stronger and deadlier. On the other hand, he might have been a more settled family man, popping out for a pint to his local on a Sunday afternoon reminiscing about the crazy things he used to get up to and shaking his head, but we will never know for sure.

I spoke with officers from Cleveland police and although a lot of them have retired, they still can't speak of Lee Duffy although they've agreed that a lot of the facts in this book are true, although I can't name the now retired officers.

Even though Lee will have been gone 27 years by the time you read this, a handful of people in this book are still uncomfortable using their own names so I agreed to change their names to protect their identity, other than their names their interviews remain 100% as they were told to me.

Every chapter, I hope, although different to one another will capture the full picture of who and what Lee Paul Duffy was about.

Happy reading and I hope you enjoy this book about the remarkable man he was either way, I've enjoyed researching the life of Lee Duffy, my overall opinion of him changed with every interview that I conducted. Now go read thirty separate people's experiences and opinions of knowing Lee and I'll see you for my summing up at the other end. Many thanks, always a pleasure, Jamie B. X

"Lee Duffy was the type of person you could take to meet your grandmother on a Monday, then Millwall away on a Tuesday".

Lee's close friend.

Rod Jones - Lee's Uncle

Not all of Lee's family were overjoyed with me doing this book and having read Stephen Richards' books on the Duff I can totally understand their point. I've read Richards' books a couple of times and whilst I agree they're accurate with the dates and the events of Lee's life, it lacked empathy and detail. I'd say 70% was on Viv Graham and the stuff that he had about Lee was only found in the Gazette archives. Many reports from the Richards books were wrong even down to Lee's children's names and pictures which claimed to be in the Hacienda when really, they were at the Marton & Country Club at John Graham's wedding in the summer of 1991.

One name I was thrilled to be able to add to this book was Lee's Uncle Rod Jones. Lee idolised his Uncle Rod as he was growing up it's fair to say and saw him as someone to look up to. Lee would constantly try to impress him and it's also fair to say that Rod has been a bit of a rascal in his time also. This is Rod's account of his nephew.

Rod said:

I'm 70 years old now and me and my Sisters, Brenda and Norma grew up just off Princess Road in the town of Middlesbrough.

The end of Lee's life wasn't fair, he didn't deserve to die among so many enemies who revelled in his demise and lapped it all up. The Richards' book are a load of shit and I think a book on my Nephew is long overdue but only if it's done properly.

Lee lived with me for a few years when he first got out of the detention centre. Brenda wanted him out of the South Bank area because he was getting up to no good, so he came and lived with me and my family in Hemlington for around two years.

There's a lot of bullshit going around that he was a boxer, my Nephew wasn't a boxer. He had the gloves on a few times and went on the pads with Blacky (John Black) and I, but he was never a boxer. I think he may have been on the pads with Shandy Boyce a handful of times, but he was never this top boxer that the papers made him out to be. Also, Shandy didn't train Lee as people think, there was nothing regular with Lee's boxing training.

I could never understand the Sayers coming down for Lee's funeral and bringing this great big bloody boxing wreath, I think even they were under the impression that Lee had been a fucking boxer, but he really wasn't. Lee's nickname was the Duffer and people used to say he used to duff them, so it was all good for him having this boxer's image I suppose.

My earliest memory of Lee is holding him in my arms when he was born, and thinking aren't you a big lad!

Lee was always bullied at school and it was fucking scandalous what the kid went through, absolutely terrible it wouldn't have been allowed in today's schooling. He was bullied until he was at least 12 years old. There was a girl who looked after Lee who did judo and she used to protect Lee. Lee used to hide behind her many times when he was younger, and she took a shine to our Lee.

One of the reasons our Lee was picked on was for looking gormless, I mean he used to walk about with his mouth open and that never changed right up until the day he died. Lee and his brother were like chalk and cheese, whereas Lee and his younger Sister were very close all the way through his life.

Lee also had a problem with his nose and he couldn't breathe through it properly which maybe would explain why he always had his mouth open, but he was also nicknamed 'Bungalow' and 'Bungalow Bill' by a lot, because people used to say he had nothing upstairs. Lee had a fight one day with a lad because Lee asked him "what do you mean by that"? Then the lad said it's because you've got nothing upstairs and Lee lost his temper and got stuck into him.

Lee didn't come out of his shell properly until he did that robbery at the Dragonara hotel (now Jury's Inn) in Middlesbrough in November 1983, Lee got two and a half years for robbery. Lee and a girl who was on the game robbed some money and that was Lee's first time away behind the door in a proper man's prison. Many times, Lee used to hang around with that girl and when she brought customers back Lee would jump out and rob them as well as give them a good hiding. Not many people were prepared to go to the police and report it because they'd have to explain what they were doing with a prostitute in the first place.

Lee wasn't a big successful criminal you know! Our Brenda used to say, "Where's all the big car's and money if he's such a big criminal"? There wasn't any! Even when Lee got with Brian Cockerill and they were taxing people, there wasn't loads of money! Lee Duffy was never taxing people for big money like Brian Charrington and Curtis Warren, they were taxing arseholes in council houses for £300 they would find in a draw.

When Lee first went inside as a YP (young prisoner) he did what he had to do to climb the ladder and got on the weights and did sit ups and that's when he first got big. Lee was always this skinny dopey kid to me because he was my little Nephew but of course he really muscled out.

One of Lee's biggest problems was his involvement and hero worshipping of Ducko when he was about 18 years old. Our Lee was easily led and Ducko was a bad influence on the young Lee. I've actually been there and seen it, and I wasn't amused at all, I saw an innocent lad walk in a room and Lee had a £1 bet with Kevin Duckling that he could knock out this kid who was just minding his own business, Lee walked over to this kid and went "ere lad" then BANG! he put the lad down. I walked over and picked the kid up and Lee and Ducko were laughing like fuck. Now to me that's not fucking funny and I stayed with this kid and took him to the toilet and I was ashamed that my own Nephew could do a thing like that. I mean, getting into fights is different, but to go knock a young lad out who was just minding his own business was fucking disgraceful and I told Lee I wasn't happy with him. Lee just laughed at me, Lee didn't do serious he never was serious at anything.

Lee was fighting his whole life against every would be hard man in the town. Every naughty man that was about, there's a story of our Lee having a run in with them. One fella who Lee was alleged to have battled with was former middleweight boxer Dale Henderson-Thyne. Word has it that Lee had a secret fight with him up Eston Hills. Dale said that Lee sly punched him as he bent down to get in his car on Pelham Street in the town.

The hardest Lee fought with was a fella I fought with and his name was Jonka Teasdale. Lee ran down from his house on Keir Hardie Crescent, South Bank in just a pair of shorts to The Jovial Monk pub in North Ormesby, which was a good two miles, and when he got there he ended up breaking Jonka's jaw. Jonka had a lot of the doors in town like The Wellington among many other places and Lee was only around 18 years old at the time in 1983. I think he made a statement doing that and it was almost like Lee saying, 'well I'm here now' you know! It was a bit of a changing of the guard if you like. The young cub beats the old lion kinda thing.

Lee worked on a lot of doors, but he never ran any like Jonka did because he never had a business brain. Lee worked on the doors at Rumours with Ducko and the Jaffray brothers from Thorntree.

One thing I will say about our Lee is, Lee wasn't having long fights. Lee was explosive, he had a big right hook which was a family thing, I had it too. Most of Lee's fights were over in seconds "BOOM" and that was it. I'm 6ft 3 and Lee got all my family's genes in that respect, my father was the same.

Lee's Father Lawrie Snr was also a right handful in his time as well as Lee's Grandfather, so Lee really came from a naturally fighting family and from a long line of nasty bastards. Lee loved his Grandfather and he used to sit on his knee as a boy and listen to his stories of how he used to fight at Farrer Street bare-knuckle to make up his wages to get back what he'd just spent in the pub on drink.

Lee's Dad Lawrie Snr was also very sadistic with his violence. My sister Brenda was with him one time when a fella who'd lent Lawrie Snr £5 asked for it back, with that Lawrie Snr beat the poor guy up and when he'd finished he ripped the £5 note up and stuck it in the unconscious man's mouth to add insult to injury.

Many times, I had to go sort Lawrie Snr out because he'd been beating my Sister up. Whenever I went and gave him a kicking our Brenda always used to stick up for him and she'd be hitting me. He didn't treat my Sister well at all. I don't think he ever had a job either and he used to drink every day.

Many times, when our Lee was only young he would be sat in the front room and he would see me giving his old man good hidings, so you could say Lee was brought up with violence. Of course, I wished he had never seen that, but I could never stand by and watch while old Lawrie gave our Brenda the hidings he did. He once even flung her out of the bedroom window and she broke several bones.

Our Lee hated a fella named Paul Sykes from his time in jail, absolutely hated him. It's been alleged this Sykes had raped many a YP in Durham jail. I myself again had a carry on with Sykes, I knocked him out in the Contessa club in Middlesbrough. A fella named Freddie Charville threatened me with Paul Sykes and he paid him to come up from Wakefield to Middlesbrough. I knew Sykesy from jail many years before, so I knew who he was. This Charville had paid Sykesy to come and take me out. It was a Friday night and I was walking in the Contessa when I saw Peter Matthews on the door. He said to me "I wouldn't go in there if I was you Rod, Freddie's got a fella up from Wakefield to put it on you". So, I went in and when I went in, Sykesy's jumped up and put his hand out to shake my hand and I've hit him with the family right hook straight away 'BANG' and a few others for good measure and he never got time to react. I was blessed with the power of the punch just like our Lee and Sykesy didn't know what had hit him. The reason I caught Sykes like that was because he knew me, but he knew me by a different name which was Don Cross, that's the name I had in prison, so I was tipped off if you like. Sykesy didn't have a fucking clue that my name was Rod Jones.

When Sykesy came to Middlesbrough to sort this fucking Jonesy bloke out, he was sat in the club and he'd had a few drinks whilst I was stone cold sober, and I left him sprawled across the floor with his senses shattered. Sykes was into interfering with lads in jail when I was there, I know that.

Sykes used to come to the Baltimore Hotel in the Longlands and get pissed in there and cause havoc by touching women's arses in front of their husbands and abusing all the bar staff in there on a regular basis. The man was a fucking total animal. Malcolm the owner used to ring me up and ask me to get Syksey out of the Baltimore which I did do a few times.

A few of my family said over the years that Lee grew up looking up to me, myself I think he probably did but it's not a thing to comment on without sounding big headed is it?!

For years I was a double A CAT and was "shanghaied" from one prison to the other which maybe Lee thought was impressive. The young Lee will have heard all about the times his Uncle Rod was on the run all over Britain when his Mam Brenda would come and meet up with me and assist me when I was "at it". I suppose you could say I was a professional criminal because shamefully I was up to all sorts when I was a younger man.

I still have a scar on my eye from fighting with Middlesbrough legend, fighting man Jackie Parsons. Afterwards he got upset because he'd bent his wedding ring while hitting me. I went looking for him with a gun after that but never found him. We later made up. I liked Jackie, he was one of the old school. That man worked the doors until he was in his 70s you know.

When Lee was living with me at number 12 Faygate, Hemlington I would have characters around the house like Davey Hugil, Keith McQuade, Brian Charrington and John Black so I suppose it could have looked glamorous to the young Lee. Blacky turned out to be a bit of a mentor to our Lee and was forever training him in the boxing gym.

I did used to look after Brian Charrington and I'd done a few prison sentences so maybe Lee was impressed with it all, ultimately he chose a similar path didn't he?!

I was partners once over with Brian Charrington and Keith McQuade in the car lot behind the Majestic bingo in North Ormesby which was closed by a major drugs bust in the early 90s. Keith sadly died a few years ago in Hull prison, he was a lovely man.

Our Lee was always respectful towards me, apart from when he was a little kid and I used to walk in and he used to jump on my back and try to pagger me, he never could.

The first time he came home from jail, he was maybe 15, I went to pick him up and the first thing he did when we walked in the house was jump on my back and try to beat me to the floor, even then he never could. Even though I was his Uncle, our Lee was always sizing me up for the right hand even as a kid. I used to know that look he got and I'd say to him "OI BEHAVE", he used to do the same with Blacky. Sometimes you'd be talking to him and he'd just adjust his feet and you could see him dipping his shoulder, I don't think he could help himself and he probably did it in his sleep. He would size everyone up to belt, even if he liked you.

Lee was forever trying to impress me. That's where he got his right hand from because I showed him, I taught him to punch from the hip. Lee used to have a terrific right hand. He was a one punch KO artist as I told you earlier on. I never boxed in my fucking life, but I can move about and our Lee was exactly the same. You've got it, or you haven't got it and Lee had it in abundance fortunately or unfortunately depending on how you look at it.

I have a lot of thoughts on fighting and I used to teach our Lee on the bag when he was just a lad telling him to hit the same spot over and over till he perfected it to a tee. I used to say that when you see these gypsies squaring up in a pugilistic manner, well forget that. Your hands should be by your side. Don't give the other guy any inclination that you're about to throw the shot. Then when you're ready, throw it from the hip and bring it up like your bowling a cricket ball and crash it into his jaw. This was something Lee became very good at. It's very hard for a man to come back from one almighty whack, then if you follow it up with maybe two more it should be game over. Many of our Lee's enemies didn't have any idea they were about to be attacked at all. Lee was just ATTACK ATTACK ATTACK 1-2-3 BOOM BOOM BOOM that's all it took. Sometimes only one was enough for our Lee.

In all the years of me knowing our Lee regarding his fighting, I don't think he took much stick back. I can never remember him with any cuts or black eyes considering he was fighting weekly.

I do feel a little bit responsible at times when I hear the bad stories of our Lee's violence because I was one of the main culprits who taught him to fight. The young Lee used to pester me constantly when he was 9 and 10 years old to demonstrate to him how to throw punches correctly. Lee was more of a street fighter than a boxer, but he could do it all. He was a tough kid and he'd done his apprenticeship on Middlesbrough's most ruthless estate, South Bank.

That night when Lee died, John Black and a crew of lads crossed the top of Marton Road, they were going to go down that way on their way back from Stockton, as they had been doing the doors there, but he changed his mind at the last minute, it would have all been stopped if they had gone down Marton Road. John says he always regrets this.

In that last fight with Allo, Lee hadn't been to sleep for days from all the gear he'd been on. Even after Lee was stabbed, the taxis drove off and never picked him up when they saw who it was lay dying. Lee didn't have to die that night.

That night when Lee died I left Britain on the ferry to France and was heading for Romania. I run an international charity taking many clothes over to Romania, in the early hours a guy came to my bunk and said, "I've got your sister Brenda on the phone". So, I got dressed and went in the cabin where the phone was and they put me on the ships line to Brenda. Brenda was frantic, and she said, "Can you come straight home Rod our Lee's been stabbed". Brenda was crying and really not making any sense and I couldn't make any of it out at first. I said," Brenda I'm in the fucking middle of the channel and I'm on my way to France now". I was leading the convoy and all the lads that were with me were Lee's mates. Many had even been in Lee's house in Eston that same week. Well we couldn't turn back and when we heard Lee was dead there was no fucking point in coming back, what could I have done! I ended up staying in Romania on that trip for the full three months and missed our Lee's funeral. When I got to Romania and spoke to Brenda, Brenda was saying that I needed to do this and needed to do that. Long story short Brenda asked me to do him and make sure he went with Lee, she wanted me to shoot Allo, that wasn't going to happen.

It was unfair of our Brenda to ask me to do that and get myself a life sentence at the same time. I also knew that if it hadn't been that night Lee died, somebody else would have got him along the line. I might as well have gone and killed half of Middlesbrough at the same time. It was very ludicrous to even suggest it, but I don't hold it against her, she was just a grieving Mother. Her heart had been broken with the loss of her little boy.

Allo used to come in my house many years before he killed our Lee as my step son Darren used to go to the football matches with him and the Boro Frontline mob. When I see Davey Allo these days I think he gets embarrassed if I see him in a bar. He can't hold my look and he looks away, maybe out of respect because he took my Nephews life, I don't know.

I was completely shattered that I was on a boat to Romania and I had my Sister on the phone telling me my little Nephew had died. The worst thing about it was Lee was going to come out to Romania on that very trip. Lee was going on about it for fucking weeks before we went that he wanted to go and help the less fortunate which is what we do. Brenda wanted me to take him with us just to get him out of the way from Middlesbrough for a short while. So, Lee was banging on about it for weeks and weeks and the last week I said to our Lee "are you fucking coming or what"? Lee's answer was "Yeah Yeah I'll sort it I'll sort it" but I knew he wasn't going to come. Anyway, when it got to about three days before I couldn't take him at his word and I took his name off the list because I realised he was never going to come with us. Had Lee decided on coming with us he wouldn't have died that night. Hindsight's a wonderful thing isn't it!

Our Lee's funeral was a huge event itself I was told. Many of the big key figures across Britain turned up like the Sayers family from Newcastle, Joel Richardson from Leeds came with Marco also.

After the funeral our Brenda used to go across to Newcastle and stay with John Henry Sayers, they did look after her and were a great comfort when she was grieving for Lee. I think it was the Sayers family who were pushing our Lee to have a fight with Viv Graham, but in my opinion that was never going to happen. I mean, where was that fight going to take place? On a field or in the street? That was only made up after Lee and Viv's death to sell Stephen Richards' books in my opinion. There was never such a thing as a fight to the death happening like is portrayed. That story has only really come to light since about 2001 to sell books. In reality the loser of that fight probably would have been shot by the other one's gang on the spot.

Lee's Mam Brenda used to go to Lee's grave and dig little holes in it and push these special biscuits that he used to like down towards his coffin. Fig biscuits I think they were called. She missed him greatly.

Lee's grave was smashed three times that I know of, and the person behind it, I know who it was, well how I've never done something about him I'll never know! That man from Eston's one vile human being that's all I will say.

Over the years I've heard so much shit about our Lee, even blokes in their 40s who should know better and they're telling people how they used to run about with Lee and it's all complete bullshit. They had never even met him.

One of the things you can't deny about our Lee, and that's everybody's still talking about him 27 years after he died. I thought a lot of Lee because I was his Uncle and Godfather, but I can't forget that he hit some people for no reason whatsoever and they couldn't defend themselves very well.

Lee would fight a hardman or a soft man it didn't really matter to Lee, but that's not right in my opinion. Lee could go knock a really hard man out like Jonka Teasdale, then he would go and do exactly the same to a young guy who was having a quiet drink. We can all do that. You can't get away from the fact that Lee did do a bit of bullying as well. It's very easy to be a big fish in a small pond, and

Middlesbrough's a small pond. To be a big fish in a big pond, well that takes some doing and Lee didn't do that.

I think if he'd have got some fucking brains and got something upstairs he could have done something, but Lee was used, he was always used. There's a fella in Middlesbrough that wound Lee up like a clockwork mouse and pointed him in a certain direction and he was off. Brian Charrington also used Lee to do his dirty work as he was being sent to various places to collect unpaid debts. He also did bits and pieces with Newcastle's Paddy Conroy, our Lee shared a cell with him in Durham prison.

Lee was a one off as a young lad and I used to always say, right from him being young that Lee was an accident waiting to happen. It turns out I was right. That wasn't the first time death had come calling. One night I stayed outside his hospital door after he was shot in the knee outside the blues protecting him because he'd refused police protection. My Sister asked me to sleep outside of his room for the four days he was in there in case the men from Blyth came back to have another pop at him. During the day when I would go to speak to him he never realised I was doing him a favour, he even told me to sit outside while he spent time with his girlfriend. His ward was the one facing the Ayresome Road in the old general hospital which has now been demolished. Lee would often smoke dope in his hospital bed.

The thing with our Lee and guns it just wasn't him. I heard all the stories about him running about with the Sayers, but I think he was just trying to play the part of being a gangster. Truth be told, there was one day I was with him and I'd been to pick a gun up from one of my friend's houses and on the way back Lee wouldn't even get in the car because we had the gun hid in the back of the car.

The amount of prisons Lee ended up doing in his short sentences must have been something because I know a few of them like Lancaster, Strangeways, Walton, Holme House, Durham, Armley, Acklington, Low Newton and Kirk Levington and that's only a few off the top of my head that I can remember.

Lee was used all his life for small change and I told him this, many times. He just wouldn't listen and if he did you'd have to explain something to him three or four times and he'd usually reply with "WHAT" while pulling a confused face.

I wish my Nephew was still here now, but the fact of the matter is he's not. He's been pushing up flowers for the last 27 years and there's nothing glamorous about that. All these young kids that look up to Lee Duffy like some kind of role model need a reality check. He should be here now for the children he never really knew and his grandchildren. Our Lee was bright enough to not live the life he did. He chose his own path and look where that got him.

"The world is a jungle, you either fight and dominate or hide and evaporate".

Abhishek Bhambure

Yvonne Cox - Next door Neighbour

Considering that I grew up in Middlesbrough I've never been that familiar with the South Bank and Eston areas. So, during the research of this book I've kind of discovered places in the town I never knew existed, places in Eston like 6 Durham Road where Lee used to live at the time of his death with his girlfriend and their baby daughter. I had time to spare one day and was with a friend of mine, Michael Costello, in his car and we went around that way to get a feel of Lee's manor. Another place that I'd never even been anywhere near was Keir Hardie Crescent which is the road Lee grew up on. I've been to see these houses and see for myself where Lee came from. The day I went to Lee's former family home on Keir Hardie Crescent was around May 2018. As I was in my friend's car driving along I noticed two ladies sat in their front gardens like people do when the weathers glorious. Now these ladies where in their 70's I'd say, so I gathered there was a good chance that if I asked them which house was the Duffy former family home they'd know. "Excuse me love, which one was the house that Lee Duffy lived in" I asked! They must have noticed this stranger walking up and down their street with paper and a pen, so when I explained what I was doing and why I was looking for it, it looked like it made sense to them. "That one over there with the Christmas lights hanging down" one of the ladies told me. She also said that the house next door to it was where a lady and her daughter lived and that they'd lived there over 50 years, now that did interest me. So, I thanked the ladies for the information and headed over to the house next door to the Duffy family home and gave the door a knock. I was greeted by a lovely lady named Yvonne who knew Lee very well indeed, I mean how could she not after living next door to him for over 20 years. I was thrilled that Yvonne was very welcoming and she told me a few things about Lee and what nice a lad she thought he was.

Yvonne told me:

I'm in my 70's now and I've lived in this house on Keir Hardie Crescent for over 50 years now. When Lee's parents Brenda and Lawrie Snr moved next door to me it was the back end of the 60's. Lee was only a little tot when I first saw him. I found Lee to be a smashing lad when he was growing up.

He was a kid who'd have done anything for anyone in this road. Lee was bullied a hell of a lot growing up around here. A lot of the times I would look out of my window and I'd often see kids maybe 7 or 8 years older than him bullying him. When he was 10 he was always getting clipped off say 19 year olds, I never knew why he was always getting hit by people. He never bullied anyone as a kid I mean he just wasn't capable of it as a lad.

Lee's dad Lawrie Snr was always having a go at the young Lee I can recall. Old Lawrie used to take young Lee out the back and bray him I often heard him getting stuck into Lee many a times. It was Lee's dad who wanted to toughen him up and he would take him to boxing because he thought he was too soft.

Lee broke his arm when he was only 12, he was climbing up the lamp posts outside our houses to decorate them for the Golden Jubilee in 1977 and he came crashing down landing on his arm then he ran in crying and my husband took him to hospital bawling his eyes out still.

When I used to see Lee about as a kid it was always mainly away from his home, I got the impression that he never liked being at home much because of his Dad, who was a big drinker by the way. Lee, out of his three siblings was closest to his youngest Sister I thought than his older Sister and his Brother.

Lee and his Brother, who was 4 years younger were completely different to each other, like chalk and cheese utterly. Lee's mother Brenda was just a wonderful person. She would do anything for anyone, but she had a hard life being married to Lawrie Snr. Many a times poor Brenda would come running in here away from Lawrie Snr who was also a big bloke. One time she was only in her bra and knickers and he'd been torturing her, so she ran out in a sheer panic. Every time we'd hear raised voices coming from next door it was always mainly the Dad Lawrie Snr, he was happiest being sat in the Albion pub all day in South Bank.

My husband didn't really speak to Lawrie Snr for several years. That was purely down to how he was treating his kids.

My husband Tommy actually saved Lawrie Snr's life because he'd put his fist through a glass cabinet and cut an artery in a bad way, he was losing so much blood but that was all to do with him losing his temper with Lee. There was that much blood in the house and the kids were screaming.

Of course, when Lee got older he was different to how we'd seen him as a kid, but he never ever brought any of it to Brenda's home or near us.

Lee was so polite to speak to always. One time he even saved my husband from someone having a go at him in a pub, that was just Lee looking out for his next-door neighbour. Lee even made the fella who was having a go buy my husband a pint for being cheeky. He always treat me and my family with the greatest of respect the whole of his life.

I'll never forget the day of August 25th in 1991. The police pulled up and all you could hear was poor Brenda screaming in sheer agony, it was a sound like no other, truly horrific. Brenda's front garden the week after Lee's death was just flowers and wreaths galore. People came from all over to place flowers in front of Brenda's house.

At Lee's funeral you couldn't fit into the church it was that packed. I had to stand right outside because there was just no getting through the masses of people that had turned up to say goodbye to him.

Lee's death completely and utterly destroyed poor Brenda, she was never the same after that I found. As well as losing her Son people were sending her threatening letters. In them letters it said they were going to go to her Son's grave to chop his head off and put it on top of the

Havana roof. Brenda was even considering removing Lee's body at one point just to cremate him because she took those letters seriously.

For the years after Lee's death Brenda was a lost woman. Brenda made Lee's old room a shrine to him with his pictures up.

I only have good memories of Lee Duffy. He never ever did anything but show me and my family kindness. Whatever he did in other places he never brought it to our doors.

"If you sit on the fence like a crow you have to be prepared to be shot at".

Lee Duffy

Alan McKittrick (Kippa)
The Fellow South Banker

When I decided to write 'The Whole of The Moon' one of my first thoughts was that I wanted it to be different. What I needed was real born and bred South Bankers who grew up with Lee Duffy before he was infamous, well Alan McKittrick is just that.

I caught up with Alan and explained what I was doing, he gave me his approval, as you can imagine not everyone that I've approached has said yes to me interviewing them which didn't come as a great surprise to me to be honest as there's a lot of mistrust surrounding Lee's story.

Alan spared me a little time one Sunday and we had a chat about the friend he'd known since forever.

Alan said:

I'm an Engineer by trade and now 54 years old. I grew up in the South Bank area of Middlesbrough.

I knew Lee very well and long before he gained his notoriety. I even lived next door but one to him at one point.

When I think of my childhood I can't ever remember a time Lee wasn't there. The stories that have been put about of Lee being bullied as a child were very accurate because I saw a lot of it. When Lee was young he was commonly known as "sniffer" because he couldn't breathe through his nose properly. He had a problem with is nose because he was beaten up a hell of a lot as a lad. Even the days he wasn't getting beaten on Lee would be picked on constantly for one thing or another.

Lee used to go down Grangetown boxing club and he was trained by Marty Turner. When I saw Lee suffering the good hidings he got as a lad, he was never actually beaten up, if that makes sense as when Lee got a kicking he'd just jump up and walk off, he was a very tough kid.

I always said with Lee that when he did get filled in he would get a look in his eyes, a look as if to say, 'one day I'll be coming back for you when I can fight!'

Before Lee got to the level he did I used to say to friends that he'd come back and get all these people who'd done him wrong which is what he did. I have no sympathy or compassion for the people I know Lee levelled out in his later years, like a friend of mine Spave, because I saw the way Spave treated Lee when we were kids.

I don't mean to sound horrible but Lee as a kid was your typical big dopey lad and a bit gormless looking, but when he got roughed up he wouldn't let the perpetrators see him hurt he'd just shrug it off and walk on usually muttering "No effect" under his breath.

Whenever I used to go in Lee's house he always had dumbbells and a curling bar laying around, but Lee didn't need to train as he had a lot of natural definition and a lot to work with right from the beginning. From day one, although slightly dozy, he was always a big strapping lad.

One day I was coming through an alleyway with a friend of mine Spave, this was the one that used to bully Lee as a kid, and it was around the time that Lee, who was in his late teens by then, was just on the rise. Well, I saw Lee coming towards us and I knew of the history between Lee and my mate. Like I said I'd known Lee since I was as a boy, so I knew he was gonna be ok with me, but my mate Lee wasn't gonna show Spave the same courtesy. Lee ended up punching my mate that hard on his forehead that it swelled up with an immediate bump appearing like a golf ball. When my mate hit the deck, Lee made a point of standing over him shouting "WELL NOW I'M FUCKING TELLING YOU"! I knew this was a reference to the bullying that went on a few years before and the tables had turned. Lee was just getting one back over on the bully that day I have to say. When I picked my friend up off the floor he couldn't believe that the big dopey lad he used to fling about had done him so much damage that day, it was like something you'd see in a film.

Lee used to come to my house a lot because I was always into motorbikes and owned a few. Lee would come and ask to borrow bikes to go on messages. What he was actually doing was going on little run outs and taxing people or he was off on drug runs. I remember one day he went over Brambles Farm and taxed somebody on a load of dope, he came back, and I had a smoke with him, which was a thing me and him did. I would get stoned with Lee quite a lot but when he started climbing the ladder I took a backward step away from him because I could see the way his life was heading.

Lee had got to the point of wanting to be up in Newcastle and on the drug scene all the time and wanting to become big time. The irony of Lee Duffy is, he should have went on to become a multi-millionaire, but he had other ideas, he wasted his potential of what he could have become.

To be honest when Lee was on the rise or doing his Newcastle thing, that's when I sort of pulled away from his company for a little while like I said. Lee's idea was he really wanted to make it to the top just like Al Pacino in Scarface. I was the opposite to Lee in that respect because I was very happy and content just getting stoned in South Bank.

The only times Lee was ever a bit funny with me was when I would lend him motor bikes. I never had anything too flash it was normally them little Granddad bikes, C90'S mostly, well anyway he was a bugger for getting anything back from once you'd lent it to him, if he liked it he would try to hold onto it.

In later life he used to be forever taking peoples cars off them and driving about streets with "The Whole of The Moon" song playing full blast with the windows down.

There was one day that Lee came banging on my door shouting "LEND US YA BIKE KIPPA". I told him the one he had his eye on in my back garden wasn't mine it was a friends. To cut a long story short Lee took my mates bike to go on one of his drug runs over Brambles Farm, but when he came back to drop it off Lee was tormenting me and driving off when I went to get it from him. Now this went on for say a good twenty minutes and Lee thought it was hilarious, I'd chased him from one end of South Bank to the other, that was until I went and picked up his dog Bulla. Lee used to have an English Bulldog called Bulla which was his pride and joy and he used to take it out on the motorbikes with him.

Now as soon as Lee saw me with Bulla I could see his face change. Now I'm not the biggest fella being 5ft fuck all, but I'd stood my ground with Lee by chasing him everywhere. Of course, we were very familiar with each other and maybe I couldn't have got away with talking to him the way I did if I was just the average guy because I've seen Lee arguing with massive men at times and if Lee said jump the big fellas would ask "How high"? By this point Lee's getting seriously pissed off with me because I'd picked Bulla up by his collar and made my way towards Redcar Road East and by now Lee's screaming "PUT ME FUCKING DOG DOWN". I just said to him "I WONT". Anyway, in all my years of messing around with motorbikes I'd never known one of them bikes to stall but it did. I then ran over and jumped on the bike landing almost on his lap. Now he's fucking towering over me here, but I was really annoyed because I'd been running everywhere trying to track Lee down. I told Lee "GET OFF THE FUCKING BIKE"! Lee then tells me that I'm showing him up! I told him "I'm not showing you up Lee, you're showing ya fucking self up"! I think the reason he never brayed me all over that day was the respect he had for me. If he'd have wanted to he could have smashed me into next week but he didn't like It that a lot of people saw me talk to him the way I did and with me being only small I think Lee thought it wasn't good for his reputation.

There was respect there from Lee for two things as far as I was concerned, one was because he obviously loved me, and two because I'd been chasing the legendary Lee Duffy all over whereas normally guys 6ft 6inches would run away from him, here's me 5ft running towards him and demanding my bike and not only that, I'd taken his prize possession dog as a hostage.

All the way through our lives together Lee never ever hit me. I think the worst thing he ever did was he set Bulla on my dog when he was around my Mams once for the crack.

I always found Lee to be a very tactile person, when he saw me he would always come running up like a big Doberman wanting to cuddle me. He never showed me the darker side to his personality, but on the same hand I've seen him slaughter people outside Just Ji's in South Bank. These days that's the new Police station.

I'll never forget when I was at Redcar with Lee one day in the early 80s when Lee was still a teenager and he just smashed this bouncer. That was over the bouncer coming up to Lee and saying, "are you the little prick who's going around fighting everyone"? That's all it was for that night. Everything from start to finish was the bouncers fault in Redcar that day, his whole demeanour and attitude, he wanted to test himself against Lee's rep, Lee was maybe 17 or 18 and that bouncer was easily into his 30s all day long, Lee's strength was incredible.

I have to say that Lee wasn't the innocent party many times though. I've been there when he's taxed people. Lee could never stand to see people making a fortune from drugs when he had nothing or hardly anything. Lee would take fortunes off people or hordes of drugs and take them all himself. He was never taking all these drugs off people and handing them into the police himself to clean the community up. Lee would take drugs off people with one thing in mind and if he couldn't sell them he'd smoke them, snort them or eat the fuckers…. If he took the money off people he just used to spend it, it was none of that "Well you're a bad person so I'll hand this, that and the other in". It was all for Lee's benefit but a lot of us were selfish in our younger years.

Over the last 20 odd years, and to be honest, even when Lee was alive I would hear people saying "Eeh that Lee Duffy's an evil fucker I saw him walk up to my mate and punch him for nothing". I'd just sit there thinking, hang on a minute, ya mates one of the most well-known drug dealers in Middlesbrough and he's killing young kids for fun. 90% of the time all Lee was doing was braying drug dealers and sniffing all their coke on a weekend with his mates, or if it wasn't a weekend he'd be in the house smoking big joints thinking he was an Indian with a peace pipe. Lee used to love his puff which is what I was very much into in them days too.

In all the fracas I seen Lee get into he was more of a street fighter. He never had what you would describe as a boxer's style, but he was physically fit with hideous strength. Lee was an expert at grappling which is used in today's fighting, the stronger you are the better. Make no mistake about it though, if Lee had a man down he'd not think twice about jumping on his head. There was just so many stories I knew of him breaking people's jaws or folks collar bones.

As I've already said Lee and I had known each other from little boys, so it makes it very special that I had seen him the night he died. I felt like I'd had the chance to say 'goodbye'.

I was in Just Ji's in South Bank when Lee came in shouting "NOW THEN NOW THEN KIPPA". I was sat there with a mate and we were completely stoned. Well the lad who I was with he had been funny with Lee when he was a kid. So, my mates feeling paranoid because although Lee had taxed his younger brother a few times in adulthood, Lee had never got his retribution with him like he had done with most of the men in South Bank that had wronged him and so now he's convinced Lee is gonna serve him up when he's at his peak in strength.

Lee came over to see me and he just didn't give a fuck. Normally in Just Ji's there would be special dancers up on tables half naked but Lee told them to get down so he could roll a joint in the pub. Another thing I could tell by a mile off was how much Lee was coked off his tits. So, now not only is he rolling joints on the tables but he's doing lines of coke on there too. Whilst Lee's doing this he's telling me how many E's he's already eaten. At the point of Lee saying this to me he'd only have around 6 hours left to live the poor bastard.

I declined all these drugs being offered to me by Lee because I'd rather just be stoned. My other mate can't sit still and is convinced Lee was about to use him as a human sacrifice to summon the Devil at any moment. I had to really have a word with my mate and tell him to act normal otherwise Lee would sense his fear and then he would get it. It can't have been much fun for my friend when I was in Lee's company for maybe an hour or so that evening. Like I said I'd always been at ease in Lee's company, but I could sense the atmosphere turn very cold for others and not just my mate when Lee was in Just Ji's. It may have been just as well for my friend that Lee was out of it that night. Could you really judge Lee for being funny with the people who insulted him though and branded him "Sniffer" because he couldn't breathe properly?!

There was a lot of people in South Bank who used to mistreat him and that's coming from me who'd known him all my life and before he was infamous.

Another couple of things Lee would get tormented for when we were kids was that he had quite thick lips and his trademark large hairstyles. He'd always had it slicked back so it would always make his head look bigger than it was.

Lee said to me he was going to The Havana and did I want to come with him and a few of his little hangers on but I politely declined. I gave Lee a hug and wished him a goodnight and that was the very last time I would see my friend Lee alive.

South Bank wasn't the only place I knew my friend Lee from. I don't like admitting this, but I went to Durham prison in the early 80's for non-payment of fines. This was the same time Lee was in there on his two and a half year sentence for robbery and he told me what went on in there. I'd never seen anyone with as much say in the prison system. You know when you watch these films and there's lunatics in there and everyone wants to grovel around them, well that was pretty much Lee Duffy in prison. When Lee first saw me in there he came running over to me, put his massive arms out and ruffled all my hair up. Then he asked me what I was in for? "Fucking fines" I told him with embarrassment, Lee laughed at me then told me how I would have no trouble with anyone because I'm a South Bank lad. Before I walked off he shouted to me "YA GOT ANY BACCY"? I told him they'd took it off me on my way in. As soon as I said that he grabbed me arm and said "OWAY WITH ME"! So, I followed him to the top landing, at the very top of the landing some of the cells merge and you can get 4 to 6 men in one cell. Well Lee walked in a cell which had 6 blokes stood in it and took baccy from each of them and gave it all to me in front of them, I thought 'fucking hell these 6 are gonna be out for my head' and quite rightly in my opinion. I was in there for another 42 days after that day, and no one even looked at me sideways because I was known as the Duffs good friend.

The most bizarre thing that ever happened to me was that one day Lee invited me to his cell for a smoke. Well I'm not sure if anyone has ever said this but as soon as I got to Lee's cell I noticed it was fully painted black. On one wall it had stars, like the galaxy, and on the other wall it had a great big full moon painted. I thought Lee had invited me up for a few rollies of baccy, until I saw Lee sat skinning up with these great big joints of dope. I couldn't believe how he got them in, I mean this was the 80's we're talking about here. So, I'd got my head around the fabulous idea we'd been lucky to have a smoke in prison and me and Lee were having a great laugh about back home and what we were gonna get up to when we were both out. Then suddenly a screw comes flying in our cell shouting "what the fuck's going on"! Well I've got to be honest with you I absolutely shit myself! Fucking hell I'm gonna get more time 'the lot. The only thing I could think of doing was staring at Lee's pile of mucky magazines. Well, you'd never have believed it, but Lee called the screw a right cheeky cunt and told him to fuck off out of his cell for not knocking. Believe it or not the screw turned around and closed the cell door behind him. By this point I was well on edge and I said, "Listen Lee mate do ya mind if we call it a night"? Lee's give it the big one and said very friendly like "Nah Nahnahnaaaah mate we'll just have a few more". Lee was just desperate for a friendly face I'd say looking back. Lee had everything in that cell loads of magazines, radio, milk and tonnes of fresh fruit.

In my time of being in prison with Lee I never saw him dish out any brutality. When Lee was walking around the yard I would talk to him because I was his life-long friend but there were the others, all these Geordie hangers on who used to hero worship Lee and do whatever he told them to do. When I used to see them being all over Lee I used to get paranoid thinking do I look like one of them?! I never disassociated myself with Lee, but I took a backward step unless we were on our own as you just didn't know what was going to happen next.

When Lee died there was a lot of happy people in Middlesbrough. Over the years I've had people shouting in front of me "I'm glad that fucking evil cunt Duffys dead". When they've said those things I've always had to jump in there and say, "Well they might be your feelings, but I grew up with that lad". Maybe I wasn't with him when he was up Newcastle giving Viv Graham nightmares, but I saw the shit he got as a kid and that he would get abused day in, day out so that's maybe why he went like that.

I went to Lee's funeral and it was chock-a-block. There was a lot of folk there who only turned up to make sure he was dead and to gloat. I know there was a hell of a lot people like me, who'd never had a problem with Lee and I thought the world of his Mam Brenda and his younger Brother. Lee's younger Brother by 4years, has really turned his life around from what he was getting up to in the early 90s. He's a very deep person and not like Lee in that respect. Me and him spent a lot of time together back in our youth. We spent many hours talking almost geek like shit and just about how deep life is. At certain times in Lee and his Brother's lives growing up they were very close, of course you don't need me to tell you Lee's younger Brother wasn't like him in some respects, but he did spend a lot of time with his older Brother at the backend of Lee's life and on that scene in general. I mean nobody I ever met was like Lee. When I've caught up with his Brother over the years its blatantly obvious that he doesn't really like speaking of them crazy times, he's very much into God and saving people so his old life has no place in what he does now. When Lee first died, his Brother went through this stage of his life where he would just be constantly partying and he went through more drugs than most people I know, so when he lost his big Brother he did take that to another level for a while until he found himself. I mean, we all grieve very differently, and I think it took for him to be stabbed himself to wake up and finally pull away from that life. I've always liked Lee's Brother but if you take how he was in the early 90s, to how he is today there's just no comparison. Not that I'm saying he was a bad person then, he just made some silly mistakes. Whereas now, the only thing he thinks about in his life is ways of helping other people. He has his own charity which he runs, and he keeps people off the streets, also away from drink and drugs. Lee's Brother has found Jesus and that man has a heart of gold.

Brenda, Lee's Mam, was absolutely beautiful. She was such a lovely lady and that girl died from a broken heart. For all the years Brenda lived after Lee was gone I always used to keep in touch with her, she'd always give me a knock and ask me to have a look at her car. She lived on for many, many years after Lee but in my opinion, she never got over losing her Son. I even spoke to poor Brenda only a few days before she passed away. She would always speak of her Son after his murder (yes murder) but as time went on she never really brought Lee up a great deal after the first few years. Not only did she lose her Son, but for years she had to endure the vile bastard's who would smash poor Lee's grave up on a weekly basis. Let me say this on that matter, because I know a bit about the sledge hammering of his grave stone because I've always been a local lad, so quite often than not, I heard about who was doing it and let me say this, that was only ever done by the fucking wankers who Lee taxed or by the ones who Lee had assaulted because of them brutalising him when he was a nipper. I know of a good few people that Lee dealt with in the last few years of his life and the cowards couldn't do anything about it. Now that he's dead, this gave the people who wouldn't face him up whilst he was alive the opportunity to think, I know what I'll do, I'll go smash his fucking grave up to get him back, that'll teach him. Well them people are beyond words, really, they are!

Today we're in 2018 and coming up to 27 years since we lost Lee and I still think about him so much. I think it's great Jamie that the page you made (Lee Duffy – The Whole of The Moon) was set up, certainly for the lads of my era. It's been bringing a lot of memories back when I've been scanning through it all.

When I look at my friend Lee on your pictures on Facebook in his shorts, the words "Awesome Potential" really shout out extremely loud for me. If he'd have taken more notice of wiser friends instead of being wayward all the time he would have given himself a better chance in life. Of course, Lee Duffy didn't do what people told him to do. Lee was a loose cannon. God, I saw him being victimised as an 11, 12 and 13 year old boy and he'd had enough by the time he reached 18. You can't keep picking on someone for years and it not to have an effect, because sooner or later you're going to create a fucking monster which is really what them bullies did.

The Lee Duffy from a man you wouldn't recognise from Lee Duffy the boy. As soon as Lee was old enough and strong enough to do what he wanted, well he just lived for the moment from that day on. He used to just shout "FUCK YA'S ALL" and that's how he lived his life for the 8 years he had of adulthood.

What I used to pick up from Lee was that he was fearful. What I mean is, he feared getting pissed because he would say that's the only chance people had of beating him in a street fight, so he never used to drink really. Well not more than two or three halves anyway. No, drugs were more his thing. That's why Lee sniffed so much coke because that stuff makes you sober! Have you ever tried getting pissed with the amount of coke Lee used to sniff? It would be impossible.

Lee had a sense of humour he used to like a laugh, put it this way, if Lee stuck his dog in your garden to antagonise your dog then that wouldn't be funny to you and nor to me, but to Lee he would find that hilarious. I saw him do that once and he was really giddy and all the time shouting "GO ON BULLA, GO ON BULLA".

In the court case itself I believe too much was made of Lee's bad reputation. They put it across that it was the only thing Allo (David Allison) could do because Allo was in fear of his life and scared beyond thinking straight. So much was judged on Lee's past that you're allowed to stick a knife in someone's left armpit and it was justified and he got off on self-defence. Well, that was fucking bollocks, that was murder anywhere else in the world. It doesn't matter how you dress it up i.e. the defences co-accused flung him the knife and then he took a life. After that it was made easy for the jury to only come to the conclusion of one verdict and that was NOT GUILTY. In the cold reality of how it was put across, whoever did this, then they had done the people of Teesside a huge favour, that was what was being eluded to in court, is what you'd have thought, if you didn't know Lee like I knew him.

So many truths were masked and papered over in my opinion so that one man got away with murder.

Even now, you could ask random people on South Bank High Street and say, "Who was sniffer"? and they'd say the Duffer!!!!

I have been to Lee's grave since he's been gone several times. The papers and books don't like to print that he's missed by people, but I know people who miss him.

I miss him terribly.

"It's better to live for one day as a lion than 1000 years as a sheep".

Tibetan Proverb

Mary - Childhood friend

Mary is 52 years old and comes from the same estate in South Bank as Lee did, she still works there today and runs a business. She met Lee when they were both 4 years old.

Mary said:

I'd known Lee Duffy from as far back as I can remember, his house on Keir Hardie Crescent faced directly onto the back of ours, so we all played tigs, rounders, beck jumping and kirby together as kids along with Lee's two Sisters and his younger Brother. Lee also had several half siblings.

The stories of Lee being bullied as a kid are very true. Lee wasn't a big character as a kid, nothing like he was when he was an adult. Lee was never boisterous as a boy, far from it, he was a very serious and subdued child, that's how I would have described him, he was a shy lad as well and he wasn't a jolly kid at all. It was only when Lee got into his teens that he started being the rebellious Lee that we would come to know.

Lee would go to approved school, some call it borstal, at around 14 years of age for a short sentence of around 6 months if I remember rightly. Lee was also into glue sniffing which a lot of kids were back then, where we lived that was the thing to do. A lot of my friends would get drunk with cider, but Lee was always glue sniffing and I suppose that was a way to escape his life at home, a release from his Dad.

When I close my eyes and I think of Lee Duffy as a kid I picture him as a big skinny lad with blonde hair who always had a snotty nose.

I'll never forget having a fight with Lee when we were still kids outside the Oak Leaf one day, Lee pushed me and pulled my hair, so I pushed him over and he landed in a bin and then he got up and ran home crying to his Mam Brenda, he was an extremely sensitive kid I thought, but we generally got on well most of the time. Lee was part of our crowd and we'd go to the youth club and the Oak Leaf discos. As a child I'd say Lee's main friends he knocked about with were Paul Reader who's now passed, Keith Carter and Tommy Bennett who's also passed.

I wouldn't say Lee Duffy was always massive, of course being 6ft 4 he always had the height, but it was only really when he got out of prison for the second time that he was muscular. That sentence that Lee did he went in a scrawny kid and came out a man, he was so broad.

When Lee became an adult, I did see him fighting a good few times yeah, he saved me from getting knocked out in the Talbot pub once. Some rowdy drunken bloke was about to run over and bang into me, I didn't even see him coming but Lee did, and he got up and lifted him off his feet that fast that the guy didn't know what was happening then Lee dragged him through the front doors of the pub and onto Eston High Street. Lee left that lad there like a dead dog on the floor with his tongue hanging out. My friend, who was stood next to me, saw it all and she told me this guy was about to glass me or pour a drink over me, something like that.

As we became adults he would still drink in our company, and we still had the same friends we had as kids. I always got on with Lee but yes, at times, when he was older he could be very arrogant and full of himself. In truth Lee as a man was very cocksure of himself and full of confidence in everything he did, that's just the person he became from about 21 years of age onwards. Lee to me was two people in one, the young kid who got bullied and then the man with the reputation, who we all know about.

I'll go on the record and I'll say one thing in Lee's defence, that lad had one rough childhood. Lee's father Lawrie Snr was a bully and he wasn't very nice to Lee's Mam Brenda. Lawrie Snr was an extremely heavy drinker who didn't really ever say much. It is well known around South Bank that he would bully all his kids to a point which was way beyond necessity. To be honest, it was just how people were in them days, you would never get away with bringing kids up like that today. In them days if your Dad was a drinker who beat you then it was just one of them things. Lee's Mam on the other hand was lovely and was always very well presented, always. That woman never got over her boy's death because Lee was her idol as he was to a lot of people and kids especially in South Bank. Lee was famous in South Bank and was spoken about very much, there was always talk of him going around about him taxing people.

Just the look he had about him, with his flat nose and he was always sniffing, he would put the fear of God into people walking around at 6ft 4. Lee always wore his hair tall as well, so he always appeared to be around 6ft 6, he was one big strapping lad and I do mean big.

After he came out of prison, after his last sentence in May 1990, I saw him in Eston on the bus. He got on and we were chatting but when I was looking at him, I just couldn't help myself but to say "oh my god where have you been" because he was absolutely huge. Lee took me for a drink that day when we got off the bus then took me for a meal in Bibby's restaurant and he was lovely. If he knew you and he liked you he was brilliant, if you'd crossed him and he didn't like you then it would be a different scenario altogether but that was who Lee had to be in his world.

I personally can't say anything bad about Lee Duffy like a lot of folk in South Bank. Yes, he did some bad things but so did a hell of a lot of the other people in South Bank. The fact of the matter is, Lee Duffy was a 26 year old kid who lived in a world of violence, drugs and taxing people. He didn't have any qualms about anything he did in life.

If you were in his company and he didn't like you, he'd make it known. I remember being in the Commercial Pub on Normanby Road the time David Tapping poured petrol on him and went to light a match, but he'd got it wet, so it didn't work. Lee ran out of the pub to strip his clothing off then ran back in and beat him to a pulp. Another clash Lee had was with a family of three brothers in South Bank called the Smiths. These guys will be quite old now but back 30 years ago they could all look after themselves. Lee beat the three of them up in one go and the three brothers were all in hospital at the same time, I kid you not.

For the rest of my life I'll never forget the day of August 25th 1991. I was in bed and the phone started ringing in the early hours, someone rang to say that Lee was dead. I was just in such a state of shock. I know what he was, but he was my friend.

This is going to sound completely crazy but yes Lee Duffy was a bully to some, but he was alright!

I went to Lee's funeral and it really was horrendous. I've never seen so many people go to just one man's funeral, it was held at St Peters Church in South Bank. The streets of South Bank were flooded with people and cars. When Lee's favourite song was played, The Whole of The Moon, it made everyone fall to bits, he was forever playing that song he loved it. His kids still play it today. Most people in Middlesbrough, if they heard that song would automatically think of Lee Duffy. That was his special song.

Like I said earlier, I can't speak a bad word about Lee Paul Duffy from a personal view. A lot of the bad he did to people was for a very good reason, that never really gets spoken about though. I knew a lot of the reasons and even in my eyes, and I'm a person who is very non-confrontational, they were good enough. Especially when people are trying to set fire to you!

There was a lot of the Robin Hood factor about Lee as far as the South Bank people were concerned. Lee just became so big in our town of Middlesbrough and it's quite a big place. He was feared but loved also. I was never scared to be around him. In fact, I used to stand up to him at times and tell him to his face. Lee used to tell me laughing, "I hate you, I wish you were a man because I'd have knocked you cold". He used to tell my husband in jest, "The only reason I haven't levelled that one out is because she's a woman".

The fucking animals who did a lot of damage over the years to Lee's grave were just hurtful, nasty, vindictive and evil scum. Just because they couldn't do it to Lee in his life time they'd go and smash his grave up at 4am with sledge hammers. All that did was crucify poor Brenda. It didn't matter what he'd done in life he was gone.

I'm in my 50's now but there's still so many people in the community of South Bank who have stayed there, and he's still spoken of today by us all. 27 years on, in our area, the stories of Lee in the pubs and shops are still very much alive. He'll never be forgotten. He has become a legend to those that knew him well. His stories will be told for many years yet.

R.I.P old friend X.

"Duffy enjoyed the fear people had of him".

David Woodier, prosecution witness at David Allison's trial.

John "Buster" Atkinson - Close Friend

There's been a lot of people I would have loved to have spoken to whilst researching the Duff. One of them who I'd have loved to have spoken to was Lee's close friend Neil Booth, Neil declined to be interviewed, he had his reasons and I've respected them but one person he did direct me to was good old Buster. Boothy said a Lee Duffy book without Buster would not be right because Lee loved his fellow South Bank friend. I was thrilled when Buster agreed to spare me an hour of his time at his home in South Bank.

Buster said:

I'm 69 now and I grew up in South Bank, I still live there today. Many years ago, when Lee was still about, I had my own taxi office in North Ormesby. I used to take Lee everywhere Sunderland, Newcastle and Durham and he always paid me. One particular time that I'll never forget was when Lee helped my Wife Dolly who had been locked up over driving offences. Lee had gone to my house, I wasn't in as I was in London at the time, but my Son was, Lee asked my Son where my Wife Dolly was so my Son explained what had been going on. What happened was that the drivers who we employed had been getting speeding tickets but chucking them away and not saying anything. Well, all our cars were in my Wife's name and the police came and lifted her. When Lee found out him and Boothy got the money together and went and got Dolly out of the cells it came to £500 in all and I never gave him that back because he wouldn't accept it. Lee said I'd done plenty for him and he wouldn't hear about it anymore. Not many people will know of that side to him but that was Lee all over, helping people.

I first clapped eyes on Lee Duffy when he was a young lad, still at school, maybe 14 years of age.

Lee was a very quiet lad in his school years because he was bullied all the way through. When Lee got older he told me he always resented the folk who'd bullied him, then he smiled and said, "They won't fucking bully me now though will they" and he was right, nobody ever bullied him again after he left school. Lee told me from his own mouth that he was the victim of bullying as a kid at school.

When Lee got to around 18 that's when he really changed to become the Lee Duffy we've all heard about. Lee didn't like seeing anyone bullied and he'd look after decent people. If Lee saw anyone bullying the people that he knew or any of his friends, he happily taught that bully a lesson.

I loved Lee even as a kid when I saw him walking the streets of South Bank at all hours. Lee didn't like being at home and would even walk over the blues parties while he was still at school just to stand outside and have a nosey of what he would control in just a few years from then. When he was 15 he couldn't wait to be 18 and out and about. I classed Lee like one of my own, that lad was a good friend to me and I took him all over, sometimes not even for money just as a favour that friends do for each other.

When Lee became 18 that's when I really became a friend to him, before then he was really just a kid, but I would go on to have some great laughs with him. The man that killed Lee, Davey Allo, I've had them in my taxi together laughing and joking and that's the truth. Those two were great friends until somebody mixed that.

Lee was extremely boisterous, and the big bastard was always playing pranks on me on the wind up. The day bloody Lee and Lee Harrison sent me to hospital because they spiked me they were shitting themselves. What they'd done was put something in my lemonade and I was walking about sweating like a good un, anyway I went up to the Duff and said, "I feel a bit funny, what was in that drink you've given me"? The Duff said "Ooh its just lemonade" but he was laughing too much, and I knew there was something up. Anyway, I must have started tripping and hallucinating because, at the time my taxi firm was quite small, I had a mini bus and about 5 cars but all of a sudden, I start thinking I've got over 40 plus cars. I was on the mic. shouting "COME IN CAR 43, DO YOU READ ME"!! I was completely off my head and I thought fucking hell what is going on here I was seeing things and my head was spinning and the two Lee's were just crying with laughter. Anyway, to cut a long story short somebody had to call an ambulance and I was rushed to hospital and that really put the shits up them. Both of them were never off the fucking phone thinking they'd killed me. I said to Lee when I spoke to him "You ya big fucking bastard I'll get ya back when I come out of this hospital"! I know the Duff didn't mean any harm it was just all a laugh to him and Lee Harrison.

Another night the two Lee's crept up the stairs in my taxi office and I was half asleep laid down on the couch and they ran in, the pair of them in balaclavas with baseball bats pretending to rob the place shouting "GIVE US YA MONEY". On another occasion Lee had got in one of my cars and told the driver to get out, anyway the driver comes running in crying he's had his car stolen. He said "Buster, this big cunt has taken my car off me outside the blues". Well I was outraged, I thought I'll get the fucking bastard on the mic. he's not taking my car". So, I radioed in to the car and it all fell into place when I heard a familiar voice shouting "IT'S ME YA DAFT BASTARD AND I'M COMING TO THE OFFICE, THAT DAFT DRIVER WASN'T TAKING ME TO NEWCASTLE, YOU ARE"! Well I ended up driving Lee to Newcastle that night. What I haven't said was, not only was Lee out partying in his usual pair of shorts, but he also was on the town with some kind of Pitbull. When Lee had got to Newcastle he walked in one of his friend's houses and put the Pitbull in the bed with him shouting "OI OI" and his usual "NOW THEN NOW THEN". That's the sort of crazy thing Lee used to do, he got me to drive all the way to Newcastle at two in the morning to put a Pitbull in someone's bed. What a funny man he was. Lee was always jovial and happy and kidding about with folks.

Boy could Lee fight as well, he'd done a few bits at the Wellington gym with John Dryden but also John Black did a bit with Lee on the pads. God could he hit but he didn't pick on people who couldn't fight, if you couldn't fight Lee would look right past you, unless you were selling drugs, but if you were a big lad he'd wanna wipe you out to be the talk of the town. Lee was a one hit fighter; one punch and you were gone.

Lee had been to my house hundreds of times, sometimes even when I was in jail. Well my love came up on a visit and told me "I'm letting young Lee stay with us because he's had a bit of a carry on with his Mam", so I've thought alright that's fair enough. Then Dolly said, "The bastards having parties every night and I have to go to work". God Lee did like his partying he did.

Lee Duffy was alright and if you were skint he'd say "Here, there you are have that"! He was very generous with money was Lee and one good hearted lad. If Lee went out with £20 it was spent, also the same with £500 he didn't think anything of buying everybody drinks.

I know he liked to play his jokes on me, but he was always very respectful to me and my wife Dolly. On a serious note he would never argue with me, never.

I do think Lee suffered flashbacks from his childhood when he became a man. There was something there maybe that was troubling him, and I think personally that it was about when he was bullied as a kid. I do believe that stayed with him. Not to mention that Lee had also had a rough time from his Dad when growing up. Lee had been traumatised by the bullying and that really shaped his life for the things to come in later years. When Lee got to around 18, he remembered all the cunts that used to bully him, and he went around the lot and got them all back.

A lot of bad things have been said regarding Lee but there were many times Lee did good when others were doing bad. I was there one night when Lee and Paul Livingstone walked in Rumpole's in the Cleveland Centre. Well Paul ordered a load of drinks and walked off without paying, when Lee found out he walked back to the bar and paid the bill, which in my opinion was never going to be paid by the way. When Lee found out he was outraged and its usually stories like that that get linked to Lee Duffy, now I witnessed that with my own eyes.

If you go to Lee's grave at Christmas, you'll see a wreath on it every year, for the last 27 years I've never forgotten him. I still talk about him to this day to his good friends like Terry Dicko and Boothy.

There was a lot of times when Lee would ring me saying he was in a bit of bother and would I come and pick him up and I never let him down, it worked both ways because the loyalty Lee gave to me and his close friends was never in question as far as I was concerned.

Lee trusted me and one day he said to me "You're the only person who knows where I am at all times Buster, if you have any bother ever then just ring me". I did call in for a favour once with Lee, it ended up with me taking Peter Hoe, Lee Duffy and Kevin Duckling to Redcar one bank holiday. What happened was that I had a lad named Mike who I had working for me and he pinched a car and pinched a load of watches. Well this Mike thought he was clever and was trying to pull a fast one on me until I told Lee about it. Lee was furious and said, "Consider it done Buster and I don't want any money". Lee found him, and it was settled that day but to cut a long story short, Lee did an extra month in jail for me.

Lee wasn't just famous in Middlesbrough he was famous all over. One day I took Lee to Watsons blues party in Manchester, well this big black man told Lee on the door that he wasn't getting in, well that bouncer got the shock of his life as Lee laid him out cold, I was there, and I said to Lee "fucking hell you're gonna get us shot here"! Lee just turned and looked at me and laughed his head off he was in hysterics.

Lee did go to Newcastle to hunt Viv Graham down a good few times because he asked me to drive him there. I took him every time he went. I used to take Lee and Lee Harrison to the Hacienda in Manchester and over to Liverpool partying, they went all over.

I went to see Lee in Walton prison in Liverpool, I visited him in Durham and in Armley prison in Leeds and many times I would take Lee's partner along with us.

Lee could have been a millionaire if he'd have put his mind to it, but I don't think he saw a future for himself as he spoke about death a lot. Lee told me several times that if anything should happen to him I had to make sure his girlfriend and the baby would be alright. I told him a good few times he wanted to pack it in, talking about dying all the time, but he knew it was going to come. Lee had a real morbid fascination and he could sense he wouldn't make 30.

Lee Duffy was his own man he didn't need a fucking army. Lee was a one-man band. Lee was my friend and I knew if I ever had any bother he'd have been there for me and he told me that many times.

On August 25th, 1991 I had a phone call in the early hours from a lad named Bob Smith who ran Romeo's Café, he rang me up and said, "Your friends died". I just broke down in tears then I went to see Lee's Mam Brenda at her home in Keir Hardie Crescent.

I'll never forget Lee Duffy until the day I die, he had a nice nature about him. The rats who say he was this and that, well he wasn't. I was very loyal to him and he was loyal to me. Lee never ever back answered me, and he treat me with respect.

There were two big coaches from Newcastle alone that made the journey to come to his funeral. Joel Richardson from Leeds came down and Marco who was a big name in Leeds then. The streets of South Bank and Eston were packed like it was a state funeral, they'll never be a funeral like that in Middlesbrough again.

All the hard cases that have come out of the woodwork in the last few decades couldn't lace Lee's boots. Lee wasn't a monster to us, his close friends, but we all knew what he was capable of.

People will never forget that man I'm telling you. His name is very deservingly etched in Teesside's folklore forever. He was a pain in the arse because usually as soon as Lee clapped eyes on me he started winding me up, but I loved him.

I saw Lee cry at times over the shootings, it was getting him down, he was fed up that there were people out there who were trying to kill him. Don't forget he was just a young lad.

The night Lee got shot by the Birmingham lads for the second time in the blues on Hartington Road, I got a call from *Maria Nasirat at the Gosforth pub over the border shouting, "GET HOLD OF LEE QUICK", I said "Why what's up"? then bang, the phone went down. Of course, the people had gone to his house at 6, Durham Road in Eston first looking for Lee. When they couldn't find Lee there they started on Lee's girlfriend and her Sister. By this time Lee's girlfriend was almost about to give birth to her and Lee's child. The people who hunted Lee were that low that they even took jewellery, including rings, from those girls then they went to find Lee. An hour later at the Blues they found him and shot him in his foot. Lee would walk with a limp after that. People say he was this Terminator who didn't feel pain, but I don't think he was the same lad after he was shot. He was nervous and jumpy but who wouldn't be?!

South Bank today is very different, but he's still spoken of. They'll never be a Lee Duffy again. I loved Lee and he was my friend I'm proud to say. He wouldn't get in another taxi he wanted me all the time. I will put flowers on Lee's grave until the day I die. He didn't deserve to die the way he did.

Derek Beattie loved Lee also and It's a shame you couldn't speak to him, but sadly he's in a coma. Derek would have told you all sorts for this book, God bless him.

God bless you Lee Duffy, you were one funny man and one of a kind. I owe him a lot I loved him, and I wish he was here today. Middlesbrough would be a lot different if Lee was here today I tell you. A lot of people in the Boro in the last 27 years have gone around in gangs, Lee Duffy didn't do that, he went about on his todd or with Boothy and that was it. Lee didn't need gangs.

*Maria Nasir was the ex prostitute/drug dealer who ordered the second hit on Lee Duffy, allegedly the payment was an ounce of cocaine. It is believed that Maria phoned Buster that night asking him to get hold of Lee because she'd changed her mind and just wanted him roughed up, not murdered. Lee's saving grace that night was that the gunman had poor eyesight and it was very dark.

Today, it is believed that the gunman is now blind!

"It is better to be feared than loved, if you cannot do both".

Niccolo Machiavelli

Robbie – Associate

I'm a 51 year old business man and I grew up in Grangetown, although I went to St Peters school in South Bank.

The first time I was to ever come across Lee Duffy was when I was 13 years old. My Dad owned the kiosk in South Bank on Normanby Road which was really the closest shop to Lee's house and I used to work in there. Lee was in most days and when you saw him, even at 14 years old, you could tell he had something about him that stood out and that he was different to the other kids. I guess my first experience of how Lee got his reputation as a bit of a fighter was about three months after I'd first met him and I was in Eston swimming baths. I was in there with a couple of my mates playing tigs or diving in, just doing what normal kids do at the baths. I'd like to point out that the kids who I was with that day, and there was maybe four or five of us, weren't what you would call fighters. For absolutely no reason though Lee Duffy came up and said to my mate Gary Downs, "what you looking at"? then BANG he battered my mate, who happened to be the biggest one of us all. I'll never forget it, Lee punched poor Gary with one punch and I'll tell you what, I've never seen anything like it, his nose just exploded and there was blood everywhere.

The pool lifeguards had seen what went on and ushered us all out, all of us including poor Gary who hadn't done anything at all.

As soon as we walked out of the baths Lee was stood there on his own waiting for me and my mates. He'd already beaten up the biggest so now I was the next in line in height and he was making a bee-line for me, so we started fighting. To be quite truthful the 14year old Duffy gave the 13 year old me a good hiding.

There was no excuse for his behaviour and to be honest Lee did this to a lot of kids growing up, and from what I've heard there was never a reason behind any of it. It was just widely acknowledged that it was just how a young Lee Duffy was.

That day I got a good pasting from him, but I did get stuck into him and gave him a go, the young Duffy wasn't really a name then though he was just a skinny lad. Lee didn't need to do that to any of us that day, we were just a few ordinary lads from Grangetown who'd never had a fight between us but of course Lee didn't care.

After my painful experience at the baths he would still come in the shop and I got to know him far better. He didn't tell me as such, but I think I gained his respect because I stood up to him that day, even though I got a good hiding. I also got to know his other siblings as well as his mother Brenda, they would come in the shop daily.

When I was 16 my Dad sold the shop and I left St Peter's in South Bank. I went into the world of employment and for a good three years, until I was around 19 years old, I had a bit of a fall out with my Dad. So off I went, and I did my own thing for a few years. It was around this time I started knocking around with a fella called Andy Bryan whose

Brother Paul was the notorious drug dealer from Eston. Pauls now doing life for double murder.

I became good friends with Paul Bryan and part of the crew through knowing Paul's brother. Paul Bryan had a group of us lads that basically went around doing things we shouldn't have done. Lads such as Mick Morley, Dave Green and Andy Delpth.

Paul Bryan used to get a bit of gear and supply Lee Duffy in the early 80s. This was a time when I unintentionally got involved in the underworld with Kevin O'Keefe (Beefy). Lee had just had a real run in with Beefy, but I'll never understand why because they were good friends for years.

What would happen in our little gang was that when one of us were in jail, all the others would chip in together to get the person some drugs in there, or if not, then at least give their lass a lift up, that's the way it was back then. People would help each other out more than they do today.

Over the years, I must admit I'd seen Lee do some naughty things. One night in Eston around '82, there was a club, it used to be called the Royale but it was renamed Oscars, we were all stood in the bar having a great time and Delpthy, who was normally one of our usual group, but at that time we weren't really having much to do with him because of his extracurricular activities such as burgling a vulnerable adults home, he was in our company though when Lee Duffy walked in the bar, it was like the scene in Legend where Tom Hardy plays Ronnie Kray. Lee had heard what Delpthy had been up to and Delpthy had his back to Lee, Lee walks in tip toeing with a bottle of

Bud in his hand and he looked at me, put his fingers to his lips and mimed "Ssssssssshh" then he fucking smashed Delphty over the head with the bottle. Lee was laughing his fucking head off whilst Delphty was rolling around the ground in agony. I know some of us thought that was maybe a step too far but none of us said anything and do you wanna know why, because Lee was Lee and we'd have been next if one of us had piped up. Lee Duffy alone was a force to be reckoned with.

I was in Jail with Lee on two separate occasions because I was a prolific car thief but before I went to Jail I had this fancy car and I'd gone down with Beefy one day to drop some gear off at Lee's house. Lee said to me as he looked out the window "Is that your new car Robbie"? I said, "yes Lee it is". Lee then said, "I'm having that". I was good friends with Beefy who was stood next to Lee, now Beefy was well known for being able to look after himself, and he had a bit of clout with Lee as they were very good friends, when they weren't fighting that was. So, Lee's told me he wants my car and that I have to drop it off at his house tomorrow. He told me that he wasn't paying me for it, he was just having it. When I got the chance, I turned around to Beefy on the sly and said "Ha'way Beefy man sort him out, he's gonna take my fucking car off me". Beefy's just shrugging his shoulders as if there's not really a lot he can do. Lee was really staring at me, then suddenly, he broke out in fits of laughter saying, "I'm only kidding".

The first time I did time with Lee was around 1984 I think. I was in Durham nick with him on B wing. When I first went in I was put into a cell with some idiot Geordie burglars.

Well after about two hours of me being in my cell I heard a knock on my door, I opened the door and there was a lad stood there with his belongings i.e. blankets, towels, toothbrush etc... The lad, who I'd never seen in my life before said "Lee wants ya"! I stood there aghast until the lad said to me "you are Robbie"? "Yes" I said, "Lee Duffy has sent me up here and you're to go down there to him" he said. I wasn't going to argue, so I stepped outside the cell to see Lee on the landing below waving for me to go down. I got down to Lee's cell and walked in and he slammed the door behind me. This was my first time in jail so it very daunting for me as it was but now even more so because it looked like I was being forced to share a cell with someone like Lee Duffy who I considered to be a bit of a psychopath! Lee knew it was my first time in jail and he put one of his giant arms around me and said, "Don't worry I'll look after ya". You can imagine my relief! After saying he'd look after me Lee pulled out a big lump of cannabis and rolled a joint.

Lee brought me into his cell because I was a Boro lad. He had known me for many years of course because of all the driving around I had done for Paul Bryan.

That first night with Lee and this long haired kid named Wiggy, who was also sharing Lee's cell, Lee told the screws to close our door and he continued to get stoned. Lee turned to me and whispered, "watch this Robbie"! Lee said "Ere Wiggy, show Robbie ya tattoo's"! So Wiggy stands in the centre of the cell and proceeded to take his top off and spun around whilst showing off his tattoos proudly. Lee smiled at me looking slightly evil and again whispers to me "watch this", "Show Robbie ya tattoo's on ya legs" Lee said, so Wiggy drops his trousers and starts parading around the cell again like Kate Moss. This lad was covered in tattoos from head to toe. Lee then said, "show Robbie ya tattoo on cock now Wiggy" So Wiggy drops his pants and shows me his penis covered in tattoo's. Then Lee stands up and shouts "RIGHT WIGGY, ON THE BED NOW"! Now I'm sat here thinking what the fuck am I about to watch here?! It suddenly dawned on me that I'm locked in a cell with Lee Duffy, a stoned Lee Duffy at that and I'm now becoming very paranoid. Wiggy started shouting "NAH LEE, NAH PLEASE DON'T"! This only makes Lee reply more firmly "ON THE FUCKING BED NOW"! his raised voice is met with more cries from Wiggy begging for Lee not to do it again. The penny dropped that whatever was about to go on had gone on before! By this time Lee's screaming "FUCKING NOW WIGGY OR ELSE" and with that Wiggy gets on the single bed, but he stands on it with his back against the wall. Then I look at Lee to see him handing poor Wiggy a pillow which Wiggy held as some sort of shield around his stomach and Lee starts pulverising young Wiggy making loads of boxer sounds with his nose. Basically, Lee was, and had been using this Wiggy as a human punch bag. I don't mind admitting at the time I was fucking petrified that something far worse was about to happen but because I was from Lee's hometown of Middlesbrough I was untouchable to him. Lee only kept them kind of jokes for the Geordies and the Mackems!

I did time with Lee a second time in the year he died. Both of us were on remand. In them days if you were on remand and you got a visit off your Mrs, they could bring you four cans of lager and 20 fags, cakes, biscuits etc... Then what was left you could take back to your cell. So normally in a prison visiting room there could be up to 40 blokes on a visit in that room and if Lee was on that visit, he would line us up before we went back to our cells. Lee I'm not kidding you would walk along that full line taking at least one thing from each of us, me included. Whenever I was in Lee Duffy's cell, there was normally just a big pile of contraband in the corner of it of what he'd stolen from people, you name it Lee had it.

When Lee was inside the prison walls he would always be in the gym. I wouldn't say the screws feared him but there was definitely a sort of respect there because of course they didn't want Lee kicking off, and Lee had a bit of control over the other prisoners. This time, Lee was padded up with a guy called 'Kid Mordie' who was a well known armed robber from Sunderland. Lee and this 'Kid Mordie' were well known for going up and down the landings pouring buckets of water under doors just to soak your cell on the wind up. I heard later that allegedly 'Kid Mordie' was killed by the regional crime squad by knocking him off his bike.

When I would see Lee on the out he was different with me, in a good way. It was if he had a new-found respect for me because I'd been behind the door with him.

Maybe he remembered the fight we had at the baths that day in Eston, maybe he thought I put a bit of effort into it when not many against him did but after I had done that time with him he was always ok with me.

I know he's done bad things because I have seen them, I remember being with him one day when he went to the home of a local drug dealer in South Bank named Glen. Lee went and knocked on Glen's door and asked, "Where's my money"? to which Glen replied, "I'm sorry Lee, I'll give you it on Friday" on hearing those words Lee punched him and sparked him out. While poor Glen was laid on the floor Lee took his rings off him. Lee then kind of livened him up by dragging him up and saying, "Never mind fucking Friday". Glen was pleading with him to wait for it until Thursday then but of course that was met with "BANG" he punched him again which sparked him out. Lee then left him on the floor and went into his house to take anything he could find of any value. On the way out, Lee copped Glen again and said he'd be back on Friday. I witnessed all this, and it made me wonder how he had become the person that he had. Was there something that had happened when he was a young lad? I've heard all kind of different reasons to why he was the way he was.

People have asked me in the past what Lee was really like. Well there must have been something wrong with him because this was a man who could and should have had everything, but he ruined it for himself.

At times I was asked to drive Lee around, sometimes he had his own car but I'm not sure that he ever passed his test. He could drive don't get me wrong, and let's face it, the police wouldn't have stopped him to ask him, they wanted as little to do with him as possible.

I'll always say Lee Duffy never really did me any harm in life. In fact, he really took me under his wing when I was in jail with him. I also go to his grave quite regularly even to this day, he's buried near another close friend of mine Wayne Watson.

Lee did a lot of harm to people during his life and that's why his grave got smashed up as many times as it did I imagine. There's some folk still in Middlesbrough that still have a lot of bad feelings towards Lee but like I said he did me no harm. Yes, I fought him as a kid, but I was one of the lucky ones regarding the way he was towards me.

If you knew him then he was loyal to you and he'd look after you. I say that as maybe it wasn't about me in jail but more to do with the fact that I was from "Boro". Out of the 700 in prison there may have been 40 odd from Middlesbrough and it was that number who were always going to be ok and safe from Lee Duffy. He was very proud of the roots he had I always got that feeling from him.

I always got the impression from Lee that Buster Atkinson played a big part in Lee's life, particularly when Lee was still a young lad. Buster had been a bit of a jack the lad and in my opinion knew the Duff as well as anyone.

Very occasionally, I'll hear his name being brought up in my place of work and the overall view people have of Lee Duffy is that he was a "wrong un". You hear more of the bad than you do the good by a landslide. Of course, I don't share those views.

From the day I encountered him at Eston Baths, that was Lee Duffy for me. Lee Duffy just liked punching people for no reason and I don't know why! I can still play that day back in my mind like watching a re-run of Match of The Day.

Lee was only 14 years old with a slicked back hairstyle. The one thing I can clearly recall about Lee was his breathing problems. He always seemed to be struggling with his breathing from his nose, maybe that came from his fighting I never got around to asking him about it.

I found Lee to be like two different people in one if I had to sum him up to you. I've been sat in Lee's house just general chit chatting and he's been one of the lads whilst he's been getting ready to go out, then when we've been out he's broke into random acts of violence for no reason at all. Then when he usually hurt someone it would make his night and he'd been giggling for most of the evening. What normally happened when Lee hurt someone, and he laughed, was that everyone in Lee's company would laugh as well because they felt they had to.

"I'll keep taking your bullets, but I'll keep taking all your money off you as well".

Lee Duffy in Ramsey's blues.

Darren Collins – Close Friend

I've known Darren Collins for almost 20 years and been in his house many times, but I never knew he'd had such a close relationship with the Duff until I spoke with Lee's uncle Rod (Darren's stepfather). After a couple of hours chatting with Rod he told me that Darren and Lee even shared a bedroom for a couple of years when Lee came to stay with him in Hemlington. I caught up with Darren after he agreed to speak with me.

Darren said:

I'm 52 years of age now and I'm from the magnificent town of Middlesbrough. I encountered Lee through his Uncle Rod who was my Stepfather. Lee came to live with us after he got out of Kirklevington Detention Centre when he was still a school kid. Lee was living in South Bank, but his Mother Brenda didn't want him going back to that area because he was getting into a lot of trouble, so she sent him over to our house in Hemlington which is the other side of Middlesbrough.

When Lee first came to live with us my good friend Stevie Adams recognised him from the detention centre and asked him what he was doing at my house. After explaining the full situation Stevie told me that in all the time he was in the there, Lee was the 'Daddy' even though he was only 15.

Lee had been in all sorts of trouble before he came to live with us but when he came to share a bedroom with me he was great. All my friends wanted to avoid him when we would go out and play because they said he was scary. Lee was a year older than me and a lot bigger, but he took me under his wing and looked out for me. Many times, we would sneak back over South Bank way when we weren't supposed to be allowed to go to the Oak Leaf youth club for the kid's disco. By that time Lee had stopped going to school. He wasn't old enough to leave but he just didn't bother going for the last two years that he should have been there. I seem to remember Lee being expelled and being told he wasn't welcome back. Even though Lee didn't go to school much he was very intelligent. He had an extremely good head on him and was naturally bright.

I always thought Lee wouldn't go out of his way to bother getting to know others well, so I think that made him appear to be a bit standoffish and he may have come across as being rude. I know sometimes my friends would avoid me when I was with Lee. Sometimes some kids even pulled me to one side at school and said "Please don't be bringing your Lee out tonight will ya" when we'd be planning to knock around the estates on a night.

I didn't know Lee around the time that people say he was bullied, he never ever spoke of that with me, but he was a fighter at 15 years old there's no doubt. Even at 15 years old he wanted to be the hardest kid in the area and I have to say he did shot his weight about and intimidate the other lads around Hemlington.

Even though we shared a bedroom together for the best part of two years, and you would have thought we would be sick of the sight of each other, we still spent a lot of time together.

Back then I was madly into football, but it wasn't Lee's cup of tea. I did drag him to a couple of games and even Wolves away in the F.A Cup, his Uncle Rod was driving the bus. We did go boxing for a little bit over the Rec in Hemlington with Shandy Boyce but that only lasted maybe two months if that. Boxing for Lee Duffy wasn't a serious matter although he's always described as "the former boxer" Lee was far more interested in getting up to mischief than anything a smelly boxing gym had to offer him.

Lee used to do alright with the girls and he had himself down as a very good looking man when we were growing up. Lee was one for always looking in the mirror and messing about with his hair and flexing his muscles. He used to say no girl on this planet would ever be able to resist him he was full of himself.

If I remember rightly, Lee went back to jail in November 1983 and didn't come out until 1985. That's when he really became the Lee we all knew, and he started his plans for world domination and Middlesbrough was to be his first port of call. It was during that sentence that Lee really worked on himself in the prison gym and where he really put on all his weight, I mean he was a big lad anyway but that's where he did his training and prepared himself for the combat which lay ahead for him in his future years.

I would say up until 1985 Lee was a normal lad but when he came out of jail his thought process changed and that's when Lee started taking over the town and striking fear into the hearts of every doorman. My step father Rod did try to speak with Lee and tell him he was going the wrong way in life, but Lee wouldn't listen to his Uncle. Lee fell out with Rod a few times because Rod was trying to talk sense into him, but Lee was his own man and wouldn't listen to anyone, he wanted to make his mark on the whole of Boro and he did just that from 1985 to 1991.

The last time Lee came out of jail after his last big sentence in May 1990 he must have thought, right I'm having this town and every man on the doors is going to answer to me. To do the things Lee did you've got to have some front haven't you?! But that was exactly what he went on to do. Even the times after he was shot he was back out on his crutches and he would make a point of everyone seeing him back out there. Lee thought if he didn't then everyone in Boro would think he was in hiding so he would make himself seen, especially in the blues parties.

One night I saw Lee having a carry on with Allo in the blues and I told Lee to leave it. Now I used to go to the football with Allo and I just knew what a fearless cunt he was, so I knew he was never going to back down from Lee. What used to seriously piss Lee off was that Allo would never bow to him like everyone in the town did. Lee wanted David Allison to bow his head to him like he was a king and say, "You're the kiddie", well that just was not ever going to happen believe me. Allo couldn't beat Lee in a fight, he really couldn't match Lee in that respect, but he was prepared to have a go with Lee every time he saw him win, lose or draw. Davey Allo was as game as they came and had never backed down from anyone.

I wasn't there when Lee and Allo clashed for the very last time but some of my mates were and they said at times Lee was letting Allo get back up then 'BANG BANG BANG' Lee was knocking him back down to the floor, almost toying with him. Don't forget Lee hadn't slept for about two days at that point and was high as a kite on all sorts. Lee gave Allo an awful beating though he really did.

Everybody says it ended with Lee King passing his close friend Allo the knife and that he got that one lucky/unlucky shot which was a bit of a haymaker overhand right which came crashing down under Lee's left armpit. Lee said straight away "You've killed me Allo", he knew he was minutes from death. Allo didn't mean to kill Lee, both were just bulls going at it.

I often said to Lee "let me manage it and calm it down" but he wouldn't listen. He just wanted to do what he wanted and with what he was doing he was bound to make enemies left, right and centre. These were enemies Lee just didn't need and they started off as people who wanted to be on his side, but he just wanted to knock them all out and be the talk of the town.

I know from being so close to him that Lee was getting into the idea that he couldn't be killed from all the failed attempts on his life. This was the time I think the film Terminator 2 was out and one of the things he would say often was "I'll be back". You could tell in Lee's character and the confidence he had that he believed he couldn't be killed.

When Lee walked in he'd have his shirt off more often than not and he walked with his head down and his shoulders swaying from side to side being full of himself. It was as if he was saying I'll go where I want, and nobody will say a word about it, that kind of attitude was Lee all over.

Now this might sound very hard to believe but Lee Duffy wasn't really a bad tempered lad. When he used to come into the Empire pub (Swatters Carr) Lee was just happy passing round the lumps of 'ganja' and the "E's" before we all went to The Havana, me and my mates never had to fear him, and we just saw Lee as one of the lads. He certainly didn't intimidate any of my crowd when he came in the blues. If you took the time to get to know him then he was ok. He also didn't intimidate any of the West Indians like Ramsey in there because they all got to know Lee when others didn't bother.

Lee more times than not would walk about The Havana in just a pair of shorts and a pair of trainers, that was Lee's nightclubbing gear. Of course, it did used to be really hot in The Havana.

I didn't see Lee fight a lot as an adult, I did when we were kids, but I don't think ever when we were grown up. Yes, if someone got in his way then he would wipe them out and he didn't think twice about showing off his fighting skills, but I never saw him start anything as adults. Lee was more of a street fighter, yes he could box but he was happy doing it all kicking, punching, head butting all of it!

Going back to Lee's death though I wouldn't hear of the news until the next morning and I was gutted, totally gutted. It hurt more because I said to Lee many, many times to leave Allo alone because he knew he's wasn't going to bow down to him.

I like Allo and he was a pal of mine, I don't hold Lee's death against him and I didn't at the time. I haven't seen Allo for years since I came back from Thailand, I hope he's well.

Quite often Allo would go to places on purpose that he knew Lee would be and if Lee looked at him he'd look back. If Lee said anything to him he would stand his ground, Lee wasn't used to that see, not from anyone in Middlesbrough and this really fucked Lee off.

The news of Lee's death spread like wildfire. There were people who were happy and could now open their mouths and say shit that they couldn't before.

Lee actually had said many times that he knew he'd die young. He knew he didn't have long after that kid had tried to pour the petrol on him. Lee knew he'd die young I think that's why he wanted everything there and then.

Lee used to be very pally with Lee Harrison and the pair would drive around Middlesbrough in an open top car playing their music loud.

Another bloke who Lee was very close to was Eston's Anthony Hoe. Lee had a lot of respect for Anthony. Now I never knew Anthony when Lee was alive but after Lee's death he became a good mate of mine. Anthony was a clever boxer. Years ago, I remember Lee having his first nice car and Anthony smashed it up. I said to Lee at the time "Why don't you go fucking kill him"? Lee said to me "I've known him years, you don't understand Darren" and Lee was just laughing. Lee and Anthony had had little fucking squabbles over the years, but Lee loved him and didn't want to go put it on him because he liked him so much, even after he'd damaged Lee's car. Lee had this unspoken kind of respect for him which I could never understand at the time.

I knew it got to Lee, the attempts on his life, but he used to deliberately put on a persona and everywhere he walked it was as if "COME ON THEN GET ME, I'M HERE".

Your normal club goers wouldn't notice Lee, but your doormen and drug dealers had problems. Lee would go in a club with the attitude of, if anyone wanted it, they could clearly see that they could have it!

It's been said that Lee used to go dig innocent people out but that was never the case whenever I saw him. Saying that, I did hear of one night when Lee was on the door for Barry Faulkner in Blaises nightclub and he went off it and put a good few men away and out of commission.

I think Lee did takeover Middlesbrough because there wasn't a door team in the town that didn't fear him, but he never used his brains. He just wanted to prove himself to be the man every weekend and he was the same in prison. He was also the same in childhood as I've already said.

He never put a plan financially into place. Lee was just having too much of a good time. He was the talk of town. When Lee died he was at the craziest point in his life there's no doubt about that. He was raving and popping up everywhere and off his head on the E's all the time, which he was on when he died. That's why he lost so much blood so quickly, it had thinned his blood.

I loved Lee and I was devastated for years after his death. The shit, all the gossip about Lee and the people who were overjoyed about him dying made it ten times worse for me.

Lee Duffy was a man who would have done anything for his family and friends. Absolutely anything. He certainly had some name and he was known all over the place, and still is to this day. Even when I had a bar in Thailand, many of the customers used to come in from Manchester and Newcastle etc and when I used to tell them I was from Middlesbrough the first person they'd usually ask me about was Lee Duffy.

R.I.P Lee

"Be sober, be vigilant; because your adversary the devil walks about like a roaring lion, seeking whom he may devour".

1 Peter 5:8

Gina – Neighbour

Gina is from Redcar and is now 56 years of age. When she had her first Son in the early 80's and was a single parent, she was placed by the council in the South Bank area.

Gina said:

The first time that I heard the name Lee Duffy was when I went around a lady's house in South Bank who I'd met in hospital, we were both pregnant at the same time and had kept in touch. Me and this girl became very friendly in the time I lived in South Bank, to be honest she was the only real friend I had there because I'm originally from Redcar which is around 5 miles away. Anyway, this girl who I was close to, her Brother was really close friends with some guy named Lee Duffy. I'd never seen Lee at this point, but I'd always heard his name being thrown around the South Bank estate a lot in 1982, that would have made Lee just 17.

I used to have a CB radio in the house and antennae outside on the roof to get a signal. Well of course some low life burglars had seen the thing which was on top of the roof, so it tipped them off that I had something worth nicking inside my house. So, one day I was upstairs, I had a little puppy at the time, well he was barking downstairs and going berserk which wasn't normally like him, so I ran down. As I got downstairs I noticed the curtains blowing wildly like somebody had just jumped out of the window, so then I looked on the side and the CB radio wasn't there, I'd been burgled. I put it down to just living in a bad area like South Bank, but I still called the police even though I didn't expect the police to get back to me.

The next day I was at my friend's house again and she asked me "what were the police doing at yours yesterday". I told her exactly what happened. At the time of me telling her, her Brother was there, and he'd overheard everything I was telling her. Anyway, to cut a long story short I got a knock on my door the next day from this tall skinny teenager saying, "Ere Mrs, is this your CB radio"? I told him "yes it was, and it was stolen the other day". He then told me "somebody told me about it the other day. I gathered I could find out who'd done it, so I went and grabbed him. Anyway Mrs, ere ya are you've got it back"! He introduced himself as Lee and said one of his friends had told him about what had happened, and he didn't think it was right, so he sorted it for me. I thanked Lee that day and whenever I saw him he was always dead nice to me and my Son. It turned into a joke between me and him and if he saw me he'd ask "Ya haven't been burgled again have ya"? and just laugh.

Lee was just a kid when I knew him, and it was years before he was really well known but it showed he had a good heart. I mean when he did that for me there wasn't anything in it for him.

Many years later I would hear all the stories about him and what he'd been up to, but he was only ever nice to me. What I did notice though just through living in South Bank was that Lee's reputation really escalated from when he was about 20 years of age. He was always in our local papers over the year's right up until his death.

"I spoke about wings... You just flew".

John Butchworth – Friend from South Bank

John Butchworth is from the South Bank and Grangetown areas of Middlesbrough and is in his 70s now. He now lives in Australia with his family.

John told me:

I knew Lee from when he was around 14 years of age, right up until the day he died at 26. I can remember my friend Lee like it was yesterday. I coached him at Shandy's boxing gym, that's how I got to know him.

My first memory of Lee was that he was quite a quiet lad, but very tall and lanky with a massive head.

Boxing wise, Lee was a natural puncher and he really mastered the basics of boxing and had them down to a fine art. I would take him on the pads and he had one hell of a right hand and this would play a huge part in his street fighting as he worked up a reputation for himself. He would really step in with that right hand and if he hit you then you were gone. In all honesty, Lee would never have competed in amateur boxing, he loved the training, pad work and sparring side of it, but being truthful Lee shied away from joining a proper gym and getting his medical. Sometimes, he'd come but then you wouldn't see him for weeks on end because he'd get distracted with something else.

In Lee's youth he was badly bullied because of the way he looked. People would torment him over the size of his head, his big lips, call him nasty names and say he looked Down's Syndrome. He got the piss taken out of him something terrible.

Lee also suffered mental abuse due to an abusive drunken Father who was violent to him, in my opinion that stayed with him. I know I would often see Lee out at all hours and even on a school night, and when I asked him why he was out walking the streets of South Bank he would tell me it was because he didn't like being at home.

At times, a young Lee of maybe 15 years old would stand chatting to me and the other lads on the doors where we worked for hours in the South Bank High Street pubs. He was such a nice kid in them days although very insecure and very far removed from what he was to become.

As Lee rose through the ranks as a teenager he was beaten in a couple of fights. Mark Johnson gave Lee a right beating when he was young, Lee hated him. He wasn't as invincible or superhuman in his teens as he was to become in later years.

There were two brothers in a nearby area who were known as a couple of the hardest around and they used to beat a young Lee up quite a bit. Lee also got into a fight with a lad who had a decent rep and lost that fight. Then the next day he went looking for the lad to have another go. I can't remember for the life of me that lad's name, but he really kicked the shit out of Lee. Lee was chasing him for ages because he couldn't cope with getting beat. He was really pissed off that he came second, he was still young, early teens. Lee always had to have the last word.

As I've said Lee wasn't always the tough guy that he became, and I think a big part of how he ended up was because he was kicking back at the bullies and people who'd wronged him. The two brothers who'd bullied Lee for a time at the start of Lee's reign, he would go on to beat the shit out of them both outside a local pub and the stories of what went on that evening went around like wildfire.

Lee used to love having push up competitions even when he worked on the doors. Any big guys who came in the club he often challenged to a dual to see who could do the most, he always won as well and for his size he couldn't half bang them out he really was so fit.

When Lee was around 17 I got him a little job in South Bank, this was before he went down the town working on Jonka Teasdale's door. I'll always remember one night in particular with Lee, and it still brings a smile to my face to this day. After me and Lee had finished working the doors one night we went into Middlesbrough town centre for a few drinks, he was in a great mood that night and was being jovial, it was a cold winters night and the road was frosted so it made it extra slippy. Lee started showing off to a couple of lasses who were present, and he ran and jumped in the air attempting to imitate a Bruce Lee/Jackie Chan mid-air kick, only for him to misjudge it and 'SMACK' straight on the cold hard floor and straight on his arse. Lee was laid on the floor shouting "John I think I've broke my leg"! Three fella's walking down the road had seen what had went on and as soon as he hit the deck they started howling like hyenas. Lee became extremely angry and jumped up still in pain but too embarrassed to be laid down like he was, you can imagine what happened next. Lee ran down the road and knocked the three guys out cold.

When I worked on the Havana door, literally dozens of people used to ask me if the Duff was in the club before they went in and if I replied yes, they would go somewhere else.

A lot of folk in Middlesbrough were just put off him purely because of his reputation and the horror stories they'd heard about him and although he was my friend I have to say the pubs/nightclubs were getting fed up because when he was in their establishments they lost a great deal of money because many customers kept away.

When Lee was in a nightclub there was an awful atmosphere and yes, he did scare people, many times for no reason other than to show off to his friends at the time.

I think the toughest guy Lee ever whacked was a fella called Peter Wilson, Wilson was a kick boxer. Lee broke his neck and ended up on remand over that assault. I was there that night and it was me who put the poor fella into the recovery position after Lee had walloped him. Lee smacked him when he wasn't looking, and it whiplashed his head back so fast it broke his neck. The guy was well and truly fucked! It was said Lee had hit him with a beer can because surely nobody could cause that much damage with a fist, but it was done with Lee's right hand, I was there and I saw it all. One thing I will say is Lee was a fucker for sucker punching! He was a master at it, hence why he always knocked people cold. He did the same to Brian Cockerill and nearly put him away until Brian had to grab Lee and wrestle him into a wall. Lee told me it was a draw, apparently they both were knackered and just gave up calling it a day.

Of course, Lee and Brian became great mates after they fought, and the pair were a couple of nutcases who bounced off each other when the two of them worked together. These two were a nightmare to the drug dealers on Teesside. Brian once knocked me on my arse when I kicked him out of a club for causing a problem. I ended up with a chipped tooth and a black eye. The next day Brian came to my front door and apologised and said how out of order he was and that he wanted to take me out for a drink to say how sorry he was. I ended up inviting him in for a drink and all was forgotten. It really was crazy times back then.

Lee couldn't end the night without sparking some poor bloke out and bragging about it later.

Lee also took poor Martin Clark's eye out and that's how he received his four year sentence in March 1988. He wouldn't regain his freedom again until May of 1990.

Lee had some mental issues in my opinion, I'm sure he had some form of ADHD or something wrong upstairs because he just wasn't normal, far from it.

One thing I remember telling him was to stop fucking picking on people and taking it too far, I said, "eventually someone is going to get to you", his reply would always be "Aah fuck em". He really didn't give a fuck at all.

He seemed tough to most people but to me, he was paranoid all the time and would always be looking over his shoulder. Lee quite often used to get one of his mates to run in the blues parties and check if the coast was clear first. Not because he was scared of anyone at the time, they'd be no man capable of going toe to toe with Lee no, it was because he was sick of getting shot and of course people were out to get him big time in Middlesbrough. No matter where he would go, folks were out to get him. Lee would get twitchy when in big crowds and he would get drugged up to ease his nerves, but then when he was on drugs he would turn into an idiot. Anybody who ever challenged him got a right hand to the jaw, that was a weapon of mass destruction on its own.

It's true Lee did go up to Newcastle to deal with Viv Graham in 1990. Lee went with around five lads this time, but he'd gone up on his own at times. Two of Lee's friends were carrying guns when Lee made his entrance to one of Viv's doors, as soon as he was in arms reach he smacked one of the bouncers and demanded to speak with Viv. Viv was one of the biggest cowards of all, he was a bully who only hit people when he had a firm behind him. As soon as Lee hit the bouncer he put him out cold and a couple of the others stood back as Lee's mates were pointing guns at them. The reason I know so much about this was because Lee stayed at my house that night. Lee told me in such detail and kept going over and over it, he was laughing his head off whilst coked off his tits. Lee would often come and stay on my settee, particularly when the police were looking for him. He would get coked up and he loved his ecstasy tablets. I preferred him sober and drug free but even when he wasn't on the sniff and pills he would be smoking big joints of dope.

He rarely went to the gym in the last year of his life because he'd done all his training during that last big sentence he did.

What I'd like to get across to the readers is that in all honesty, it wasn't until he got out of prison at almost 25 years old, that he really built up the Duffy rep. Yes, he always was a tough fucker, a really scary tough fucker but the last year of his life he went to another level. In that one year he really kicked the shit out of everybody in Middlesbrough. He built his rep and then got killed. I'm telling you now the Duffer rep was built within that year before his death.

Lee did have a decent side to him though, he did love the people around him. I know Lee was a good Dad and he was very respectful towards his girlfriend, he just wouldn't settle down because he enjoyed being the tough guy too much. He liked people talking about him.

He could never hold a job down because he hated being told what to do.

What you must remember is that at times in Lee's life he had nothing else going for him apart from that he could fight. He had no money and hardly any clothes, nothing. So, when the whole of Teesside started talking about his weekend missions he liked it and it obviously made him feel important.

He would do anything for his family and friends, he just should have done more for himself that's what I think. He had the potential to be somebody better, but he just loved that atmosphere in the clubs of Teesside. He was a young fit, ridiculously strong lad full of confidence and talent, but he pissed it all away, and for what? That image? To be stabbed at 26 and buried in a cemetery in Eston? He knew it as well, as did many others in Middlesbrough, it was going to happen at some point, but he just wouldn't leave people alone.

Bullies always get what's coming to them in the end, always.

That tragic summers morning in August of 1991 when Lee was stabbed, I was at home and I got a call in the early hours of the morning to say Lee had been stabbed and it was serious, I just went to bed and didn't think anything of it because he'd been shot a few times and always managed to come back like the Terminator. I thought this would be no different! Oh, how wrong I was. That do Lee and Allo had in the car park of the Afro-Caribbean wasn't their first, on and off they'd been at it years and Lee always had his number. Lee punched the living daylights out of him around a fortnight before that as well.

I know I seem critical of my friend Lee but what I tell you is the truth. If I've said anything negative about my mate Lee, then I'm sorry but I won't lie. Lee was my good friend, but he was a bully to a lot of people around him, he had a huge ego.

If my chapter ruffles a few feathers, then so be it but I only speak the truth. He was my friend and I so often tried to offer him advice like to stop picking on people because it would come around. Lee would get drugged up and corner people in the Havana nightclub demanding money or he would do them in etc... Just random people who were walking past or in the toilets. He would bully them for no reason other than to prove he was a hardman and how feared he was. Lee was also ordering people to get him food, he just seemed always hungry.

One of the biggest tragedies of the Lee Duffy story is he never even got to his prime years. Can you imagine what he would have been like at 30-35? I like to think he'd have moved away and made something work long term, of course we'll never know now will we.

I used to tell Lee many times to get into boxing seriously because he liked fighting so much. It was the strict discipline of a fighter that didn't excite him though. Boxers can't hang around illegal blues parties in the early hours taxing drug dealers of their ill-gotten gains! By the time a boxer was up at 5am for his morning jog Lee would be just going to bed. He wasn't somebody you could say "No, No Lee, do it like this" because he would just tell you "GET FUCKED"! The amount of times he told me to go fuck myself I lost count.

Another thing that is true about Lee is that he was a bugger for pulling guns out in clubs. Men who are fearless don't need to carry guns with them, which is exactly what Lee did. I suppose in his defence if I'd have been shot as many times as him or had the attempts on my life like he had I'd have done the same. People knew you couldn't beat the Duff in a fair fight so of course they would use the guns on him.

I do have fond memories of my friend the Duff. He was always good to me but one thing that did used to piss me off about him was he was never on time for anything. He was also a horrible bastard on a morning after he'd been on a night out, he'd come around my house on a morning and empty my fridge at will. He'd down pints of milk in one like people would down pints of lager on a night out for a laugh.

In the mid-eighties I did time for armed robbery, I'm not proud of it and it's something that is now well behind me. I was in Durham prison when I would meet up with Lee again and the prison legend ex-heavyweight boxer Paul Sykes. There were a lot of real hard men of that era like Gary Nelson who had a fearsome reputation inside and out of prison. Colin Gunn of Nottingham was another very feared and hugely intimidating man who had a documentary made about him. For me though, in my life, I've never met anybody who is as much the real deal as Paul Sykes was. If you put every hardman of that era in a room, then Paul Sykes would have walked out on his own in my opinion.

When Lee was in the nick the same time as Sykesy they were watched like hawks because the screws knew there was tension between the two of them. Lee absolutely hated Sykes because of the rumours about Paul Sykes being a prison rapist.

Paul Sykes was a real legend to many and he was the main man in every prison he went to, so you can imagine this didn't go down well with Lee. Paul Sykes was a real hard man who'd been a professional fighter whereas the Duff was feared due to his bullying ways, but to my knowledge it never went off between the two.

Many years after prison I would become good friends with Paul Sykes and I'd go through to his house in Lupset, Wakefield to have a good drink with him. Lupset was a right rough shithole.

Me and Paul always had to go drinking in Dewsbury because he was banned out of every pub in Wakefield. Paul used to have me in stitches and he could burn your ears off he talked that much, he always had to be right even if he wasn't.

I liked Paul and I still have a copy of his book Sweet Agony signed. Paul would have kicked Lee's arse and the Duff knew it. I'm not saying Duffy wasn't a hard bloke because we all know he was, but Sykes was a trained pro fighter who'd fought John L Gardner for the British and Commonwealth titles and could have gone far if it wasn't for his drinking and his jail time. Paul wasn't afraid of anybody.

In the past the Duff always made a play for any of the top guys in the prison, but he never did that with Paul. I would say Lee was cautious around Sykes for sure. He had the opportunities to have a go at Sykes but he never, Sykes ran the joint when I was in there with them both.

Paul Sykes would easily have knocked Lenny Mclean out in one round the time they were supposed to fight, only for it to fall through because Paul had had a fight in some pub pissed and got a cut above the eye, so he had to pull out of the fight he was supposed to have against McLean in 1979.

Paul was such an intelligent man as well when you got to know him. That man had some fights inside with some tough blokes.

Both Sykesy and the Duff would do some serious training when they were inside. I was in the gym when they were both in there but to be honest they never paid attention to each other. When Lee and Paul were in the gym together there would be a wall of screws separating them. It was certainly the tensest situation I've ever seen inside prison walls.

They don't make them like Paul Sykes and Lee Duffy anymore that's for sure. Men these days are turning into women. What I loved about Sykesy and the Duff is they weren't afraid to be themselves and go out of the norm to create some fun and make someone laugh. Neither gave a fuck about anybody or anything.

Lee has become somewhat of an urban legend over the years. Yes, he was a nutcase in a fight but a lot of the stories I've heard regarding the Duff have been greatly exaggerated.

I do think that now it's only right that his life is being documented because a lot of people don't really know what went on with the Duff. I think this book needed to be done so we could show him in a new light. I'd always hoped over the last 15 years that this would happen and I'm only glad to contribute. I think most of Lee's family just wanted it all to go away when Lee passed but, he's still very much spoken of today and I'm in Australia speaking about him still.

I still have connections to Teesside but usually my only way of contacting my old friends is through social media, but I've always kept a close eye on my old friend Lee's legacy.

This book is a long time coming and I'm very pleased about it. Teesside will never forget that man.

R.I.P old friend.

"It was Lee who got bullied and beat up. There was always gangs of lads chasing him, always someone waiting to pick on him or tease him. When Lee was younger people made his life hell. No wonder he grew up the way he did. I went to school with Lee, from juniors to seniors, and most of the time that Lee got into trouble it was because there was always someone pushing and daring him to do something. In a place like south Bank you have to learn to stand up for yourself and learn to fight, so Lee ended up with a reputation. Even if Lee wanted to settle down, no one would have let him. I remember Lee from the soft and gentle boy to growing up to be a hard but gentle man, he was really a nice guy. It's his Mother who I really feel sorry for, having to go through what she has and still is, but no matter what Lee did or didn't do, he's still her Son and I think every mother will understand what I've just said".

An old school friend, Sharon, The Evening Gazette, February 1993

Harry - Close Friend

I'm 59 years old now and I grew up all over Middlesbrough.

From around the time I left school to my early thirties I led a very different life. A life that took me to many different prisons across the country. I have a lot of friends from my crazy days, I keep in touch with them because I'm a very loyal person, but my life is completely different now. I wouldn't want my Grandkids finding out some of the things that I did in my past.

Lee was a very good pal of mine. I first met him when he was just a boy of maybe 13 or 14 in Masters nightclub (later to become Rumours). He was in there because his Mam Brenda used to take the money on the door. I knew Brenda and I knew her brother Rod (Lee's uncle) who still has a shop on Acklam Road today. Lee would always be in and out, in and out of the nightclub as a kid and drinking coke. The young Lee was always in good spirits and I used to say he was obsessed with wanting to know what me and my mates were up to. Obviously, it wasn't even legal for Lee to be in the pub, he was only in there because his Mam brought him to her work, so she could keep an eye on him.

Lee couldn't wait until he was older to be in places like that, he wasn't interested in doing things that your typical teenage boy was in to, he was in a rush to grow up. He was just so keen and eager to find out what the older lot were doing, the generation above him. Of course, I was maybe 8 years older than Lee, but he was always very respectful to us, we were adults in his eyes when he was still a schoolboy.

Lee would see me and my mates in the club and to put it bluntly, we were a bit crazy at times.

As he got older, the respect he had for me and my group stayed. From the day I met the young Duff, I always described him as a stallion. I knew, even when he was a kid he was going to be something different something special.

Lee, even at the young age of 15 had this aura about him and he was wild! I could see that the teenage Duff was going to be a stallion and as he developed into a young man he surpassed that and became that and more. I knew at the end of the 70s that you couldn't have put a saddle on Lee Duffy. Lee was just a special, one off kid and we did a lot of good things together.

I became really close friends with Lee when he started boozing around the age of 18. He kind of latched onto my little circle of friends, the same friends that he'd stood back and watched from being a schoolboy.

A few times the young Duff came out on what was called "The black un" with my circle. We'd normally go out at 12.30pm and start at the Masham pub, which was just outside of The Hill Street shopping centre, and we'd drink right through the day until we lasted. I knew then that Lee was coming through the ranks, and I certainly won't mention any names, but there were lads in our group who were, sort of the boys at the time, or thought they were and Lee was already challenging them in the way he was talking or the things he was doing to them. I know a few of them who could really have a fight quickly gathered that Lee was going to be too much for them to handle, he just had too much about him to sit on the side-lines.

Lee never had any fear! The one thing that came across if you were in Lee's company was that he was fearless. Nothing or nobody fazed him. As he got older that stayed with him because I remember talking to him one Sunday morning in one of the pubs over the border. Lee was in there on crutches because he'd been shot in the foot the week before. I used to meet Lee and my friends every Sunday to talk about the previous nights events from the Middlesbrough night scene. Lee had this thing on his foot and he pulled it off and said, "Ere have a look at that"! It wasn't good, there was a complete chunk of his foot missing. I told Lee he shouldn't be out, and he should be at home resting. Lee was there in his usual shorts and t-shirt. Lee agreed with me but told me "I am what I am, and I do what I do". Lee put his arm around me and gave me a kiss, as lads do. I just told him to be careful. At that point, another kid came over to us and said to Lee "You shouldn't be out"! Lee then looked at him, pointed his crutch in his face and said, "You don't fucking dictate my life" and this kid literally shit himself. The kid quickly skulked off to the toilets. I said to Lee "there was no need for that" Lee said, "but I was only joking with him" and he was. That kid thought he was bullying him but that's just literally the way he was, you were always better to know Lee, that was his sense of humour.

Lee was a phenomenon in every aspect of his life. He didn't worry about anything, money didn't worry him because he never had anywhere to put it because he was always in shorts. He was never money orientated.

I'm sure the attempts on his life didn't faze him either. Lee even told me a few times that somebody would get him in the end, I told him not to talk like that, but Lee said, "That's the way it's gonna be" and how right he was. Lee knew the life he was leading, and he'd crossed the paths of some dangerous people and that wasn't just in Middlesbrough, that was further afield too. Lee was well known all over the place, I had many nights with Lee where we'd just jump in a taxi and go off to Sunderland or Newcastle.

I've read a lot of books over the years and Lee put me in mind of big Frank Mitchell who ran about with The Krays, everywhere we went people were frightened of him. What Lee Duffy was capable of really oozed out of him in abundance, he was so powerful. Of course, with Lee he didn't just have the physicality, but he had the no fear factor.

Everybody has said Lee Duffy was this big ex-boxer but in actual truth that was crap. Yes, Lee had been in a few gyms and punched a few bags, but his biggest asset was his power. He had the power and no fear and when you put them two together you've got a dangerous man. He was just an all round natural big man, I've never seen legs on anyone else like Lee Duffy's in my life. My sister has photos of him sat in our back garden in shorts and they were tremendous. Like tree trunks. He wasn't a boxer for one reason only, it was because he lacked the discipline. Lee really trained everyday so who's to say that if he'd have had a different mindset he couldn't have become a champion boxer! He was so powerful with great balance, anyone with two tree trunks for legs was always gonna be powerful.

Another thing that people don't link with Lee Duffy was he had a heart of gold. Me and my Brother used to graft, but sometimes if the money wasn't there Lee was straight there to look after us.

What does stick in my memory is on his 21st birthday. Lee had a big party arranged upstairs in the old Empire pub but me and my brother hadn't been grafting so went to his Mam's in South Bank with his birthday card. We told her we were skint and couldn't make the party. By the time we got home Lee had left a message with our Mam to make sure we turned up, we did and the first person at the top of the stairs to greet us was Lee with a little envelope and a big smile. "Enjoy the night boys" he said.

Lee did have a mean side to him though, one day I'd been out walking with him and his English Bulldog Bulla. Well there was this old Alsatian barking, so Lee picked Bulla up and shot it in the garden with the dog barking. I said, "Fucking hell Lee, Bulla will kill it". Lee just said, "Well I'm sick of it fucking barking".

One memory I have of Lee is of him coming to my house in his usual shorts and t-shirt and telling me his Sister was having a problem with an ex-boyfriend of hers. This lad was one of the well known local hard cases at that time. Lee was still very young, but he told me he was going around to sort him out. I told Lee to maybe think twice because the fella in question wasn't half a big lump, he was also a real knockout merchant himself. Of course, Lee wouldn't listen and said to me he was going to give him a talking to. "I'll come with you then Lee" I said, he told me in no uncertain terms that I must not move from my front room, and that he'd only be five minutes. Lee put his glass of orange juice down and off he went. He told me he'd only be five minutes, well he wasn't even that! He'd been and ironed out this really big man on his own, and he was only a kid then as well maybe 18 years old if that. Lee told me he'd sorted the problem out and told me to get ready because we were going out to a few pubs. I'm not going into what that was for, but that guy got a hiding off Lee and it was quite deserved, he'd done something pretty bad.

A lot of people used to hear of Lee's acts of violence but let me say this, a lot of them were justified in the sense that people had done things to people that they shouldn't have, and Lee just wouldn't tolerate peoples shit.

Another night that I had with Lee and one of my Brothers was very strange. I was in his house in South Bank when he pulled this thing out. Now I'd never seen anything like this before, this was still the early 80s remember, it was a big kinda pipe. Something like what you buy in the shops for bongs. Well I told Lee I didn't do stuff like that, but he insisted. He wouldn't leave me alone until I'd had a go of this big bloody Indian pipe thing. So, I have a go to keep

Lee quiet and straight away I could feel my fucking head going all over the place. So, I'm getting completely spaced and Lee had been taking his turn as well. He was a bit of an expert in this field. It's crackers what happened next, but Lee left his front room and went and brayed on his next door neighbour's door, this was about 11pm as well. Lee made his next door neighbour drive me, and my Brother in this pickup truck down town to the old Middlesbrough police station. As soon as we get to the station, Lee starts singing songs as loud as he can. The police came out, saw it was Lee Duffy and went back inside away from him. He didn't give a monkey's toss!

I did go to see Lee at Walton prison in Liverpool on his last sentence. I'd taken his girlfriend down and when we were in the visiting room waiting for him to come in, one of the guards came to our table and told us that they'd been an altercation only moments before, Lee wouldn't be allowed any visits and he was now down the block. The staff of Liverpool nick wouldn't tell me or his girlfriend anything else, so we had to make the trip back to Middlesbrough without even seeing Lee. When Lee did finally regain his freedom, he told me what had happened. Lee said that just before he was about to see us, he realised that there was three 'nonces' on the same visit as him so he went over and "took one of them out" I think that's the way he put it.

Lee had an awesome reputation from the age of maybe 18 years old.

What I will say is when he came out of Walton nick in May 1990, it was a month before his 25th birthday, so in the last

16 months of his life his rep rocketed. Having a rep like Lee had was what Lee wanted. He was never a person to be sat in the house watching the soaps and settling down with a pipe and slippers. He was only a kid himself and he'd got famous in the town of Middlesbrough and beyond, Lee knew what he had and the power he had.

I bet you'll speak with others and they'll tell you that Lee used to walk in places and bully people, well people felt intimidated for no reason by him at times.

Intimidations a funny thing! People felt intimidated because they heard Lee Duffy was in the vicinity, they didn't have to feel intimidated personally, he wouldn't have done anything to them for nothing. It was his name, and then he'd come in looking the way he did, and the place would empty. There was no need for the place to empty! Lee didn't chin people for nothing, it was the name and the reputation that emptied rooms, not Lee himself.

When you got to know Lee Duffy, he was a gentle soul, he was good craic and he'd always kiss you goodnight if you were his friend. That was the Lee Duffy I knew, and he was a nice person. I knew him a lot of years and we didn't have one crossed word, he was my pal.

They'll never be another kid like Lee Duffy. He was a one off and we'll never see his like again, he was a wild stallion and you could never put a saddle on him. It didn't matter what age he might have got to 26 or 56, there was never going to be a saddle on him. He was a wild horse and he could never be tamed, I just wish he was still here now.

His name will go on forever in Teesside, my Grandkids will hear of his name. How and why will his name live on forever when he only lived to such a young age? He was just that wild kid who made his name and shot to stardom.

For the right reasons or the wrong reasons, he was what he was, and he'll always be spoken about. The people that knew him and really loved him, are very different from the people who didn't know him but hate him. Listen I have no doubt there's people out there who he fell out with and he punched and there's probably genuine reasons for that, but for that single incident they hate him for the rest of their lives, but I never saw any of that. He was just a young kid who got too much and too far in such a short space of time. The song by the band The Specials 'Too much too young' sums my friend Lee's life up for me perfect. He was my pal and I loved him.

R.I.P Lee X

"I saw the rain dirty valley… You saw Brigadoon".

Stephen Lenaghan – Fellow Bouncer

Stephen Lenaghan is from Berwick Hills, Middlesbrough and is now 55 years old. He's a painter & decorator by trade but he worked the doors and had done a bit of boxing in his time, he can clearly remember, to this day, how he took a young Lee Duffy on the doors with him.

Stephen said:

I'd never heard of Lee Duffy until the night he came to work on one of our doors when he was only around 18. I was on the doors on the old Albert pub on Albert Road across from what used to be the Wellington but is now Flares. Around that area you'd have Rumours nightclub, the Old Mint, the Royal Exchange, Henry's and Wickers World, they were all rough pubs to drink in, in the 80s.

That first night that he worked the door with me I looked at him and thought what a big lad he was at 6ft 4, he was just so tall and muscular, and he had a very smart appearance.

My Uncle whose door I ran had told me some kid called Lee from South Bank was coming down to work with me for the night. Within minutes of him being on the door I could tell he was a bit naughty. He told me he didn't like football, all he liked was boxing and fighting, that's what he told me his interests were.

The first night he was on I could tell he was checking all the other bouncers out over the road at the other nearby bars. Because I'd been there a while Lee was constantly asking me who he was, or was he hard or could he have a fight etc... Over the year I figured out what he was doing, because when Lee asked me if this fella was hard and I'd said yeah, he'd end up wanting to go and knock them out, so I got wise to him and when he used to ask me if that fella or this bloke could fight I'd always say "No Lee he's a quiet lad" and that would satisfy him and then he'd ask about somebody else.

Over the months of working with Lee he went on to fill a few of the other bouncers in. One night in the Albert, a big gang of lads had come in and started getting rowdy, Lee came over and banged this lad who must have been easy 20 stone, he hit him that hard that when the guy fell on the brass foot rest on the corner of the bar his head put a dent in it. From that night in 1983 onwards when I worked the doors with him he wanted to be the man.

Lee would become sort of a mate of mine and we would work together for a year but there's no getting away from it he was a naughty lad. Anyone who said anything other than that about him are talking crap! Lee also went on to work the Blaise's, the Welly, La Roche's and Rooney's doors for my Uncle but wherever Lee went in them days there was trouble.

When Lee would work the doors with me he'd often just have a sit down and roll a joint in the pub and didn't care who was watching. As I got to know him through working with him I can say he always treat me with respect, but everybody in the town was terrified of him there's no doubt about it. He was taxing people and he was such a bad lad with it, he just wanted to kill everybody.

I've never seen anything like that lad in my entire life and if he walked into a pub it would go silent. Even a few of the lads would tell me when he was in the gym sparring with them in the Welly, he didn't want to fight you, he wanted to kill you. He wasn't a loud person by any means either as you'd expect, but he went around things quite quietly and coldly.

I know when he was on La Roche's door he'd have a bet with whoever he was working with about who could knock the most lads out in one night. Lee would win them games all the time by a landslide I'll tell you. One night I worked La Roche's door and Lee was playing that game with big Mac, as I went in Colin Bacon was also on the door and he told me we were expecting trouble from a few lads from Whinney Banks and Parkend. Colin showed me this big box from behind the counter full of baseball bats and coshes, he said if it gets too much just use some of these.

You wouldn't believe what you could get away with in them days. When Lee worked the doors in the 80s it wasn't like today where it's all SIA licences, them days if you were violent it helped you get the job. Middlesbrough was a mad town and if there was any violence at the time it used to be just a "free for all" and the bouncers wouldn't hold back. There were some handy lads in the town at the time like little Kevin Auer and Boola who were lunatics, and sadly both dead now God rest them.

Kevin had a few goes with Lee Duffy, Lee sorted him, but that man didn't take a backward step from anyone, Boola was a knife merchant who'd stab you as soon as look at you.

Like I said Lee always treat me with the greatest of respect from day one when he came to work on our door as a young lad and I showed him the ropes. He never forgot it. Yes, he was an absolute lunatic but luckily, he liked me, and I knew him quite well but there's no denying what he was, he was a bully. Of course, he was badly bullied as a kid, so I'm told by the people who grew up with him.

After he left and was no longer working with me I would see him over the years and hear of what he was getting up to and I could see the path he was going down. Every weekend they'd be a story that he'd knocked this bloke out or taxed that person or that he was doing things with drugs.

I think there was something wrong with Lee because of the way that he wanted to hurt people all the time, that's just not normal is it?! He had such a short fuse and you could see his anger came like someone had switched a light on, it came that quickly.

One night, Lee was on Charlie Parkers door next door to Blaises and a fight broke out. A big gang of lads were fighting, and Lee ran into the middle of it, grabbed this lad by his long hair and dragged him across the dance floor all the way up the steps at Blaises entrance and flung him outside, I've never seen anything like it. He was quite sadistic when it came to hurting people. He wasn't too bad in Rumours nightclub for some reason, but there were some handy lads on Rumours door though like the Moloneys and the Jaffrays, it was probably the toughest nightclub in the town at the time, the music was great in there and anybody that was anybody went in there, Lee was forever knocking people out everywhere else in the town though.

Lee was quite a serious person looking at his personality. His aim in life was to take over the town of Middlesbrough which of course he did. He was always sizing men up if they were anywhere nearby, and from 18yrs to 26yrs old he definitely put his stamp on the town.

Lee, although he had his good friends like Lee Harrison and Neil Booth, very much did things on his own, he was never bothered about anybody. I mean I live in Redcar now and I heard about all the stories of Lee going to Redcar on his own and doing all the door staff, he'd fight three or four at once I'm not kidding you. Lee had no fear and that was what got him killed in the end.

Lee got shot a few times and he'd always say like the Terminator "I'll be back". It's healthy to have a bit of respect for people in a fighting sense because he'd done a bit of boxing and he could fight, he was the fastest and most powerful man I've ever seen even to this day, I've just never seen a man in my life like him who didn't fear anything. I could see it coming when Lee died, he was always going to get killed in the end and he got involved with too many bad people.

A few years after Lee died I was working in Stoke, I was on a site doing my painting & decorating. Now there was a Geordie fella on site called 'Tiny', he must have been about 6ft 8 and 25 stone all day. So, one day on a lunch time he started telling me about when he was working on Viv Grahams doors in Newcastle, I told him I did the doors as well. 'Tiny' then goes on to tell me about the time he had had a "do" with a lad from Boro, as soon as he said that I knew whose name he was about to say, "They called him Lee Duffy have you heard of him Steve"? Of course, I told him I knew him, "What happened then 'Tiny"? I asked, he went on to tell me "Lee came up from Boro on his own and starting demanding to know where Viv Graham was", he told me "he knocked me out then he went in the club looking for Viv". I don't know how true it is, but this 'Tiny' told me Lee got Viv that day in the club and done him. I don't know why he'd lie because he didn't know me obviously, we were just on a shop fit and started talking about doors. That was Lee all over he'd go anywhere on his own.

Fighting wise Lee could do it all, street fighting or boxing he knew what he was doing. What a powerful lad he was, and he could hit like a heavyweight boxer with either hand. He knew that people were petrified of him, he thrived off it and loved it.

I was in the Albert bar during the day with Lee when he pulled a gun out and pointed it at his mate John's head. Lee put one bullet in it and spun the chamber and pulled the trigger, of course it didn't go off, but he was playing Russian roulette with his mate's life there and he had a one in six chance of killing that poor fella, the lad ran out of the bar shitting himself because he knew there was a bullet in it.

Another night I went in the Madison with Lee and a load of other lads including Kev Ducko. My Uncle had all the doors in the town apart from the Madison. One night about five or six of us went around the Madison because one of their bouncers had had a go at one of ours so we went around to sort it out. Lee and Ducko ended up giving some poor fella it that night as well.

He'll never be forgotten in the town of Middlesbrough, it will never ever see a lad like him again, not in our lifetime.

When Lee was about in the 80s that was when Middlesbrough was the roughest place in the country. I've travelled all over the England working away and I've never seen anywhere as rough as Boro was in the 80s.

Lee Duffy really is part of Middlesbrough's history there's no denying that.

I met the kid on the door and although I wouldn't say I looked after him as he didn't need looking after but I showed him the ropes if you like and he never forgot it and seemed to like me. When I worked the doors, I wasn't a bad bouncer, I was firm but fair, but all Lee wanted to do was hurt everybody.

As I've said he was always ok with me but believe me, you didn't want to get on the wrong side of that lad because he was really bad. He was cold and calculated with it as well. I don't want to call him but that saying of "You live by the sword you die by the sword" well that sums Lee's life up well for me. I knew he was going to die long before he did I'm afraid. Lee just wanted to be the main man in the town, end of.

If Lee had had a business brain he could have been a multi-millionaire by now, but it was never about the money for him. He wanted to be No.1 and he attained that notoriety in the end, but it cost him his life. He paid the ultimate price and ended up being a very young man in a grave in Eston. Lee made that many enemies in Middlesbrough and when he died people where having parties everywhere in Normanby and Eston because he'd hurt that many different people during his reign.

"There won't be another bloke like Duffy, he was a one off".

Detective Chief Inspector Brian Leonard

Reuben – A Man of Duff's era and a Mine of Information

Reuben is a Middlesbrough lad born and bred. He is now 48 years of age but is a very well connected man with a wealth of knowledge regarding Lee Duffy. Of course, that was his generation and he grew up in the heart of Middlesbrough.

Reuben said:

My Brothers were around 4 years older than me and I can remember them coming in talking about the name Lee Duffy. I was only 13 or 14 but both my Brothers were Lee's age and went to the places Lee did i.e. The Havana, Blaises and Rumours like the rest of that generation. Back at that time the place to be was Rumours nightclub because it was rough as fuck. Middlesbrough has always been a hard place to grow up in anyone's generation.

At that time in Rumours the bouncers were lunatics and the place was heaving with so called hardcases. Rumours also had its fair share of cranks and weirdo's my Brothers used to tell me when they came in.

At the time I was just a young nosey inquisitive boy listening to their stories of what their night was like. Listening to my Brothers' stories I just couldn't wait to be another few years older so I could find out what the fuss was all about. Until I was at an age where I was legal to go out I would be brought up on stories from my Brothers of Ducko and Lee Duffy. My Brothers told me one night

Ducko knocked a fella out, and how that Lee Duffy would stand there with that big fucking chin on him, bulldog face and chewing chewy with just a vest on saying "Alright"? to everyone whilst looking them up and down and if they were a big lad they'd be given the "death stare" by Lee.

For years I was told those two were horrible people and my Brothers warned me to keep away from them when the time came for me to go out drinking. Duffy and Ducko were a very naughty pair indeed and the people who were around Middlesbrough at that time will be nodding their heads in agreement at reading this.

Kevin Duckling from Berwick Hills was a big hitter back in the day and he's who Lee Duffy modelled himself on. Its common knowledge that Lee idolised Ducko and wanted to be exactly like him.

Middlesbrough really was full of supreme hard bastards, I mean why do you think, for a little town, the Boro Frontline (Middlesbrough F.C hooligan firm) were so feared and had the biggest rep in the country in the 80s?! The Boro frontline would travel all over the country 150 mob handed and clash with any firm in the country. All the big city firms like Everton, Leeds, Swansea, Cardiff and Chelsea have had many infamous battles with the Frontline for decades. Middlesbrough as well as Redcar, Thornaby, Billingham and Stockton are fighting dens for men as tough as they come.

When I first started going out drinking it would be in a place called The Roseberry in Whinney Banks when I was around 17 years of age. Like a lot of my mates, I would use fake I.D to gain entry to these places. So, one night I was in the Roseberry when there was a guy who went in there called "Fatty Clarkson". Fatty was a big 6ft 3inch lad around 20 stone who was a little slow. Well Fatty was known to be capable of having a bit of a fight with anyone. He did the doors and had a good name in the town, because of his good name Duffy, I was to hear, had clipped him a few times.

Most weekends in 1989 when I would go in the Roseberry people would be talking about this Lee Duffy and he wasn't even at large. Lee was serving a 4 year sentence and wouldn't be released until May 1990 but all the same people never used to shut up about Lee Duffy. Well one night I was sat in the Roseberry with Fatty Clarkson when I just couldn't stop myself from asking Fatty "What's this Duffy like"? At the time I'd been getting into scraps myself. Fatty turned to me and said "PHWOOOOAR, he can't half fucking handle himself yeah but he's a bully".

Lee did a bit of boxing training in the Roseberry boxing gym in Whinney Banks with George Unwin. George now lives in Spain.

Back in that time in Middlesbrough around 1990, people on a bank holiday wouldn't go out on the Sunday, everybody waited till the Monday. Well I remember hearing from Fatty a tale of Lee going in the Acklam pub and flattening a fella called Richie Kieron (now sadly passed) and Lee was getting irate because he couldn't put him away.

The weeks prior to Lee getting out in 1990, the whole of Middlesbrough was talking about it. Lee Duffy's name in jail was bigger than it was in Middlesbrough and of course he went around every prison making his brand bigger.

One night after Lee's release and out of sheer nosiness, I was blind drunk so that helped with my bottle, but I went in Rumours. Now Rumours had two floors, upstairs was where the DJ box was, so I was on a scouting mission to be honest. Up until then I'd never seen Lee Duffy in my life, of course I'd had years of being told the horror tales that he would walk in The Trooper pub and make all the drug dealers empty their pockets on the pool table, but I'll never forget looking over to the DJ box and thinking, that's got to be that Lee Duffy! Now I'm 6ft myself and around 17 stone so I suppose I was in danger of been confronted by Lee, as I was looking over I could see it was Lee because I'd heard he had a flat face and a boxer's nose and hair combed back. So, I was getting closer and closer almost starstruck if you like looking at this man I'd heard of for the last god knows how many years. As I was getting closer I popped to the bar to get myself a half, then when I've turned around Lee Duffy's stood over me like fucking Count Dracula staring at me. Immediately, I've sobered up and the only thing I could think of was, FUCK ME HE IS A BIG LAD! He was a good 4 inches standing over me and the one thing that struck me was how lean and alive he was. Not just big like your normal looking weightlifter, it was as if Lee had the leanness of Thomas Hearns with it. I really was just a bit numb and Lee looked at me and shouted, "ALRIGHT MATE"? I just muttered something back through sheer nerves and quickly moved away and that was the very first time I would see the legend that was Lee Duffy. I knew it was Lee before I knew if you know what I mean, he had a special aura about him if that makes sense.

I would go on to see Lee Duffy very close up over the next year in The Havana. I even saw him in there a few times after he got shot when he was on crutches. Many a time Lee would be stood in the front door way of The Havana. I'll never forget going in with a big group of lads from the Parkend estate and one of the lads had one of them lighters which was a gun, anyway you fired the gun and a flame came out. Well my mate said "I'm gonna go pull this out on Duffy", I said "don't you fucking dare you'll get us all killed". Anyway, he went up to Lee and pulled the gun out on him, Lee laughed it off and told the lad to put his lack of chest away, as the lad was shirtless.

I would hear of the tales at that time of Lee going looking for Viv Graham. I know that Lee went up Horden and gave a few of the doormen up there a whack just to wind Viv up.

Another night Lee went up Horden to a social club where Champion Bodybuilder Eddie Ellwood ran the door. Well one of the doormen was a well known 6ft 3 18 stone bodybuilder called Clip, Duffy got out of his mate's car, casually strolled over and said "You are two big lads, I'm Lee Duffy" then banged the pair of them putting both of them on their arses. Afterwards the whole club came out and picked the two doormen up and chased Lee and his friend John Fail all over. John said it was like a scene from the film American Werewolf in London where the full village were chasing the wolf, only it wasn't a werewolf they were after it was Lee. John Fail said Lee nearly got him killed that day and he'd not even done anything.

Another night around 1987 at Bentleys over Stockton, there was a few bits of nasty bother with Lee again throwing his weight about. The club owner got one of Viv Grahams best doormen from South Shields. Yet again I won't name him, but he was a well known hardman up there and a British judo champion and the other was a well known boxer. After the trouble erupted that Lee had started, the two men decided to escort Lee from the premises. Both had Duffy by each arm, but he charmed them into letting him go and with that Lee clattered the pair of them.

There's a fella called *Rob Doneathy and he's a 6ft 5, 22 stone bodybuilder. Rob lives down the South West now. Back in the day in 1991 he used to be on one of the doors over Stockton when Duffy walked over with boxing boots and a vest on, he stood within touching distance to Rob and said "You are a big lad, I am Lee Duffy and I'll be back to see you" then walked off. Rob and the rest of the doormen were just stood there in shock, all of them. The reason Lee never did go back was because he was murdered that very same week.

These are not rumours, and many people saw these accounts of what I'm telling you for this book.

Another one of my friends who was the head doorman of the Theatre and Club M was sporting two big black closed eyes around 1990. When I asked him what had happened he said, "That fucking Lee Duffy from your way has been through causing trouble", I never asked anymore questions after that.

I knew Peter Wilson who Lee hit in Wickers World in March 1990, now I'm not saying he would have beaten Duffy, but he'd have given Lee a go if he never hit him on the sneak because Peter was a decent kick boxer. What Lee did to poor Peter really took its toll on the lad physically and mentally.

*NOTE FROM ROB DONEATHY "Lee did come down to the Mall door which I was on. Lee was dropped off by a fella named Craig Howard. Lee came towards us door staff in boxing shorts and boots. As soon as I saw this big figure I asked my pal Micky who the fuck he was, and he said "It's that lunatic from Boro Lee Duffy". Lee came towards us as far as the reception then he walked back to the front door. He put his back to the wall and started asking us why he was barred out of the club as well as out of Tall Trees! Ali Johnson a Grangetown lad spoke with Lee while he walked him back to the front door. Lee shouted he was Lee Duffy and he would be back. He never came back as he was stabbed and killed that very same week. Lee wasn't happy and told us because he was barred out that it made him look weak to the people of Teesside. I think the fact Lee only ever came to our door once was down to Ali's brother Mark Johnson than anything else. Mark had also knocked Lee away from Tall Trees. Lee Duffy should have been worth a fortune to be honest, but he had too many hangers on and they were using his name for their gain. That's just my opinion of course".

Duffy worked his way up the ladder of hard men of which Jonka Teasdale was one of the biggest names for a good while, then in the end Lee belted him and broke his jaw.

Lee clashed with Ducko and Elvis Thomo in the Cleveland pub in Linthorpe, but Elvis didn't want to know. Lee and Ducko would always be squabbling amongst themselves as to who was going to be the first to do their next evil act. Lee and Elvis later made up while doing time together in jail. Lee and Ducko did have a big fall out but I never did find out what that was over.

The Nivens family and their Grove Hill gang were feared all over Teesside in those days they were all very violent. One day Lee walked in the Empire pub (now Swatters Carr) on his own and said to Terence Nivens "Fuck off out the pub and take your cronies with you". Terence and his gang walked straight out of the bar with their tails between their legs.

Lee also gave a couple of lads it who had come from Leeds and were in Ramsey's blues. Boro had played Leeds United that day at Ayresome Park. There was something like two thousand Leeds fans in the away end that day and they'd been hell on at the match. At the end of the game the Boro and Leeds fans clashed badly on Clive Road outside the ground, so there was already a bad atmosphere around the place. These two fellas had turned up to the wrong party and Lee made a mess of them both. One of them lost an eye and that's why Lee received his 4 year sentence.

Every time I was to see Lee, he was always on his own and wearing shorts. I never saw Lee engage in any violence but one night in I was to see Lee and Molly Jaffray marching out of Rumours looking very angry and pissed off with each other. It was clear they were about to fight each other. The pair disappeared into Middlesbrough train station, but I never knew what happened between them. I've spoken to Michael Jaffray, Molly's Brother, about it and he confirmed they were about to fight but he never went into any great detail with me.

People used to say Lee and Ducko used to stand on Rumours door betting each other a fiver that they couldn't knock out the next punter to come through the door. In all the times I was to spend in and around Lee Duffy's company he was always very nice to me. Even though I was a big lad and would fit his criteria for someone to wallop, Lee knew I was maybe 4 or 5 years younger than him and I think he could sense I was just a kid compared to him.

Lee Duffy didn't always have it all his own way though, I know a few of my mates like Peter and Danny Wood have had run ins with him and stood their ground. Don't get me wrong Lee Duffy was formidable and my mates Peter and Danny are old men now but when they were on the Bongo door he never got all his own way in there with them two. One night, Lee came to the Bongo door and old Abduli said to him "Nah Lee ya not getting in man".

For years old Abduli carried a knife in his pocket purely with Lee Duffy in mind. Abduli had already killed someone by stabbing them in London many years ago before he came to Middlesbrough.

Peter and Danny were stood there and Lee out of the blue swiftly upper-cutted little Peter and then Peter hit his head on the glass counter. Peter and Danny then got stuck right into Lee outside the Bongo. Then a couple of weeks after that Lee came back around with one of the Teasdale's and there was another mass brawl.

The Wood Brothers had a few good scraps with Lee Duffy and his gang. What Lee used to do is get people to drive past the Bongo and he'd point his fingers at them both like a gun. It was happening all the time, Lee would go around the Bongo and Peter and Danny would get stuck into Lee. One night, Lee went around the Bongo and chased a fella called Tommy Stevenson from South Bank, who I believe killed himself a few years ago. Anyway, Lee was torturing this Tommy and he was cowering like a dog in the corner and Danny said, "OI FUCKING LEAVE HIM ALONE DUFFY MAN HE'S PETRIFIED OF YA" then Lee's shouted back so Danny shouted to Lee "do you want me to take his place"? and Danny ran straight out with Peter, and Duffy fucked off that day. The Wood Brothers put it on Lee loads of times.

The biggest battle I think they had was when Duffy, Johnny Fail, Sean Day, Fraca, Elvis Thomo and Chrissy Duncan went into the Bongo and there was literally hell on. The two Woods Brothers, Abduli, Mardy and little Alan massacred them, absolutely smashed fuck out of them with weapons. After that John Fail said he was in hospital for a fortnight and John Fail tells the truth, he said, "I was laid on the floor getting smashed with hammers by little Alan the Somalian, who was lifting my trousers up to smash my ankles". Duffy's gang all made for the doors because they were getting murdered. Little Peter Wood completely laid Fraca out across the doorway so the doors wouldn't open. It was like something from a horror movie with hammers and blood was flying everywhere. Afterwards people had fractured skulls, fractured skulls galore. That night in the Bongo was as violent as it gets on this planet.

Little Peter Wood who's only 5ft 6 had a few run ins with Lee. Little Peter even went around the Welly one time on his own and pulled a knuckle duster out on Lee, that day Ducko got in between them. After that scene Peter stayed in the pub and played dominoes with all the old men.

Duffy often used to go around the Bongo shouting the odds at the Wood brothers and another doorman called Camelot, but they weren't mugs. The three of them would be armed to the teeth with bars and other stuff. Those three wouldn't have given it a second thought to do Lee in and Lee wasn't stupid and always made sure it was more of a slagging match than anything else a lot of the time.

Now Camelot was game, nothing to look at but a dangerous bastard. The Bongo has always had real tough men on the doors. Even after Duffy got killed there was all kind of trouble brought to the Bongo door.

One night I heard Abduli tell one of Lee's henchmen that he wasn't getting in, one of the doormen stepped in and tried to help by just standing firm and saying "Listen you aren't coming in mate" he never manhandled him or anything just showed him the door. Then 30 minutes later the guy comes back with a sawn off shot gun loaded up and tried to shoot Abduli and the doorman but Abduli managed to get it off him but only because he thought it was a stick and not a gun Abduli said afterwards, and then they both went to town on him. That guy was out to murder them until his gun cartridges fell out, he really got the beating of his life after that. Afterwards the police got me in for questioning as I'd witnessed it all, but I said I couldn't remember and didn't know who it was because I wouldn't grass him up. The first question the old bill asked me was "was it Keith McQuade"? The barmaid who worked behind the counter in the Bongo did make a statement to the police and the lad got 3 years for it. That all escalated from Lee Duffy, he started it all.

When Lee got out in May 1990 he went to the Bongo again and started demanding to get in with Abduli. Abduli said no to Lee and that he didn't want him in. That's when Lee was shouting that the Bongo needed to show him some respect as no door in the town ran right without Lee Duffy's involvement, that was why he punched Peter Wood on the chin as I mentioned earlier and Danny and Peter were into Lee like terrier dogs. The word around the town the next day was Danny Wood had done the Duff. From that point on Duffy kept turning up in cars working himself and being confrontational. Also, Danny Wood used to stalk Duffy in his car around South Bank and it was doing Lee's head in. Danny's car was always getting smashed up and he had Lee Duffy and Terry Dicko as prime suspects. It's a good job Lee and co left Danny's car alone after that because Danny started going to work with a garden folk in the back of his car. Peter and Danny didn't give a fuck about the Duff and Lee knew it.

Danny Wood had one hell of a battle with Lee's mate Elvis Thommo after Elvis offered him out four times. Now, Danny's a quiet man and declined but flipped when his brother Peter said, "Get out there and give him it"! Elvis was boxing Danny and Danny just covered up until Elvis gassed and when he did he picked him up and bounced him off the floor then punched him twice and split his head open. That's when his brother Peter pulled him off saying "you'll kill him".

Danny Wood was an old fashioned weight lifter in his day and in Durham jail he held all the records for weight lifting until Paul Sykes turned up. Danny could bench 350, 560 dead lifting and a 500 squatting. He was one fucking strong man and in them days not many people could lift like him.

What I will say about Lee was he was always respectful to the older generation. I'll never forget one day when I was in The Green Tree pub in the town and Lee came over and sat with the old boys like Macca Harding and the legendary JP aka Jackie Parsons. Little JP was a proper fighting man back in the day and had a huge name as Middlesbrough's top fighting man. I wasn't sat at the table, but I was next to it and I saw Lee come over with a round of drinks for all the old gents. Lee lent over and said, "Can I ask you something Jackie" Jackie said. "of course Son", Lee said "was my old man a hard case or not"? Old JP smiled at him and said, "Do you want the truth"? Lee just nodded, and Jackie told him "your old man was just a big shithouse Son". Lee just nodded and said, "Fair enough" and carried on playing dominoes with them. Lee was in awe of even being around old Jackie that day and wouldn't let him buy a drink all afternoon.

Another thing about Lee Duffy was that if he was in a pub, he would stand on the front door as if he was running it. Even if he had fuck all to do with the place or the bouncers he would stand there like he owned the place. The bouncers would still let Lee do what he wanted and never said anything, unless it was the Bongo door of course!

Peter and Danny knew Lee from being a kid because they used to work on a place called Masters (before Rumours) and Duffy used to go in there from maybe 14 years old with his Mam Brenda. Lee was a kid and full of himself Peter told me, even at 14 years old he'd be taking his top off in the pub shouting "LOOK AT MY SIX PACK". Peter and Danny told me they'd think what an ugly looking little bastard he was, and he was a bully even then! It was around that time when Lee was approximately 15 years old that he gave his old fella Lawrie Snr a good pasting, Brenda told a few people about it.

What you've got to remember was in the 80s Teesside was one rough place with some seriously hard men like the Stockton lads. Lee was forever over Stockton in the nightclubs and had his clashes with "Oathead, Smiter and Smiggy. Them three lads were part of a gang called The Wrecking Crew but there was maybe twenty or thirty of them in total and they were all dangerous bastards who always caused mayhem in Stockton.

Lee was close to a lad named "Ginger Maca" from Thornaby but really, he just took the piss out of him. Maca was selling the gear at the time and Duffy used to go around his house and bully the life out of him, give him a slap, tax him and sleep with his girlfriend.

Another thing that not many people will know, but I can confirm was that Lee Duffy used steroids. Lee Duffy was fucking full of them! A bodybuilder called Craig Howard (now sadly passed) was the original bodybuilder in Boro and he openly admitted to me he got Lee on the juice. Before that, Lee was maybe 14 and a half stone and really lean like his Brother. Then when he came out after his last sentence that's the time he became fucking massive and put a good 4 stone on from what he usually was. What I will say is Lee did well on the gear, some lads have a natural infinity to it, some have natural genetics to neutralise it, he did. Lee had huge thighs on him with a very small waist, huge traps. He was the most perfect build for any boxer I can tell you. Lee's huge right hand was really spoken of when he would get into these fights which have now become something like urban myths. Lee was always on the lookout for big units, so he could bang them out and build his rep, it was a big stage.

Lee knew he was the best fighter in Middlesbrough but as for him and guns, I didn't see that with him until he got in with the Sayers from Newcastle. I think he thought well I'm a gangster now I've got to do it, but Lee Duffy certainly didn't need any guns. Guns weren't really him that was all for show firing through doors at blues parties or firing through taxi roofs. Lee Duffy was a fist fighter and his thing was to go around smacking people for anything.

One night I was out with a load of Eston lads on a bank holiday weekend and we'd been all around the town, we were having a meal in the Estedia (was the Europa) and one of the lads who we've recently just buried, a lad called Paul Robinson aka Popeye, great kid wouldn't hurt a fly, he left us to go to the Belmont which was located on Southfield Road at the time owned by Freddie Vasey. I pleaded with Popeye to stay in our company, but he wouldn't listen and off he went. Anyway, I bumped into him the next day and the poor fucker had his jaw all wired up. It turned out that Duffy had walloped him for nothing. Now Popeye, you just wouldn't start with him because he was a lovely lad, he'd never had a fight in his life.

After he hit poor Popeye I know that some lads went to see Lee's close friend John Fail the next day. They asked John "Have you heard what he's fucking done"? Cut a long story short John went to see Lee and said, "You're out of fucking order there Lee he's a great lad him". Lee told John that he was sorry, and he'd shake his hand, but it was too late by then he'd broke the poor lads jaw. Poor Popeye died only about 8 months ago.

Duffy was also seeing a girl from Whinney Banks named Leslie. Lee, I must admit was a hit with the opposite sex, girls just love a bad boy don't they and he was as bad as they come. Well, Leslie had an ex of who was only around 5ft 3, Lee ended up breaking his jaw also. The amount of jaws Lee must have broken in Middlesbrough was staggering, literally it happened on a weekly basis.

That was also around the same time Lee set about Davie Bishop. Davie had a bit of a go back with Lee but Lee was too much for anyone.

Lee did another dirty trick with the big scaffy Paul Salter when he smacked him in the toilets of the Havana nightclub. He never laid Paul out, but Paul said he was not having a go back that night because his legs had gone.

Another time Lee walked in the Madison nightclub and told all the bouncers "For the next 15 minutes nobody comes in here or goes out", now the Madison had some fucking hard lads on the door like Paul Manders and various other martial arts fanatics etc, but you know what, they did exactly what Lee Duffy told them. Of course, the reason behind Lee doing this was because he was paranoid that the enemy was in town. This was after the time that Lee had been shot to the knee and the foot, twice on separate occasions, within only a couple of months. Lee went around the Madison that night obviously searching for someone.

The Madison at that time used to house over a 1,000 people but Lee's word went so you can understand the fear this man could instil even into the hardest of men. Nobody in the town on any doors stood up to Lee Duffy apart from the Bongo lot. Even old Abduli carried a knife at times prepared to do the Duff in, he wouldn't have fucked around either. It wasn't only the Wood brothers that Lee met his match with.

A fella named Marconi from Leeds came through looking for the Duff also an ex-boxer named John Depledge from

Harrogate had started running the doors in Boro. The word at the time was that Duffy and Ducko were trying to muscle in on his doors, or at least knock a few doormen out. Marconi came through and called a business meeting with Lee and Ducko. I heard from good authority that they basically took Lee Duffy and Kevin Duckling somewhere and pulled guns out and threatened to kill the pair, it was said they got the message. What is a fact is that Ducko bumped into John Depledge a while later in the Bongo (yes that fucking place again) and Depledge started on Ducko, this ended up with Kevin Duckling laying him out in the club and then outside again in the car park. John Depledge used to have the door in the Trooper (now Camels Hump) near the student area.

Another fella who the Duff had a few rucks with was David Fields aka Fieldsy who did 20 years. He had killed a man and done a lot of time but although he was half Lee's size he didn't give a fuck about Lee and had a go with him.

The Hoe family from Eston had many a clash with Lee as well, they'd have their own stories on their clashes with the Duff.

I'll never forget the morning of August 25th 1991. I walked in the Roseberry pub that Sunday morning and all the old boys were sat talking about it. Now there was an old scaffolder in there called Alan Round and he shouted over to me "ERE, HE GOT DONE LAST NIGHT EH, I KNEW IT WAS GOING TO BE A FUCKING SCAFF". Of course, David Allison (Allo) was a "Scaff". All them scaffolders have their own craic and most consider themselves hard cases.

To be honest I was taken over with emotion and so was the whole town of Middlesbrough. I was stood at the bar but all that was going over in my mind repeatedly was FUCKING HELL DUFFY'S DEAD. I will say one thing that fucking knocked me sick that day was I know loads of people in my town of Middlesbrough who had parties. Even my closest friends were but I never agreed with it because its fucking terrible. Take it from me Parkend was booming with joy.

As I've already said Lee Duffy was a formidable force but no way invincible. It's widely known Mark Johnson from Grangetown got stuck into Lee outside a pub up there and Duffy's pal had to pull him off Lee.

One tale of Lee Duffy will always make me smile was of him driving through the pit villages in Durham with the roof down and shouting to all the doormen "THE DUFF'S IN TOWN, THE DUFF'S IN TOWN LET EVERYONE KNOW THE DUFF'S IN TOWN". One of Lee's favourite things when he was in Newcastle was to walk up to a door and say, "I am Lee Duffy" and walk off, or say "I am Lee Duffy" then flatten whoever was stood there.

Keith Mensworth who was a big 6ft 3 18 stone doorman once asked me "Who's this Lee Duffy from Teesside"? I just laughed and said, "Why what has he done"? Keith said he was working on a door one day when he came up to him and said "I am Lee Duffy" then laid him out and the fella he was working with. Poor Keith said when he woke up he was just looking at his other injured door mate in disbelief thinking what the fuck has just happened here.

As much as Peter and Danny Wood had their run ins with Lee what I find extremely admirable is Peter, who's now in his 80s still lights a candle and says a prayer for Lee today. He is still plotting his revenge though on Elvis Thomo 28 years on from a confrontation he had with Elvis and big Brian Cockerill outside of Steel City gym on Marton Road.

Middlesbrough in the 80s was a ridiculously violent place but it was only ever business for the people playing at the time. It was the world they chose to be in. Peter and Danny Wood, Abduli and even Mardi were all brave warriors against Middlesbrough's typhoon which was Lee Duffy and they took no shit, just the cuts and bruises.

Peter and Danny are two old school hard men who kicked it in Durham jail with Frankie Fraser, Paul Sykes and John McVicar. Both were in Durham nick when the last hanging ever took place. Danny even battered Newcastle hardman Fred "The Head" Mills inside a prison workshop. Mills was shouting "GET HIM OFF ME"! Danny nutted him a dozen times and Danny was there when Billingham's Alan Cowley stuck the head on prison legend Paul Sykes. Alan stuck the head on Sykes and had him out of there, Sykes didn't get a chance. Cowley ended up in a wheel chair, he continued his bullying ways way's over Stockton until one day a lad took him out with a brick and finished him.

Lee literally fought every hardman or would be hardman in Middlesbrough through the 1980s. Never again will planet earth host a man who fought as much as Lee Duffy did.

From when Lee Duffy was 18 until his dying day at only 26, them 8 years were filled with regular violence and chaos. The "Battle of the Bongo" which was reported in the Evening Gazette was all started by Lee Duffy and finished well after his death leaving four hospitalised.

Lee Duffy never had what you would call a gang because everybody in Middlesbrough knew he was a one-man army. What Lee did have was a good few hangers on. If you look back at what really started the "Battle of the Bongo" off, it was because Lee Duffy one night was made to pay, and he didn't like it! Nobody got in that Bongo club without paying the door staff made sure of that.

That first night Lee turned up with Dale Henderson-Thyne and Terry Dicko and just demanded to be let in but that was never going to be the case with old Abduli who only died a couple of years ago aged 104. After that night Lee caused havoc as I've already said, turning up with the Hoe family from Eston and Paddy Moloney and it went on and on for such a long time. So many times, the blows never rained but it would always lead to a big fucking Mexican standoff with Lee and the Wood brothers.

Another well known face Lee didn't get all his own way with was with a fella named 'Podgie' Foreman. Podgie was another who'd done a bit of time on the Bongo door and like them all, had a go with Duffy. The only way you got on that Bongo door in 1990 was if you could really have a fucking fight! That was the only door in the full town of Boro that would stand up to the Duff ask any of Lee's close friends. There was no divvies on that door let me tell you. Everybody paid, the occasional Rumours staff like

Molly Jaffray were allowed in but that was pushing it. Going back to Podgie though he'd had a ruck with Duffy on the Bongo door alongside the Wood brothers.

When Lee was drinking in the Sporting club in South Bank with Derek Beattie one Sunday afternoon, he invited him and Podgie to a stoppy back in the Ship Inn which was over the border in Middlesbrough. Anybody reading this will know Podgie was an all day drinker and he just used to go for it when he was in a bar. This day ended in Duffy smacking Podgie in the back of the head which laid him out cold. I couldn't tell you why, he just did! This was still when Lee was a young lad, he was maybe 21 or 22. Of course Lee was very well known at the time, but he wasn't as ferocious as he would become at 25 and 26, but he was still a big young buck working his way up the ladder of the Middlesbrough crime world. Podgie woke up the next day without a mark on him, but he had been put out and that would happen if Lee Duffy decided to lay one on you. The next day Podgie went looking for Duffy asking his sidekick Kevin Duckling where he was, Ducko replied to Podgie "Go home Podgie ya blind drunk, you won't catch him drunk even if you find him because he always stays sober"! Lee Duffy never used to drink much because he knew he was gonna be fighting all the time.

A month after Podgie was put to sleep he was to come across Lee again at 2pm in the afternoon. Podgie was walking through the train station coming from the Bongo to go into the town and who did he bump into but Lee again. Now Podgie was a man about 5ft 8 and 16stone, just a little chubby lad but strong as hell, never trained or anything but well made. As Podgie saw Lee he shouted, "Ah just the man I wanna see" and with that, words were exchanged which led to the inevitable which was the pair of them getting torn into each other. Podgie, to be fair lost the fight but he ended up getting a good few blows stuck on Lee which Lee didn't like. When you get a 16 stone lad who isn't scared like Podgie wasn't, well he gave all the trouble to Lee that day. At the end of it Podgie said we were both "paggered" but Lee shouted, "Have you had enough" and Podgie said "if you've had enough I've had enough but I'm not bothered". After the fight I'm not sure if they shook hands but Podgie said to Lee "You don't like being hit you do ya son" and he didn't.

Now I've spoken to Lee's close friends in the last four maybe five months and it ties into what they said about Lee. They said that they saw Lee Duffy knock some big meatheads out, but I've seen him struggle with dickheads and people who were not in his league. You've gotta understand the last time Duffy got out of prison in May 1990, there was lads in the town that fucked off to London and stayed there until he was dead. A lot of so-called hard cases in Middlesbrough kept well away from anywhere the Duff ever frequented i.e. The Havana etc... Lee Duffy didn't care about anybody in Middlesbrough, even when they were trying to shoot him. I won't mention any names, but I know a few other lads who were planning on shooting him if he'd never have died when he did. These men were that fucking sick of what he'd been getting up to for the last 8 years.

From when Lee Duffy came on the scene in around 1983, until his incarceration and his eventual death it seemed that the town of Middlesbrough had been holding its breath, in 1991 a lot of people sighed a huge sense of relief, his hold on them and the town was over.

"I saw the crescent, you saw the whole of the moon".

Mike Scott

Terence Nivens – Associate

Terence Nivens is from the Grove Hill area of Middlesbrough and is now 55 years of age. Terence now works for Middlesbrough Council but back many years ago, in the time of Lee Duffy, Terence himself had an awesome rep as being a fighting man. Terence is now well away from that life and is a quiet family man, but I'm pleased he spared me a bit of time and gave me his views on the Duffer.

Terence said:

The first time I was aware of the name Lee Duffy was in the early 80s. I was working on the door of The Masham and everybody spoke of this kid from South Bank who had a great love of punching people. Even though at the time he may only have been around 17 or 18 years old and still only a very young lad he was game as fuck and people told me he was a total maniac.

I wouldn't go on to meet Lee until I worked on Blaises nightclub door for Barry Faulkner. Barry said he had some young kid called Lee coming down from South Bank to work alongside me and a former middleweight boxer named Dale Henderson-Thyne, this was about 1985. Working alongside Lee, my first impression of him was that he was a fucking lunatic. I used to say that Lee couldn't go to sleep on a night unless he'd hit someone that day. Lee was one of them people who hit people for nothing. One night I saw him hit a lad in Blaises and a big fight erupted, well there was one lad stood with us doormen just watching the punches flying, he was called Begley and was from Easterside. Now this Begley was going to help us break the fight up, but Lee just turned around and hit him for no reason whatsoever and down he went unconscious. Lee would just punch anybody who was there. I tell you what also, that lad couldn't half fight. He really could have a scrap! Lee Duffy was one big strong lad, but he was so quick with his hands that he could literally throw an overhand right from his hip before they got their hands out of their pockets. The consequences of Lee hitting someone was that he would cause maximum damage. He had a nasty streak about him though, to the point that if he thought they were about to get up, he had no problems volleying them in the face. I saw him do that a few times but not many would get back up from his punches. Lee could do it all, not just the boxing but the street fighting as well.

When I worked alongside him for the time that I did, cor I did see him smack some big men. Actually, the very first night I ever worked with Lee, some lads came down from Berwick Hills and Parkend as well as Kev Hawkes and Kevin Auer. It was Kev Hawkes who was the main instigator, he was looking for a fight with Lee. That night Lee asked me to watch his back and of course I did. We all went around the back of Blaises, when we got around there the first thing I clocked was Kev Hawkes stood with his hands up ready to fight and he was walking towards Lee, with that Lee let two punches go 'Bang Bang' and down went Kev he hit the ground already unconscious.

Immediately after that little Kevin Auer tried to attack Lee but I grabbed Kevin and stopped him.

I must have worked with Lee on the doors for almost a year until I went to jail a few times for various things. When I came out of prison I ended up back on the Blaises door for around 12 years for Barry's brother Roy who'd bought the place from Barry.

Over the years I still had a lot to do with Lee when he would come to Grove Hill. I saw Lee a good few times around the Broadway car park, it would be during the day and he was always on his own, I just thought he was, more than likely, up to no good. He was probably taxing all the drug dealers over there because that area of Middlesbrough was one of the worst for drug dealers selling gear around that time. Then Lee would come in Blaises on the night, he was forever ironing people out.

Lee once borrowed Roy Redshaw's XR3i and he was driving about in it for months. When Roy went and asked for it back, Lee knocked him out and drove it until it was a wreck. Also, people used to pay Lee money just to be seen with him many a time. I know the Stockton bodybuilder Craig Howard once paid Lee a lot of money just to hang out with him. Craig was having trouble with someone and he just wanted to be seen with Lee because he knew nobody would bother him while he was out with him. Lee himself told me that Craig gave him money for that reason alone.

I did get on well with Lee, but I kept him at a distance. I didn't want to hang around with him, but I fought alongside him a good few times on that Blaises door.

I suppose I was very close with him when I did jail with him in Durham nick a few times as it's the norm that all the Middlesbrough lads would stick together. Paul Sykes was in there the same time as Lee but when I was in there Sykes was kept in the block because he was too mad for a normal wing. I never ever met him. Also, the prison didn't want him and Duffy clashing which is what would have happened if they'd have bumped into each other.

One day in Durham, I'll never forget it, there was an incident with Lee. There was a little lad from Sunderland who Lee shared a cell with and Lee was taking his drugs off him when he was coming back from visits. This little lad from Sunderland had promised the drugs to another guy, so one day this monster of a man came up to the metal fence when we were on exercise on B wing, which was for remand prisoners, when he shouted, "Oi Duffy you cunt", I was stood with Lee at the time and we both looked around to see this huge ogre stood at the fence growling. Now this man must have been not far off 7ft tall and looked like a grizzly bear. He was fucking huge with a big black beard, long dark hair and was scary looking. Rumour has it he was doing 15 years, but I never found out what for. When he got Lee's attention he shouted, "You bother my little mate anymore and I'll pull these bars off (from the fence) and fucking eat you". Now this man looked more than capable of pulling them bars off and doing exactly what he said, I've still yet to see a man as big as him even to this day. I turned and looked at Lee and said, "Who's that"? Lee looked a bit gobsmacked, but he just laughed and said he didn't know who it was.

One time when I was on my own in the exercise yard of Durham, Lee's little pad mate from Sunderland came up to me for a bit of advice. Now Lee used to walk around the yard with Me and Patcho but this particular day he wasn't there, so this little lad came over to me and said, "Can I have a word please"? I said, "Of course you can", he said "can you have a word with your pal Lee for me please"? I asked, "Why what's he been up to"? He went on to say that Lee was making him wrap a mattress around himself on a night and was using him as a punch bag! So, when I saw Lee I said, "Ere Lee what the fuck you doing to your pad mate"? He said, "What do you mean"? I said, "You're making him put a mattress around him and using him as a punch bag at all hours". Lee's reply was a very funny one, he said "Well what am I supposed to do" like it was normal. I just couldn't stop laughing but that was Lee all over. He had some very funny ways.

Lee's reputation inside the prison walls was huge. Everybody knew who he was in prison and what he was about. Quite often when lads came back from their visits, Lee would walk up and hold his hand out and they'd give him the drugs they'd just had smuggled in, or he'd punch them. I saw Lee walk in a few people's cells and hit them for various reasons. Sometimes I wasn't there but I'd be laid on my bunk and I'd hear the shouting from the other prisoners that Lee had banged this guy or that guy etc... I know Lee was having trouble inside of prison with the men from Birmingham who shot him. It's quite surreal that they were even kept in the same prison as him, but they were.

I'll never forget when I got the news that Lee had died. My best friend Patcho Stanley rang me up to give me the news, my mate saw it happen as he was there. He told me on the phone that Lee was dead! I said, "What do you mean dead"? His answer was "I've just seen him being stabbed, he was laid in the middle of the road screaming that he was dying then he fell unconscious and he was picked up and taken to the hospital". This was still in the early hours at maybe 6am. Patcho told me Lee had battered the life out of Allo until he got lucky with one stab which ended it. What always stuck in my mind when he was speaking to me was when he told me Lee stood up after being stabbed and blood came gushing out of his armpit in pints. He said the blood was hitting the floor so heavy it was making a swooshing sound, like rubber hitting the floor.

The next day I went into the Porthole Café opposite Albert Park that morning about 11am and there was a big gang of lads who said they'd been celebrating. All of them were clearly coked up and they said they'd had 12 bottles of champagne between them and they were celebrating the news that the Duff was dead. I thought you pack of shithouses. These guys were all happy as can be because a man had lost his life at 26! Absolute shithouses.

I wasn't happy when Lee died, yes we'd had our arguments, but he'd never done anything wrong to me and I never minded him. I knew he was a maniac, but I liked him. That Sunday morning, I was in a bit of a state of shock as was the whole of Middlesbrough.

Lee wasn't this ugly looking character you know! His pictures don't do him justice as I always thought he was a big handsome man. When you look at his pictures you think he's got a bit of a pug nose, but he didn't in the flesh, if that makes sense. I know Lee was a hit with the ladies, although some were fucking scared of him because of his bad boy image.

I can remember working in the Masham and you'd hear the regular drinkers whispers of "Ooh Lee Duffy's in the town and he's coming around soon". All the doormen in the town would be bracing themselves for what inevitably was to come. Many bouncers were all terrified of Lee coming in their establishments in case he embarrassed them, which he was more than capable of doing.

One time the word was going around that Lee was passing about fake £20 notes in every pub in the town. Anyway, when Lee came into Blaises the manager, Peter Fox, came to me and said Lee's on his way round and he's passing fake £20s so get ready. Anyway, when Lee came in I said, "Oi Lee, give it a break with them notes"! Lee just laughed and said "Aah yeah I will do, besides I've done every fucking pub in the town". He just didn't give a shit.

When Lee walked in a room he had this effect, when he came in anywhere with his hair slicked back like Dracula, everyone parted like the bow of a ship parting the waves of the ocean. My friend even mentioned that to me the other day when I told him I was being interviewed for this book and it brought back my own memories of seeing it happen.

Not many people know, but Lee smoked a lot of crack cocaine towards the end of his life. I went around a lads in North Ormesby and Lee was in there. Him and this lad had about an ounce of crack and together they smoked the lot. It was him doing stuff like that, along with the possibility of an underlying mental illness, that made him go around hitting people the way he did, he started to get completely out of control. Normal people just don't do that do they!

"I once watched Lee on the bags and he did look classy. He really could throw combinations and boy could he punch. Considering Lee had never competed as a boxer he did look like a million dollars in the gym. Not only that but he was awfully fast for a big man".

2 x ABA Champion, Commonwealth Gold Medalist and Middlesbrough boxing legend John Pearce.

Jack - Middlesbrough Man

Jack is 55 years old and grew up in the town of Middlesbrough. He still lives there today. By his own admissions he hasn't always been on his best behaviour and has, a handful of times, found himself in prison due to things like football violence whilst with the Boro Frontline.

Jack told me:

The first time I ever heard the name Lee Duffy was in the early 1980's. He arrived on the scene in the town when he was about 18 years of age. He quickly became a name that people would always be talking about in every pub I would go into.

When Lee was 18 he started hanging around with another Teesside hardman Ducko (Kevin Duckling), Lee used to idolise him and copy off him in everything he did. Ducko would wear his shirt loose, not tucked into his jeans in jail and to follow suit Lee would do the same, Lee followed Ducko all over like a lost puppy at times.

Lee was the same as a fella I used to train with called Paul Debrick (The Brick) who was also a bit of a fighter. Of course, Lee was forever fighting and when he reached 18 he started getting his man strength. Lee started knocking people out, when he first started going out, he thought he could do it to everyone he came across and most of the time he could.

When Lee began going to the town drinking most of the time it would be with John Fail and Kevin Duckling in the Clarence club (now Dickens Inn) on Southfield Road. Everybody used to go there because the other pubs wouldn't be open all day, so when places like the Masham closed at 3pm people would go to the Clarence club for a game of pool and it was a cheap pub and open all day. Lee, Ducko and Johnny Fail would, more often than not, be in there playing cards on a Saturday. I'm sure I can speak for the whole of Teesside when I say when Lee and Ducko were together, somebody always ended up getting a clip. I was in the Masham one day and my mate Brian who was mates with Ducko was in the bar. Now this day Lee and Ducko were also in and my mate Brian pulled me to one side when I was coming back from the toilet and said "Looka Jack you need to fuck off over the road to the Shakey (Shakespeare pub) because I've heard Duffy and Ducko saying they're gonna give you it, they're looking for someone to batter". By this point every cunt had already pissed off as soon as they'd seen them two come in. He went on to tell me what Lee and Ducko had been saying about me "Who the fuck does he think he is walking to the bog like John Wayne". So, I thanked Brian for the heads up and took myself off out of the way from them both because I didn't want them two picking on me.

That day they'd come in the pub looking for someone and obviously they never showed up, so somebody was going to get it, that's the way them two worked. What you've got to remember with Lee Duffy is, when he died he only had 14 criminal convictions, although Cleveland police had had over *90 separate complaints registered on their system against Lee Duffy. *This was confirmed by a retired police officer.

One day I was in the Clarence bar playing snooker with a couple of my mates minding our own business when Duffy, Ducko and a few others walked in the bar. Now Duffy and his gang of henchmen sat down playing cards for money near the pool table, one of my mates who was with me that day was a guy called big Davie Hodds. Now Davie didn't know of Duffy, but I did. So, as he was going to take a shot he said very politely to Duffy's table, do ya mind if you move for 10 seconds so I can take my shot please? The next thing anyone knew was that Duffy got up, whacked him and had him by his throat on the deck. As this was happening another mate of mine Andy ran over to Lee and said, "alright Lee leave him now he's had enough" and Lee let go, which took us all by surprise because Lee wasn't known to be a reasonable fella in these situations, so everything went calm. That was until daft Davie Hodds jumped back up and shouted to Lee Duffy, "alright then, me and you outside"! I just couldn't believe it, I was thinking you idiot you don't realise what you've done now. So, Duffy took his top off and walked outside and he really gave poor Davie a battering in the Clarence car park. This will have been around 1985 so Lee was still only around 20 years old. Lee was moving in the car park like a boxer jabbing away making them noises with his nose like boxers do. Lee moved around effortlessly jabbing Davie's head off with his long reach, he knocked all poor Davies teeth out and his face was a right state.

When you saw Lee fighting you could tell he had fantastic basic boxing skills, but he was also a tremendous street fighter on the floor. What I didn't like about Lee was that when my mate was trying to get up off the floor Duffy kept running over and kicking him in the head, that's when I ran over and said, "Leave him alone now please Lee he's had enough alright mate"! Again, I was surprised when Lee looked at me and said, "Yeah no bother" and walked away. So, me and my mates have picked poor Davie off the floor and took him into the toilets to clean him up. We hadn't realised but Lee had followed us into the toilets to have another go, I pleaded with him just to leave it and then he started on me and my other mate saying, "do you want some as well?" I said to him "no Lee we don't want any trouble we're just here to clean our friend up". As I looked around the corner I could see a few of Duffy's henchmen like Terry O'Neill and John Fail standing guard in case anything went off. Lee then told me and my mates to "fuck off" and smashed poor Davie's head into the sink and made a real mess of him.

As far as I know there was only one man who ever testified against Duffy in court and that was a fella called Martin Clark from Yorkshire. Duffy had smashed this guy's eye socket whilst they were in the Speak Easy and it resulted in him losing an eye. Lee got a 4 year sentence for it. Other than that, there were dozens of people who were warned off from taking Duffy to court. Lee had a way of getting messages to these victims who he'd done things to saying that he would get to them if they went to the police.

If ever Lee Duffy and Kevin Ducko walked into a pub nearly everyone in it would fly out the fire escapes. I saw this happen so many times even when it was just Lee on his own.

The thing is Lee Duffy would always want to go for the big lads. I had a mate who used to run a blues party named Stewie Campbell. Stewie was about 20 stone but he was like a baby elephant, fighting wasn't his thing. One of Lee's favourite sayings was "how many punches do you reckon it'll take to put him down"? Lee walked up to big Stewie and said, "You're a big lad aren't ya"? then followed him out of the blues and started punching him for nothing. Even Lee's mates joined in, but nobody could put poor Stewie down. In the end a few of Duffy's mates started kicking his legs to get him down and they did leave him in a right mess. The next day I had to go see Stewie in the hospital. Stewie told me that the police had already been to see him, and they wanted him to make a statement against Lee Duffy. Straight away I told him "no you can't"! I told him that he needed to put it all down to experience because it would be worse for him and his family in the long run. Months later Stewie thanked me for the advice I'd given him in his hospital bed because he realised Duffy and his mates wouldn't have left him alone.

Another big fella Lee gave a hell of a beating to was Mark White in the bogs in Bennetts night club in South Bank. I'm not sure there was a reason for that either, only that he was about 18 stone and it would enhance Lee's reputation.

The bottom line is, in my opinion, Lee Duffy picked his targets very well as far as I'm concerned. He'd always make a play for the big lads but more the big friendly giant type. Lee knew he had the beating of these people before he got into a scrap with them.

One story that's been well documented is the time David Tapping poured petrol over Lee in the Commercial pub in South Bank. What many people will not be aware of is the reason why Tapping did what he did. It was because Lee had been torturing his Brother for months and bullying him. After Lee beat Tapping to a pulp in the bar he dragged him outside and placed his head behind a car wheel and was planning on getting someone to drive over him. Tapping was only not murdered that night because someone saw his unconscious body and dragged him out of the way!

Lee didn't always have it his own way though because one night I saw him and Ducko fighting outside of Rumours with a group of squaddies, now the squaddies were getting the better of them two until Molly Jaffray had to come out and intervene.

I had a feeling that there would be certain people that would have declined to be in this book because they had helped Lee do some evil things.

There was a big split in Berwick Hills, Parkend and Pally Park because a lot of lads were on Allo's side, and a handful were on Lee's. Allo would knock about with Joe Livo, Lee King and Kev Hawkes and he would never ever give up in his fights with Lee Duffy. For a good few weeks running before Lee's death they were clashing. It used to start with Lee picking at Allo and Allo was like a Rottweiler and wouldn't back down. So, when Lee came in wide eyed on the night of his death everybody knew it was going to be kicking off. My Wife's Sister was there that night and she watched the full thing unravel in front of her.

Lee and Allo had so many fights, Lee always got the better of him, but he'd never give up and would just keep coming and coming. In fact, they had a fight only around 2 weeks before Lee died, and he didn't half give Allo it.

On the night of his death there were rumours that Duffy was going around with a gun on him, now these stories, to my knowledge, turned out to be false.

My Sister in law told me it was Lee King who stabbed Lee Duffy in the back when he was punching fuck out of Allo, that's how he got him off him in the first place. That was never mentioned in court but that did happen because my Sister in law watched it happen. That made sense as to why Lee had a stab wound in his back which was discovered whilst the autopsy was being carried out. When Allo got up off the floor it was Lee King that handed him the knife and said "There ya go Davey finish him off" and of course Allo plunged the three-inch blade into Lee's left armpit and severed the artery. If it wasn't for Lee King, then Lee Duffy wouldn't have died that night. I'm sure he would have met the Grim Reaper on another occasion not long after though, because the way Lee was going on somebody was going to kill him sooner rather than later as he'd started to get reckless as his drug habit took over.

Davey Allo never put any of this in his statement to my knowledge by the way, he never grassed Lee King up. If he hadn't have done what he did maybe Lee would have killed Allo, Lee King certainly did enough with the knife to get Lee off Allo that's for sure.

It is true that when Lee was dying in the road screaming for help that people were shouting "DIE YA BASTARD" because them people just viewed Lee as an evil bastard I mean it was only thirty minutes before that that he'd turned up shouting at people to "MOVE AND GET OUT OF MY WAY". The people who were there that night said it was a great night until Duffy and his gang turned up to poison the atmosphere.

The reason Lee died was that after he was stabbed, no taxi would stop because they saw it was for Lee Duffy. It took them a good twenty minutes to flag a taxi down because Lee had got in that many taxi's over the years and refused to pay. Lee even shot a bullet through some taxi drivers roof once.

An awful lot of lads left Teesside just because of the Duff you know. One guy named Kirk Garland who used to be a bouncer on the Masham well, he left Boro and went down London for 3 years because Duffy said he was going to kill him. Kirk was a South Bank lad as well and only came back after Lee died.

When I used to talk to Lee in the Clarence club you couldn't really have a proper conversation with him. He wasn't the sharpest tool in the draw let me just say. Lee would always ask me to play cards with him, but I'd just make an excuse up. A few of my mates used to get involved with the card school and I used to look at them and shake my head. Even if they'd win they were going to get battered here. Duffy and his mate used to take all the money off the table.

On August 25th 1991 I was working away in Scotland when I got a call from my Sister in law saying, "you'll never guess who's been killed tonight"? my first guess was "Lee Duffy" she said, "how do you know"? I just said, "it was always going to happen sooner or later". That night when Allo and Lee were fighting it must have been about the third fight they'd had that year. It was written in the stars that eventually one of them was going to die a young man.

I sometimes go working all over the country and when someone asks me "where are you from"? and I mention Middlesbrough, straight away they normally mention Lee Duffy.

The problem with Lee, I always thought, was that he wasn't well educated. When he died all he had to his name was £60, which was soaked in his blood, in his pocket. He should have used his fucking loaf right and made a few quid but instead all Lee wanted to do was go out and hurt people.

I would be out every Saturday when Lee was about, and you could be in the town minding your own business, then you'd hear a tale that Lee Duffy had just knocked so-so out or cracked a bouncer. You didn't need social media in them days, the news would travel far and fast.

Why Lee Duffy became what he was is beyond me, evil is not the word.

"No one heals themselves by wounding another".

Ambrose of Milan

John Dryden – Boxing Coach

John Dryden's is a hugely popular man in the town of Middlesbrough. I dare say he'd be the most protected man in the town if ever he had a spot of bother due to him running the Wellington ABC gym for several decades.

John's gym is in the heart of Boro and is still going strong today. It has kept many an undesirable off the street and saved them from a life of crime with his guidance in between the ropes.

There's many coaches out there today, many I wouldn't let train my dog, but John actually was an England advanced coach, which you couldn't become if you weren't any good at coaching, only the best are England Advanced coaches.

The reason I wanted to chat with the likeable old rascal John Dryden was to find out how much of a well-developed boxer the Duffer was.

Anybody who knows John Dryden will tell you he's a very straight-talking guy. I've had the pleasure of knowing John since the early 90's and if Lee wasn't up to scratch, then John Dryden was definitely the man to tell me.

John said:

I remember Lee Duffy in my gym very well. He first came in when he was around 16 when he was carrying a bit of weight. John Black used to bring him down our gym now and again just to train. Lee never boxed but he was good enough to. Lee was very strong, and he could wallop alright don't you worry about that. Lee came down again when he had just got out of the nick and that time he seemed to have lost all his weight and turned it into muscle. I'm convinced without a doubt Lee could have become a top fighter if he hadn't have decided to become a villain. He just lacked the dedication that a fighter must have because he wanted to be what he became.

Lee would have made a perfect amateur boxer, nice and rangy and standing at 6ft 4 with not an ounce of fat on him the last time he trained in my gym, and he was 16 stone then. Of course, as I said he decided to choose another path but even the Geordies admired Lee and not many men from Boro are well liked up there because of the rivalry we have always had between us.

I will say that in all the time I had Lee Duffy in my gym he showed me the greatest of respect at all times and to others in the gym also. For what he was, which you've all read about, he wasn't bad to have in the gym. He wasn't loud, but I think a lot depended on who he was talking to. I couldn't say anything other than I found Lee to be the perfect gentleman as a person and as a fighter, well if only he'd have channelled it into the right path instead of what he became. It's was a great waste of talent it really was.

"As a child he couldn't handle himself, kids used to bully him. He wasn't a hard child who grew into a hard man, he went on the club doors and that's where it first started off. There was a real loving side to him, a caring side".

Brenda Duffy, 1993

Donald Wright – Rumours Customer

Donald Wright is now 75 years old and he originally comes from the Carlton in Glasgow. Donald came to Middlesbrough in 1963 to work on the Billingham ICI plant but never left. Instead of setting back up the road to Glasgow, wee Donald met a woman, married her and had children. I'd known Donald for many years myself from drinking in the White Rose pub in the Longlands area of Middlesbrough, but I'd never spoke of Lee Duffy with him before, not until I'd decided to do this book.

Donald knew Lee from his days when he was just a young bouncer on the doors of Rumours nightclub.

Donald said:

I first met the young Lee Duffy in 1982 when he was working on the doors in Rumours. I frequented Rumours most weekends for many many years. His Mother Brenda already worked there so I think that's how he came to get the job in the first place.

A lot of people in the club spoke of this young underage kid of Brenda's working the door, I mean he was underage at 17, he shouldn't have even been in the place let alone be fighting grown men, there was always a lot of fighting in there, but Lee quickly put a stop to most of it with his fighting skills. At times there were multiple bodies laid about outside of Rumours, Lee left them where they fell.

If you want the honest truth of what I thought of the young Duff, I think he was an arrogant bully, nothing like his Mother Brenda who was a lovely lady.

The most heinous act by far I ever saw Lee Duffy do was when he filled in a little guy in Rumours called Dennis. Now Dennis wasn't all together mentally but Lee filled him in for nothing at all. Even though his Mum Brenda was my friend I was fucking disgusted by what Lee had done and for leaving poor Dennis in the state he did, I told Dennis to go get himself a good solicitor because he'd be due a massive sum from the criminal injury bureau. After the beating Lee gave poor Dennis he had to endure going through a great deal of rehabilitation just to get himself back to the way he was. I have no reason to speak ill of the dead but the number of beatings I saw Lee give out to people in Rumours was into double figures.

Many times, I saw him battering people for nothing at all, or if he didn't like the look of someone it was 'BANG' of course in them days if you were a bouncer you could get away with it, not like it is today. I've even seen Lee hit fellow bouncers on the door in Rumours, violence was just what he did.

If Lee was ever in Rumours when he wasn't on the door it would be with Kevin Duckling and Molly Jaffray, Molly wasn't like Lee in the respect that he was a very fair and likeable man.

As I said I was in Rumours most weekends, but I always avoided getting into conversation with Lee. The times I did speak with him he was funny with me, he always loved to call me a "Scottish Bastard".

I believe from what I saw of Lee's short life it was all about who was the top man. I even saw Lee fighting with the bouncers from the nearby pubs, he was crazy.

Lee also used to frequent the old Empire pub.

I also knew the black guy Leroy Fischer from Birmingham who shot Lee. Leroy used to spend a bit of time in Middlesbrough and it was him who got a little firm together and who shot Lee to warn him off, that was over drugs.

I know this is going to sound horrific, but I don't have anything good to say about Lee Duffy for this book, I never saw any good points in him at all. I was very sad for my friend Brenda who lost a Son, some of the saddest words I've ever heard were when Brenda told me "Donald I always knew I'd lose him one day, but I just didn't think it would be so soon. I thought he'd have at least gotten into his thirties".

It's very sad to say but Lee brought it all on himself, you reap what you sow is the saying I'm looking for. I've seen Lee Duffy just being horrible to people for nothing, just to assert his authority and say "I'm a big man" that's the way he was I tell no lies.

Today he's still remembered but, in my opinion, the only reason he's remembered is for being horrible to people.

Even when Lee was dead and buried, people came to his tombstone with a sledgehammer. It's horrendous for me to even say that out loud but that happened for the people that don't know. It was done a good handful of times by people in the dead of night. What really sickens me is that people were even phoning Brenda's house saying "Mam, It's Lee, I'm speaking to you from the grave". It was all the more damaging for poor Brenda to go through, that poor broken woman.

"Live by the sword, die by the sword"

Gospel of Matthew

Peter Appleby (Appo)
Middlesbrough Clubber

Peter Appleby is a painter & decorator and is now 56 years old and grew up in Middlesbrough town centre.

I'd known of Peter for around 20 years from the Middlesbrough pub scene myself. When I was growing up he seemed to be in every pub I ever went in, but I know Peter was part of Lee's generation and seemed to know everybody.

Peter also had a photo of Lee that he had taken, he put it up on Facebook and not even Lee's family had seen it before, it was that that led me to Peter. The photo was of Lee in Bennett's nightclub in South Bank from around 1985, Lee was sporting blonde streaks and a moustache, I don't think anybody was going to tell him he looked ridiculous though, do you? I suppose it was the 80s though!

Peter said:

The first time I ever came across Lee Duffy was in the old Empire pub in the early 80s. This big strapping rough looking lad walked in with a black string vest on, his hair spiked, and he had a bit of a flat fighter's nose. I could sense something different with this guy instantly, he had a presence about him even back then, the kind of presence that tells you that he was different to others, his vest was the kind that Rab C Nesbitt wore but obviously a different colour. If he wasn't so big and moody looking he'd have been hammered for wearing something so ridiculous. I could see people looking at his vest like WTF, but nobody said anything to him.

Lee walked over and introduced himself to the table I was sat at and started talking away to everybody. Every time Lee came in he'd come over to my circle of friends and that's how he started hanging about with us, this was really when he wasn't as famous in the town.

Funnily enough that very first day I met Lee, he had me and a lad named Kevin O'Neill doing press ups outside the pub seeing who could do the most. I know it's a bit mental doing press ups in the street when you're out drinking but we were only young lads back then and it was Lee who was orchestrating it.

The other lad Kevin who I was with could really look after himself but on another night him and Lee were gonna have a fight and believe it or not, it was over press ups again and which one of them was doing them right. Now Kevin was only small, but he was a hell of a fighter and he ended up facing up to Duffy, but it never went off. Kevin would have had a go with anyone but that day he just said Lee was too big and they never locked horns, it was more handbags if you like.

After my first meeting with Lee in the pub when he had us doing press ups his name started to come up more and more during conversations. This was the 80s and there was no social media, people in them days were lucky if you had a landline, but you'd be constantly hearing his name in every pub you went in for all kinds of different reasons. If you were in a nightclub, you could normally tell Lee was in the building before you even set eyes on him just because of the way people were acting. Lee's whole demeanour was scary, he wasn't the kind of guy who would walk around being loud and brash, but in my 50 odd years on this planet I've never seen anything as scary as him even if he wasn't speaking.

I'd say the only time Lee was funny with me was one night in Rumours nightclub. Now I've never drank, and I've always been into my training and looked after myself physically. So, one night I was in the bar and I could tell Lee was checking me out because he'd been staring at me. I was talking to a girl called Debbie at the time and her face just changed it was then that I gathered Lee was stood behind me. I could see his huge intimidating figure hovering about as I could see him in the mirror, but I was trying not to notice him. He then came over and said, "Ere you, you don't smoke, drink or take drugs, well I smoke, drink and take drugs and I'm bigger, fitter and stronger than you". I just said, "I can't argue with that Lee" and went to the bar. I didn't think he was fitter than me at the time, but I wasn't gonna tell Lee that, I just kinda laughed it off and agreed with him.

I know Lee put that on me looking for a reaction but of course he never got one. Maybe he was being funny because of the drugs he was on, I certainly used one of my nine lives that day. I stayed in the nightclub for the rest of the night and he never bothered me after that. I wasn't that scared of Lee because I was used to seeing him in Bennetts nightclub in South Bank and I was familiar with him which I think was the key. Lee was always better for knowing I always found.

Lee was very competitive, I mean he couldn't be beat in a fight, but he also didn't like people looking smarter than him. One night I was in Bennett's in shorts and shades and I could see him again checking me out. Then he left and came back ten minutes later in tennis shorts and his massive legs out and shades himself. Of course, Lee only lived around the corner from Bennett's in South Bank.

I never saw Lee causing any trouble in there and he was always in when I was in, that was his patch, and nobody started anything if he was in anyway. The doormen pretty much gave him a free reign in there to come and go as he pleased wearing whatever he wanted.

Lee broke Jonka Teasdale's jaw outside the Jovial Monk pub in North Ormesby, and he used to work the doors for him! Lee had walked in the pub and asked Jonka if he could have a word with him outside. When they were outside Lee told him he wasn't happy with the way he'd been treating his Sister. Jonka told Lee to fuck off and went to walk back into the pub, only for Lee to crack him one. I saw Jonka when his jaw was damaged and all that was was Lee wanting to be the main man. Lee was only still a teenager when he did that to him and Jonka had been one of the main men around, he had a lot of doors. Afterwards Jonka moved away to Nunthorpe and out of the limelight and for a quieter life.

Over the years I've done a bit of door work myself. Around the time Lee was running about I was working with a big fella from Hartlepool called Bob Raw. Anyway, as it was getting closer to finishing time and it was entering the hour of the Duff, which was the hour before closing time, as Lee liked to come out late for a few then go on to the late blues parties. Bob knew this and was getting twitchy. The rumour going about was Lee was going to come down the club we were working on and this was the time of night he normally showed up. Cut a long story short, Bob turns around and says, "fuck this I'm shooting off now" I asked him what for and he replied, "well I've heard the Duff is coming down tonight and I'm the biggest aren't I, when he comes down he's gonna knock me out first". The poor bloke had built it up that much in his head that he panicked, and he's done his own head in with it, so he pissed off. I can't even remember if Lee came that night but like I said he'd built it up all night so much so that he didn't even wait about to find out, poor Bob didn't even know Lee, but his emotions were running riot to the point that he couldn't handle the suspense of whether Lee was going to turn up that night or not.

To me, Lee Duffy wasn't about money, cars, fancy clothes, women or the doors, he just wanted to destroy everyone. There was no business brain in Lee's head he just wanted to find top fighters, so he could knock them out. If you were hard or you had a name, then you were getting it. Average blokes 5ft 6 sat in the corner minding their own business never had anything to worry about from Lee Duffy unless they were a drug dealer.

Every single day Lee wanted to knock somebody out and when he'd knocked out a big name in the town, he was like "Who's next"! You just don't see people like Lee was, it doesn't happen.

The people I know who've had reps, when they get them they want to live off them for the rest of their lives. Well Lee wanted to prove it every day, and he walked the walk and talked the talk.

One of the most hard-hitting memories is being sat next to him in a party after we'd been out. I must have been sat there at 4am when I just side glanced and saw Lee's big head next to me, my leg touching one of his massive thighs. I just remember looking down thinking how different he was. Not like a bodybuilder, more athletic and just completely different to anyone I've ever seen in my life and it wasn't because he was big, I've seen loads of big lads, but Lee had a real aura I've never seen in anyone else.

Physically Lee was invincible in a fighting sense, but he had all the other ingredients like will, heart, tenacity and desire.

When he died I was shocked because he just couldn't be beat. I know this might sound crazy but when I got told Lee had been killed, in my head it was like a prime Mike Tyson being beat by James Buster Douglas. It's the biggest news Middlesbrough's ever had before or since.

I don't believe Lee could have changed his ways, the way he ended up was his destiny it was in the stars. He was only here a short time, but he lived his life in the fast lane every time I was in his company. Looking back with hindsight, it was always only ever a matter of time until he was going to be killed. If you live by the sword you die by the sword and Lee would go looking for it most days.

I don't believe Lee had any mental issues because he was switched on and very sharp, I just believe it was in him to be who he was. He started off as a 17/18-year-old and it just snow-balled until the day he died at 26.

Lee, in my opinion was crazier at the end than he was when I met him all those years before that. Normally a lad settles down, well Lee didn't. Lee morphed into the fearsome figure that he became, and it was all done in 8 years by him alone and 90% of it in just a pair of shorts.

People like Lee Duffy just don't happen normally, turning up in big cities wanting to fight the main men. He went through all the hard men of Middlesbrough like dominoes, then when he'd knocked them out he'd move further afield and find more to knock unconscious.

I hear the stories of Lee bullying taxi drivers or some other innocent party, well I've no doubt they'll have been the odd casualty, but the Lee I knew, he was only interested in you if you could fight or you had a name, so it could enhance his reputation. That's what kind of animal Lee was, he was a lone wolf. Lee lived through the years of a prime Mike Tyson and like Tyson, Lee was a master of intimidation. He knew how to scare people. Lee knew the threat of violence was far greater than the act. Fear begins in people's minds and once they are genuinely scared of you, like they were of Lee, then they'll run from you forever or behave sheepish which people did around Lee. I used to see Lee doing it to people all the time.

One Sunday afternoon I was in the back of the old Empire pub which was called the Cyclops. Lee was in there on his own and he had had trouble with three of Allo's mates who ran with Allo on the Boro frontline (Middlesbrough FC hooligan firm). Now these three blokes were game as anything and never ran from anyone. These fellas could really have a fight, but that day I was in there I saw Lee on his own and he was chasing these three fellas' around the pool tables and they were trying to get away from Lee. I mean there was pool cues and a table full of balls but none of them picked them up to use them and they didn't get together and gang up on Lee. These lads would have fought anyone else, but they didn't wanna know with Lee that day and Lee was teasing them trying to cut them off with different angles. Lee didn't like anyone who had anything to do with the Boro frontline because they fought in numbers, whereas Lee was always on his own.

Of course, Lee's main rival David Allison was really the main man of the Boro frontline and pretty much the same mould as Lee, Allo would fight anybody win, lose or draw that's how he was.

Apart from the time Lee was a bit funny with me in Rumours I never had a problem with him. I think that was largely because I never thought I was anybody or wanted a name for myself. I trained but I wasn't into the life Lee was into.

I never actually saw Lee do anything violent with my own eyes, I've been in nightclubs when poor unfortunate souls had been knocked out by him, but I never witnessed the scale of his brutality first hand. Lee did say to me one night that the reason he preferred shorts and trainers in nightclubs was because then he was ready to fight. He wasn't one for wearing all top designer gear like his best friend Lee Harrison. Lee Harrison was always the best dressed man in the town, the Duff was always trainers, shorts and vest 90% of the time, he was ready to fight as he said. Lee stood out just because he was Lee Duffy but the way he used to dress meant he would stand out even more and that's what Lee loved.

The Lee Duffy era was the best time of my life and when he died it was the end of an era in Middlesbrough. The partying, the music, the girls and that feeling of youth between 1985 to around 1991 was such a special time for me.

As I said I met Lee in 1983 and from that day in '83 until '91, he never ever changed. If anything, he grew psychically and in attitude and temperament.

I would have imagined if Lee had never been killed when he was so young that he'd have only gotten worse in the things that he was getting up to. The game would have become madder and he'd have expanded but of course we'll never know now what would have happened if Lee had reached his thirties. If Lee had reached an older age he wouldn't have had to lift a finger because his name was that big and carried so much weight. Saying that Lee liked that side of things and hurting people so I'm sure he'd have still done it, but that's just my opinion.

The lads who hated him and didn't like him were the ones doing bad things themselves. I wouldn't have had a problem with Lee if he'd have still been around because of the way I live my life.

In the years after Lee's death I went to Gran Canaria back and forth on a good few holidays. At least three different times I've met three different Geordie lads and as soon as I'd said I was from Middlesbrough the first question they all asked me was "did you know Lee Duffy"? Honest to god!

One lad told me they remembered him coming up to Newcastle on his own hunting for Viv Graham. That just shows you the interest in him and how much his name was known doesn't it! Newcastle is a huge city with some seriously naughty people there as well and that lad told me everybody in Newcastle feared Lee when he used to go along in just a pair of shorts and trainers. Lee's name in Middlesbrough will never be forgotten ever.

"I treat good people good, and bad people bad".

Lee Paul Duffy

Terry Dicko - Close friend

I first heard the name Terry Dicko around 1995. Largely down to him running an afterhours club called 'The Steam Packet'. It was a place that people went to when they weren't ready for the night to end. The place was usually full of non-desirables and it was the right kind of place to go to if you wanted to purchase drugs and there was usually a wide variety of them to choose from.

Terry's parties could go on for days and if you wanted a place to find trouble then that was the place to go. This was the kind of place Lee Duffy would have felt right at home in if he'd still been around taxing young and upcoming drug dealers. I myself ended up at Terry's parties maybe a dozen or more times from 1997-2003. I'll never forget once pushing my luck with Terry in the Steam Packet when I was around 19 years of age. I was with a friend of mine called Danny Marlowe (God rest him) and I was way way gone. The only reason I remember this story is because my sister Samantha and Danny were there to remind me of it the next day. I was just your typical chewy little teenager and I remember calling Terry's name maybe five or six times. Each time Terry replied "what"? I would shout "fuck off". My Sister told me that my one saving grace was my own stupidity. Although I deserved a kicking, Terry could see I was just a young kid who'd had one too many shandys among other things and the only thing I needed right then was putting to bed.

Can I just say, writing this now how thankful I am that Terry's a decent person who could see me for what I was, a drunken little prick.

The majority of people in Middlesbrough have heard all the stories of Terry Dicko aka the mad axeman. I'd seen him on Donal MacIntyre's 'MacIntyre's Underworld' alongside Teesside's Brian Cockerill, Terry was doing his best catalogue pose.

I'd seen him so many times around town and I knew what he was about, well I thought I knew him before I interviewed him for this book. My view on him was he was a nasty little bastard. He maybe only around 5ft 6 and looks like a Mexican, but he can really fight if needs be. Not to mention he's an extremely well-connected man in the Middlesbrough area.

Whilst doing one of my other interviews for this book I was asked, "Have ya spoke to Dicko yet"? I was aware of who Dicko was, but I didn't see the connection between South Bank's Lee Duffy and over the borders Terry Dicko, and I was told "Whatever ya do ya must speak to little Dicko because Lee loved him". I said I'd love to speak with Terry, although I wasn't really jumping through hoops. My only experience of Terry, as I mentioned earlier was of me telling him to "fuck off" numerous times, so I was hoping he didn't have a good memory for faces! I asked how to get in touch with him and an hour later a text came through with Terry Dicko's phone number. Great I thought, I wasn't going to mention my encounter with him in the Steam Packet right away, not until I was more familiar anyway.

Terry and I exchanged messages for a couple of weeks then I arranged to meet him in Isaac Wilsons for a chat about his friend Lee Duffy.

Terry said:

I'm 61 years old now and I'm proud of being brought up "over the border" as that's where Middlesbrough began.

In 1859 in a local newspaper article it described 'Over the border' as a mere colony and gathered there was the vilest of the vile and that made me chuckle, I've always remembered that but I'm very proud of my border roots.

When I was a kid I'd climb for pigeons and my dad was the same. I was pigeon daft. I'd climb the gas works and I'd climb Teesside Bridge for pigeon eggs. I loved climbing I was never afraid of heights as a little lad. Me and my pals used to race up the Teesside Bridge to see who could catch the most pigeons. We were basically risking our lives for fucking skem. You only realise how dangerous it was as you get older.

Me and Franny Duffy used to catch Koi Carp out of the gas tanks. Even when I was young, it was about never giving in. I've got enormous determination it never ever lets me down.

It's fair to say I've been a bit of a "bad un" in my time. At times I've been a pure bastard and many prison sentences have come and gone because of it. I've never been a bully in my time though. I'd like to think if I'm in the wrong I'll put my hands up and say sorry whereas people in our world don't say sorry.

Many years ago, over the border in Middlesbrough there was a lad who had just come out of the Fleece pub, now I know I shouldn't have done it but this drunk walked by, and I was having a bad day because I'd lost my little dog at Whitby, I was heartbroken so I wasn't in the best of moods anyway but I could tell this fella was effing and blinding saying I'd nearly ran him over. I couldn't understand this as I was parked up and hadn't moved, so I just ran him over! I think about that and I ask God to forgive me for that and all the other times that I've done things that I shouldn't have done.

Lee was only a kid when I met him, his Mam Brenda worked the cloakroom at Masters nightclub and used to take a young Lee with her sometimes. Lee's father Lawrie was actually at sea with my dad in the Merchant navy.

I suppose I never really took much notice of Lee until he was maybe 17 or 18 years old and frequented Rumours nightclub.

A lot of people will remember the Duff from being in The Havana and he used to love going in at times on a Sunday night when it was a member's club. You had to have your photo taken to be a member, so you could gain entry and so the police knew who was in. Well this Sunday Lee walked in and Jack Wardell from behind the counter said, "I'd like to see your picture please"! Lee stood there and just said "FUCK OFF"! This went on for a good few minutes and each time Lee's reply was always "FUCK OFF" anyway, everybody in the whole club knew who Lee Duffy was so he didn't really need to see his picture. So, Lee shouts, "I've had enough of this, get me a fucking taxi now" and walks out. To cut a long story short, Lee walks back in 4-5 minutes later demanding to know where his taxi was! Jack told Lee "there's a load out there on Linthorpe Road Lee"! Lee then responded by saying "I've asked you to get me one" as he said that, Lee slowly lifted his jumper up to expose a gun tucked into the top of his jeans and gave Jack a smile. Jack's then said to Lee "You're not gonna shoot me are you Lee because I can't get you a taxi"? and this made Lee laugh and he replied "YES" while laughing like a school boy, but they knew each other very well because not many people would be that familiar with Lee Duffy if they didn't.

Actually, Jack and Lee were great friends, one night they even shared a taxi home together and Jack told me that Lee was in the back of the taxi when he said to Jack "ere, have ya seen the air conditioning in these cabs Jack"? Jack said, "What you on about Lee"? Then Lee pulled out a gun and just put a bullet through the roof of the car! Lee shouted "THERE" whilst laughing his head off. Lee was like this big naughty schoolboy who would be constantly doing mad things around the town.

One thing that used to keep him entertained was finding a garden that had a dog in it then putting his dog 'Bulla' over the garden wall, Lee and his mate would go around the estates looking for dogs to put their dogs up against, then they'd stand like kids peeking through gaps in the gate!

Lee Duffy, if I was to sum him up was "radged" full of energy and full of fun. He pushed me over one day in the Madison nightclub and I chipped my elbow. I thought you fucking bastard and I ran at him, but he just started laughing. Then I laughed back.

Lee was my friend and all I can say is good things about him. I once saw Lee stick a £20 note in some old fella's pocket, the old guy didn't know he had done it and when he next went in his pocket he pulled out £20 and he was completely at a loss as to where it had come from saying "eh, I didn't know I had that, where did that come from"? See, that gave Lee a good feeling in his heart he used to say.

One night over the border I was with Lee and a few mates and it was Christmas time but everywhere was shut. So, we couldn't get in anywhere for ages. Anyway, we tried a side door to the Old Robin Hood pub. Lee walked in shouting "Oi Oi" but nobody answered. I think Reggie had it at the time, but nobody came out. We all started making ourselves at home and what I'd noticed is one of the lads started taking the piss downing shots thinking it was gonna be a free for all. At that point I shouted, "You can fucking pack that in now, you're all fucking paying for those drinks"! Lee said, "Ya right Terry we've all come in here to get out of the cold, we're not gonna fucking rob him as well so get ya hands in ya fucking pockets".

Another time I was in the Green Tree pub with Lee when he asked the landlord Frank to lend him £130. To be honest Frank gave Lee the money thinking he'd never see it again, but Lee was true to his word came in the next day and repaid him, as well as telling everyone in the pub to behave for Frank or they'd have him to deal with.

When Lee had his fall out with Dale Henderson-Thyne I was the mediator. One night, Lee came around my house shouting he wanted to fight Dale. To be honest that's how I really got to know Lee through knocking about with Dale, in the end Lee came around my house three times asking me to arrange a fight between him and Dale Henderson-Thyne. What had happened, Lee told me, was that Dale had been to Lee's girlfriend's house when he was in prison to ask for £130 that Lee had owed him. Now this fabulously offended Lee he was raging when he found out, "Please Terry can you sort a meeting, please Terry I can only ask you" he begged. I didn't want to get involved because they were both my friends. In the end I said I'd go and see Dale and with that Lee hugged the life out of me like he'd won the lottery and was shouting "THANK YOU THANK YOU TERRY I FUCKING LOVE YOU TERRY" and flung me in the air like a little fucking ragdoll, still going on. Anyway, I went around to Dale's house and found him there, he'd been digging an extension with big Woody at his house all day. Now I didn't know how to approach the subject, how did I break it to him that basically I'd come around to be the bearer of bad news and tell him that Lee wanted to fight him. I think if I remember rightly even Dale said, "you're very quiet Terry", but I didn't want to say anything in front of big Woody, so I asked if we could have a word in private. When me and Dale got some privacy, I was thinking there's no easy way of telling him, so I just came out with it "Looka Dale Lee Duffy's been around my house three times, on three separate occasions telling me he wants to fight you"! Dales response was "Go get him"! I said, "Look Dale you've been digging holes all day leave it till tomorrow". Dale was insistent though and told me to go get him right then. I tried to sort it out with the pair of them as I didn't want to see them fighting. I told Dale "we're all friends together" but his reply was still "Go get him". So, I did as I was asked, and I went and found Lee at his girlfriend's house. I knocked on the door and I could hear Lee coming shouting "OI OI". Lee stood back, arms folded and asked me what had went on! I just told him "he's told me to come get you" and with that Lee starts shouting "AAAAAH MATE THANK YOU" whilst picking me up and throwing me in the air. Lee was ecstatic and said about a dozen thank you's as if I'd given him a Christmas present. Lee was hugging the life out of me and calling me his best little mate in the world.

At the time Lee had this Mark 1 Granada so he set off to follow me to Dale's house. Anyway, we arrive at Dales, Dale comes out and him and Lee went off ahead of me and around the corner. Afterwards I asked Dale what had happened when they were both out of sight. Dales words were "I wouldn't like to go for another walk with him, he was just too strong.". Lee said something different to what Dale said but I never commented on it.

It's been 27 years since Lee Duffy died and people are still talking about him, because he was the monster of Teesside, but he was a good-hearted monster.

When Lee walked in the pub the rats would walk out. What hurt and annoyed me is the amount of crap people said about him only after he died.

Lee knocked Micky Salter (God rest him) out outside The Havana. Lee didn't half crack him and I went and picked Micky up, Lee was shouting "Leave him Terry" but I couldn't. I picked Micky up and rested him against a shop window for him to regain his senses. Afterwards Lee said I was too soft hearted and was laughing at me.

Lee also knocked Podgie Foreman out in The Ship Inn. As soon as Lee saw him he said "Ooh look who's here" then hit poor Podgie that hard he came back on himself, going full circle and then hit the deck out cold.

I saw Lee hit some poor fella outside of the Bongo because he was having some trouble with the owners of the club. As soon as the club shut down I went over Petch's yard to get two full drums of red diesel, I also got a load of concrete to cover the doors of the pub and pulled the signs down and I let rocket flairs off because Lee was my pal and I was supporting him, loyalty means everything to me.

Derek Beatty was driving over Ormesby Bank in Middlesbrough that night, about four or five miles away from where I let the rockets off. Derek saw them and said to the passenger in his car "Dicko must be kicking off again over the border" and he was right. I was barred out of the Bongo for 14 years over it!

There's people that might disagree, but Lee's father Lawrie was a hard case you know! I introduced Lee to my old man and told him that he was Lawrie's boy because my old man had been such good friends with Lawrie from their travels around the world.

Lee's death hit me very hard. When he was laid in his coffin at 6, Durham Road in Eston I said to his Mother Brenda, "I'm not being rude or disrespectful, but Lee wouldn't want Davey Allo doing life for this, I hope to God I haven't disrespected you". Brenda told me she was glad I had said that and that how much their Lee loved me, and Lee told her I was the most genuine man he'd ever met. Brenda even told me she was going to write a letter to the judge to say that Lee wouldn't want anyone doing life for his murder. For me to go in someone's house and say what I did to Brenda whose son was in a coffin, that was straight from the heart and she could have maybe taken it very differently, thankfully she didn't but I also told her I loved Lee and he was my good friend.

I've been good friends with Davey Allo also over the years. I caught up with him only a few years ago in The Zetland pub doorway. I said to him "do you know what your problem is Davey? It's that you're too predictable". Davey then said to me "Do you know what your problem is Terry? You're a psychopath"! (laughs) I really like Davey Allo and it's been very unfortunate he's had some awful luck at times himself.

Davey told me he didn't want to kill Lee, he just wanted him to go away, which of course Lee was never going to do unless he was unconscious. There's few that know this, but Davey still lights a candle in church for Lee to this day.

In the last couple of years, I've only found out I'm some kind of relation to Davey and when we see each other we say, "Now then cuz". Davey's a great lad and I know my friend Lee would have forgiven him for what happened, it was just an accident.

It was nothing to do with Davey, he wasn't celebrating by any means, but when news of Lee's death got out around Middlesbrough the town was alive with joy. All the shithouses were having "The Duff is dead" parties. I know of a few people who had done that, and I thought 'you scumbags'. They were all little rats who came out of their little hiding holes now that Lee had gone.

He was my friend and I loved him, I even said to him one day you know to be careful because he was gonna end up dead. Lee just stood up in a big pose like He-Man like he'd just won the Olympic Gold and shouted as loud as he could "I LIVE BY THE SWORD AND I'LL DIE BY THE SWORD" whilst having a right giggle.

I still have arguments today with people because he was my friend. I'm just not going to sit and have people call him because he's not here.

People only know about Lee Duffy what they want to know, they don't know the loyal friendly Lee Duffy. Lee could be soft hearted, he had a really good heart. For years I put flowers on Lee's grave. Buster Atkinson still goes to this day. There's one story I'll tell you about old Buster whilst were on the subject. Well Lee Duffy and Lee Harrison once spiked Buster with acid. Buster's always had a taxi firm but at that time I think he only had around five taxis'. Well the two Lee's got Buster that off his box he was shouting in the pub "COME IN CAR 43". Lee Duffy and Lee Harrison were crying with laughter. Lee Duffy was always spiking people. At John Graham's wedding at The Marton & Country Club he spiked Brian Andrews with a couple of acid. I was there. Lee had a tracksuit on at one of his good mates' weddings. That was Lee.

Lee used to love a dance in The Havana nightclub and to be honest he wasn't the greatest dancer. His best friend Lee Harrison was, god he was smooth and had great rhythm but when I would watch Lee on the dance floor, usually on his own as it would clear sharpish when he got up, he reminded me of a new-born giraffe trying to walk for the first time.

Lee never spoke to me about being bullied as a child. Looking back with hindsight I don't think he could tell me because he had such a macho image, but I could sense there was something in his eyes regarding his past. Saying that Lee was capable of showing his emotions because he came up to me in the Mayfair club in Newcastle in tears one time. The week before this we had been out, and I lost a chain which was of great sentimental value to me, Lee had found it, picked it up and flogged it but at the time he didn't know it was mine. A week later he came up to me totally distraught and crying saying, "please forgive me Terry but I found your chain and I sold it". Lee didn't even have to say anything because I'd never have known that he was the one that found it but he was in bits because of what he'd done. I told him he didn't need to express his emotions to show how genuine he was, and I gave him a cuddle and told him I forgave him. I owed him £250 but he said, "Keep it Terry it will make me feel better".

Lee Duffy was a cunt for winding people up. He pulled my best mate, a fella called Nosha Howard, in the passage way in The Ship Inn over the border and said, "I've heard you've been saying things about me Nosha is that right"? Immediately I've jumped up and shouted "Woah, Woah Lee leave it, don't you fucking dare Lee he's my best mate leave him alone". Lee turned to me and smiled and said "Terry I'd never fall out with you. Anyway, I'm only winding him up". By this time poor Nosha's heart rate had gone sky high and he didn't know if he was coming or going because he thought he was about to be done in by Lee

Duffy. Lee hadn't even any plans on doing any such thing it was just a big joke to him.

Another favourite game Lee used to like playing was smashing half pint glasses over my head when I wasn't looking. One night in The Ship Inn over the border Lee smashed 3 glasses over my head from behind, each time he said "AND AGAIN" whilst laughing his head off like a school kid, my response was "Aah ya big bastard" while rubbing my head and laughing along with him. I know that might sound crazy to some people, but we were just young lads and we used to do crazy things to each other.

One night in the pub after Lee had been shot, he was half asleep with his head resting on a table and I made a big bang by throwing a lighter in the fire and Lee shit himself thinking he was under attack again, it was just after he'd been shot for the second time and he was on his crutches, I couldn't stop laughing and he was calling me all the little bastards under the sun while hobbling around the pub on one foot chasing me.

Funnily enough I was talking to a lady only the other week and she was telling me how she once went on a date with Lee. She said Lee was a charming gentleman and told her to sit down and that nobody would bother her that night. She told me for the full date people in the pub were getting up and shaking Lee's hand it was crazy. She'd never seen anything like it you'd have thought he was royalty.

If you want me to describe Lee Duffy to you, he was just one big tornado in Teesside. He was this big boisterous lad capable of battering people and full of fun with it.

I miss my friend greatly to this day and I pull people up sometimes when I hear them slating him. It was only the other month that I heard some little scrote slagging him and I said, "Hang on a minute son can I just stop you there, did you know Lee Duffy"? To cut a long story short this lad was 3 years old when Lee died, and he was just jumping on the bandwagon like the rest of the fools in Teesside.

In the early 90s when Lee's grave was getting smashed up I saw one of the culprits in the Madison Night Club. The Eston man came up to me saying "Alright Dicko"? I said "Don't you alright Dicko me you cunt! You and your mate smashed my mates grave up". He was giving me a load of excuses as to why he did it, but I told him to fuck off away from me. I'm as upset about that still today as I was about it when it was happening on a regular basis.

Lee did make me laugh when I walked in a pub with him though, he'd stage whisper to me "Ere Terry watch this" and as soon as people saw Lee they'd get up and run to the doors like rats up a drainpipe. In the end it would get to the point where it was just me and him sitting together drinking. I said, "ere Lee where has everyone gone you've emptied the full Empire pub". Lee really used to see the funny side to everyone scattering away from him and it made him laugh. Lee used to do a running commentary like you hear when you're listening to the horse racing "and he's almost there now at the final fence, but here's another coming along at the far end and he's at the finishing line of the front door and he's out of the pub and home to win the cup" etc... He was a funny funny man without him even trying to be funny.

Lee Paul Duffy is fucking irreplaceable and the loyalty I've shown my friend this last 27 years is a testament to the love I had for the lad. They say if you speak about the departed, it keeps their spirit and energy strong. My fucking friend will be here forever, and my friend Lee would be absolutely loving this book, it's a long long time overdue. This book tells the true story of who he really was and what he was about and it's not by the fucking gobshites who'd never met him and only judged him on his reputation.

Friendship and loyalty mean everything to me. Sometimes in life you've got to dig through a mountain full of shit to find good folk. When you find them you stick by them, well Lee was good folk.

Sleep well my beautiful friend. You were the monster of Teesside, but you were our monster.

R.I.P Lee XX

"In South Bank, you learn at a very young age that if you want something you have to fight for it".

Lee's brother in the Sun newspaper 1993

B–Friend and Fellow Prisoner

I'm a 53 year old man from Middlesbrough but I want to remain anonymous so for the purposes of this book I'll go by the initial B.

I first met Lee around a mutual friend's house in the early 80's. We both used to go around to smoke dope and chill out. Lee was there quite often.

The very first time I met Lee he asked me to get him a kilo of dope, which at the time, was something that I could do so I agreed. There was another guy around this house in Middlesbrough so we borrowed his Cortina and we drove over to Darlington. Lee insisted that he would drive and as we were both high as kites and off our heads I didn't think it would matter who drove, but he drove like a man possessed, he was driving through red lights, straight over roundabouts, literally, and laughing his head off all the way. I'm sure my life flashed before my eyes many times on that journey, it was certainly a rollercoaster of a trip.

The return journey was even worse as on the way back Lee knocked a geezer off a motorbike. Lee stopped the car to check if he was ok, he was and we both just looked at each other and pissed ourselves laughing. It was really pissing it down and we couldn't see the roads even if we'd have been straight headed. When we got back Lee passed the keys to the lad whose car it was and never said a word of what had just happened. That was the very first time I met the Duff.

I would meet Lee many times up in Newcastle because we had a lot of mutual friends there. I'd often call around his Mams for him and we would get up to more crazy things.

I wouldn't only be close to Lee on the out as I also ended up in Durham jail with him for many months, although we were on separate charges.

By this time Lee Duffy's name was notorious in the North East of England. We did have some laughs in prison. In them days though it was the mid 80s with slopping out, no association, gym only if you were lucky and television only on a weekend it was pure bang up.

Me and Lee used to smoke with a handful of lads at the time. Our visitors used to come up together. Me and Lee were always overjoyed to see our mates wife because she always brought us a parcel. In them days you were allowed four cans if you were on remand and me and Lee used to neck Carlsberg Special Brew when they shouted us to get back to our cells, by the end of the visit we'd be both fucked trying to walk back to the cell we shared.

Being in jail with people builds bonds and trust and I got to know Lee more when we were inside than I ever did on the out. We were both young and ambitious yet on very different paths. Many times, our court dates were on the same day, it was called "production". Down in the old bridewells at the magistrate's court we'd be wrestling all day. Lee was so hyperactive and would always be flinging me about like a rag doll. I used to say to Lee "you better not punch me"! I'd land punches on Lee if I could and he'd just start laughing. He'd land a few but only touching me but he was more interested in doing wrestling moves on me all day. Big Daddy and Giant Haystacks were popular at the time.

One memory I have, which I'll never forget, was when I was trying to have a piss in Durham Prison toilets. Well Lee came over and started shadow boxing in my face, but he accidently caught me with an uppercut and my teeth clattered. I just turned around and shouted, "WHAT THE FUCK DO YOU THINK YOU'RE DOING YOU BIG PRICK". Now there was a load in the toilets, but it went extremely silent. Everyone was thinking the same thing and that was that they couldn't believe I'd just spoken to the daddy of the prison like that and they were all making for the doors ASAP. Lee just grabbed me in a bear hug and started laughing and banged a spliff in my mouth and cuddled me some more. We walked out cuddling back to the exercise yard. One thing Lee did do was blatantly flaunt joints in the screws faces. That was Lee all over.

I got banged up with this kid one night. He was on production to Teesside to give evidence against Lee, who was only banged up in the 8-man T-piece around the corner. Lee had hit him in the blues and smashed his eye socket with one punch. That was how he received his 4 year sentence in 1988. Martin Clark was the lads name and he got swagged (moved) in the middle of the night once the screws cottoned on to the history between the two.

Every single day in prison I spent with Lee I would see him sparring with his pad mates if I wasn't in with him. Lee always asked me to move to his cell if I wasn't padded up with him already but although I loved him, he did my head in wanting to play fight all the time, besides I used to get enough of him when I was in the bridewells.

Another memory I have when I think of Lee Duffy was when a lad, who didn't realise who Lee was got cheeky with him. Lee really battered him, broke his jaw, knocked his teeth out and afterwards Lee shouted "unlucky mate" then Lee just cracked on walking as if it was nothing.

Lee's fighting prowess was awesome, and he should have been pushed into a legitimate way of letting off steam like boxing. However other people had their needs for Lee Duffy in Middlesbrough and he was used.

I've met some hard men/wannabes throughout the 20 year sentence I've just finished but none have come close to or stood a chance against a 24 year old Lee Duffy. I've seen a hell of a lot of so called hard men breakdown behind the prison gates. Just the thought of prison can break many a man, but Lee revelled behind the door, he just didn't give a fuck about anybody or anything! That was Lee.

There were times when no one even came to see Lee in jail, but the same people that forgot he existed when he was in jail would use him on the out. I would even give him things because he had nothing but also to stop him taking things off other people because at times he had fuck all. I had to talk Lee out of doing a few crazy things over the time that I knew him. Lee would never listen to anybody because he was his own man, but surprisingly he did trust me and took my advice sometimes on not to act out some of the things that he wanted to.

I was in Crete the night Lee died. It was sad because he was alright you know. I had a lot of memories with him and we made some money together and we had some fabulous laughs that will stay with me forever.

I didn't have anything Lee wanted and vice versa but we had a mutual respect and he was never a bully towards me ever. In fact, in the early 80's me, Lee and another lad were all seeing the same lass. The house rule was whoever got to her house first was buzzing and the others waited.

R.I.P Lee we had some great times together.

"If you turn and face the other way when someone is bullied, you might as well be the bully too".

Unknown

Gram Seed – Associate

What can I say about Gram Seed that I haven't already said in my other books?! Gram is the only person I've ever met in life that I've been star struck by. Yes, I was in awe of Frank McAvennie when I was 8 while asking him to sign my autograph book. Yes, I've been star struck meeting Glenn McCrory at amateur boxing shows as I was growing up, but Gram Seed is the biggest star I've ever met, and I'll tell you why.

I've known of the 6ft 5 larger than life man since the late 1980's. I would often see him around town intimidating people, usually for money. I would also see him a few times at the old Ayresome Park were the Boro played their matches. My Uncle, Michael Parsons would take me to a handful of games and in the pubs beforehand.

As a child it was very black and white with me, I would look at someone and think they were either good or bad and, in my mind, Gram came into the bad category as I saw him walking around very menacingly, to me he looked the epitome of what bad people looked like. Whenever I saw Gram he was usually doing something anti-social. So, imagine how petrified I was when one day, at the back end of 1996, I saw Gram laid on his usual bench outside the post office on Grange Road in the heart of Middlesbrough, Gram had a bottle of White Lightening in his hand and he looked my way and shouted, "Ere kid, come here I want ya"! I was only still a school boy and I clearly remember thinking at the time, what the hell does he want with me maybe he's a kidnapper! Needless to say, I never went over to see what Gram wanted but that memory has always stayed in my mind.

Most people in Middlesbrough know the story of Gram falling into a coma and nearly losing his life. The most ironic thing in all of this is that now I'm proud to say Gram Seed is my hero. I've had the pleasure of being in the company of Gram and his lovely wife Natasha several times and Gram now runs a church in Stockton called Sowing Seeds Ministries and spends his time helping those people less fortunate and more in need than himself. Who'd have imagined that that big scary drunken tramp, 20 years later would be someone who I looked up to?! Life's a funny thing isn't it?!

Anyway, I wanted to ask my good friend Gram Seed what his memories were of "The Duffer". I knew Gram would have come across Lee because Gram is very much part of that Middlesbrough era.

Gram said:

I grew up in the Berwick Hills area of Middlesbrough and I'm 53 years of old now. I first started hearing the name Lee Duffy when I started going to the football matches, I will have been about 17 years old.

I was about 19 when I got to know him, every week I used to chat to him in the nightclub called Rumours, its long gone now. Then came the nightclub Blaises and he was forever in there.

When you went in Blaises and Lee Duffy was about you knew he was a real force. Lee always used to stand at the front of the door, like he was a bouncer, even though he wasn't working, he was always a very confident lad, he had a certain swagger about him.

Lee was often in the Fountain pub and the Little Ormesby Institute. One funny story I remember being with Lee was when we went for a game of snooker in the Little Tute. Of course, with places like that and the old social clubs there's committee men and they have rules. Well this day we had gone to play snooker, there was a doorman on who must have been about 5ft 4 and not a day younger than 88 years old. This committee man didn't take any rubbish and he was telling us about his days of fighting for our country. There was around five of us playing snooker that day, but Lee wasn't a member. So, as we came in the committee man put his hands on Lees chest and said, "Where do ya think you're going son? Ya not a member". Everybody turned to look at this old short guy, putting a big 6ft 4 Lee in his place. This old fella wasn't bothered about Lee Duffy or his reputation, he'd been in the war he was telling us. Lee just laughed and did as he was told. We laughed about it for years afterwards. I'll never forget that committee man, all he was interested in was the rules.

Lee wasn't into the football fighting scene at all, but a few times like when there was a big fight outside the Empire pub he was handy to have around. There was a massive brawl with a few Chelsea supporters and he put a few away.

Lee told me more than once that he was picked on as a kid and that he'd now found that he was good at fighting, so he was never going to allow people to do that to him again.

I saw Lee fight five men once at Blaises. Five of them had come to "sort him out" and keep him out of the club. I saw Lee kick one of them at the top of the stairs, then he went down and went through the lot like a hot knife through butter. He absolutely brayed the men, then cockily went into Blaises and waved at the men who didn't want him in there.

I've also seen Lee fighting a well-known face in Middlesbrough called Kev Auer (God rest him). Kev fought Lee and wouldn't give up. Lee knocked Kev Auer down several times, but every time Kev got back up, you have to admire him for that. In the end I think it was Lee who said, "You're obviously a nutter just eff off".

Another time I saw Lee have a fight was in the Speak Easy on Linthorpe Road. Now these lads where from out of town and had actually started on him, Lee didn't want any trouble he was saying to them, then 'BANG BANG BANG' Lee finished it before it even got started, against three lads. One of them tried to glass Lee, but Lee put him on his backside instantly.

One night in early 1988 we were in Rumours, Lee came over and bought me a drink, and the people who I was with were like "wow that's Lee Duffy"! I don't know why but since the day I met him he was always ok with me and I don't understand that because I'm 6ft 5 and everything

Lee Duffy would normally challenge. I spoke with him and he treat me well, I never had any fear in Lee's company and I took him as he was.

One night I gave Lee my tracksuit top because the police were going to arrest him. Lee was about the same look as me then as he had short hair, bald at the sides and we were both big lads, so I gave him my tracksuit top. All my friends were saying I was a nutter because this top was really expensive, it had Olympic rings on the back and it was one of a kind. You couldn't even get that top in England as it was American. I was very passionate about my clothes then. I used to think if the outside looks good, I'll then be good on the inside. All my mates were laughing like a pack of hyenas saying, "You'll never get that back". About five days later I was in the Market Tavern in North Ormesby and Lee Harrison came in and said "Ere, Gram there's ya jacket back from Lee". All my mates were in disbelief. One of my mates said I must have got another one (Gram laughs). I said how can I get another one, it was one of a kind.

You know what! It's a tragic situation because I'm sat here 53 years old and when I first became a Christian I thought I wish I'd have met Lee during my new life. It's been very difficult following Jesus over the last 22 years. I'm now a witness for people to give them hope and the one person who came to my mind when I started on my new journey was Lee Duffy. The bible talks about two of his disciples becoming fishers of men and them being the real testimonies. I mean who better man than Lee Duffy to change his life and speak to the kids who looked up to him. I heard from a genuine honest South Bank lady that Lee was seeing a vicar only three weeks before he died.

In my job I visit a lot of prisons and I meet a lot of people who are really tormented inside. I've seen thousands over the last few years. I've been to Frankland, Whitemoor, Wakefield and Belmarsh, the top category A prisons. The people I meet are so troubled inside, they're almost wanting a way out.

I met a big fella on one of my prison tours. He'd been part of the ICF (West Ham hooligan firm) in Shepton Mallet in 2001. Shepton Mallet is a lifer's jail and this guy was a big massive man who'd been part of the firm. Well when I'd been there for 3 days, he shouted out of his cell window, "Do you know what you are Gram"? well I expected a load of abuse but what he said was, "You're hope on legs"! I've never forgotten it because that's what I've always wanted to be! I just want to help people like Lee Duffy. I believe in the light and the darkness and in the bible it says the darkness can't put the light out. Where the light is there can't be any darkness. I think Lee was thinking about changing his life, he would maybe have had an impact in Teesside and maybe throughout the country if only he'd had enough time to turn that corner.

I spoke with Lee after he was shot in the knee, he was in the pub on crutches. Lee told me that he had to do a back flip over a car, but as he did that he was shot in the knee. Lee told me there was three of them and as he was getting back up, they screeched away in their car as fast as they could.

The stories that went around the town were massive. So many stories of how someone had tried to kill Lee again.

I believe Lee had three attempts that I know of on his life, and if you look at it, it was all in quick succession really! Them stories were so big around Teesside, if the internet and Facebook had been around at the time of Lee's life then he'd have been viral.

The day Lee died I remember it very well. I was on bail from Leeds crown court and I was living in a Bed and Breakfast on Borough Road. I'll never forget going to the local shop on that warm sunny morning in August to get some fags. When I was going back to the B & B a lad walked by who I knew and said, "Have you heard what's happened"? He said "someone was killed last night on Marton Road. I don't know who it is but apparently its someone famous". I remember walking into the B& B really wanting to know who it was. Of course, there was no mobile phones in them days, so I thought the only place you get information is in the pubs. So, I walked into the Laurel pub on Borough Road and the first thing I asked was "does anyone know who got killed last night"? and they said, "yeah Lee Duffy"!!!! Well I was just in disbelief, this guy must have got the wrong end of the stick, surely, he was mistaken. He can't be, was what was going around in my head! Because people had tried to kill Lee before and had failed it wasn't feasible to me that someone could have killed him. I think even Lee thought he was invincible like the Terminator, and I think a lot of people shared the same opinion as he did. Everywhere you went that day, Sunday 25th August 1991, people were talking about it. I had no plans to go anywhere that day, but I just couldn't stay in. No matter where I went in Middlesbrough the subject was Lee Duffy. Of course, in a couple of hours it went around the town who was supposed to have done it. At the time I did feel sad because I knew Lee well. I didn't hang around with him, but I'd always enjoyed his company and never ever felt threatened in his presence. I just felt so sad the full day.

When I was in the pubs that day I was listening to all sorts of rumours of what had supposed to have happened, but such is the way that what people don't know they make up. The Police aren't daft in Middlesbrough, quite often they were in the pubs listening undercover. That day, although I felt so down, I couldn't help listening to people around me and thinking of how much utter rubbish people were talking.

Lee got a name for himself doing what he liked doing. He was fighting constantly, then people were trying to kill him and the whole town of Middlesbrough was bad mouthing him.

I never ever classed Lee as a bully, but because of the things people were doing to him and saying about him, he may have hit people for what appeared to be no reason at times. Lee probably thought he had to keep this awesome reputation that he created as the top lad of Teesside. I've always said when people say "oh he's the hardest in Middlesbrough", or such and such is "the hardest in Manchester" that actually you could look at a quiet family man who is having a meal with his wife and he could be a killer, all it would take was for someone to hurt his daughter or wife then the killer could come out of him and then he becomes the hardest man in the town. I think a lot of it depends on the circumstances someone finds themselves in.

I did thirteen prison sentences myself when I led a very different life to what I do now.

Lee Duffy's name was bigger in jail than it was on the out if you could imagine that. When I used to travel to different jails all around the country Lee's name was brandished around. People used to ask me "Do ya know Lee Duffy"?

My Grandfather always brought me up with the attitude of, that "If you go on someone's reputation then you'll get beat straight away"! I always like to meet the person and judge for myself.

Lee Duffy was a statistic of a society of growing in South Bank. A lot of people put him up on this pedestal. When I think of Lee Duffy now, after 22 years of being a Christian, I think of a troubled young man who lost his life. A Mam lost her son, brothers and sisters lost their brother, young children lost their father. Lee would have been a grandfather now too.

Lee was a good friend to people, people like Lee Harrison and Neil Booth so they lost someone so close. You've got to look at people as individuals, I look beyond peoples troubles now. I meet loads of people these days who are fighters, some of them are my closest friends like Chris Crossan. I also meet people who can't fight their way out of a wet paper bag, but the thing is, you've got to look beyond what you see with your eyes. You must look with your eyes into their heart. Forget their problems or their mess.

My mentor Patrick Hilton said "You've got to look beyond warts and all. There's a person there, who might have been saying "Help me"! Who knows that Lee Duffy didn't go home on a night and think deeply about things, maybe not at the beginning when he was a proud young lad, but who knows whether the reason he started going to see the vicar was because when he went home on a night when he was sober, or when he was holding his little daughter, how do we know he never thought 'can I change'. The difficulty will have been though that when he walked out of his front door, someone of his reputation wasn't allowed to change, people didn't allow it.

Lots of people in Middlesbrough beat Lee Duffy in a fight, but it only came out after he died. Some people in the Boro are full of it.

Another thing I'd like to say is, who really wanted to know Lee Duffy when he was getting bullied for fun? Nobody. Now how many people wanted to know Lee Duffy when he was knocking people out for fun? Everybody! Lee Duffy didn't have many true friends, lots of hangers on but very few real friends. Sadly, lots of people in Middlesbrough were happy that Lee had died.

There's a famous quote I always give to these kids in prison and its worked well, it is, "Go tell people about the gospel, and sometimes use words". I don't tell these kids anything. How can I tell someone who'd eat me alive in a fight to change? I can't! How can I tell a multi-millionaire they have to change? What I have to do is I have to become words to them. With Lee Duffy I wouldn't have said anything to him, I would have showed him acts of kindness. I would show him unconditional love.

There's a famous story about David Wilkinson and Nicky Cruz. Well Nick Cruz was part of a gang called the Mau-Mau in the New York Bronx and he was the warlord. He was the one who picked the weapons for the rumble. Well David Wilkinson was a guy who set up a famous Christian rehabilitation called Teen challenge. Nicky Cruz told David Wilkinson, "If you tell me that Jesus loves me one more time I'm gonna slice you up". David Wilkinson said to him, "If you cut me into a thousand pieces, each piece will continue to tell you that Jesus loves you". What he was saying was that Jesus loves unconditionally, it means whatever you do to me I will still tell you that there's hope. Now that is what I would have done with Lee Duffy if he was still here. I would tell Lee Duffy without words.

There's a friend of mine Chris Crossan and he says, "There's no point being the fastest runner in the world in Holme House prison, or the best fighter in the graveyard". Well Lee Duffy unfortunately is the best fighter in the graveyard.

Would you rather be on the front page of The Gazette or the back page? By far you're better off being on the back page. The sportsmen on the back pages, well people remember them, and they look up to them. Kids who are growing up now don't know of Lee Duffy or who he was. They know who Anthony Joshua is. I say to these young angry kids in prison, "do you want to be remembered as a tough guy for a spell or a gentleman and good role model for a lifetime?! I get these kids thinking you see and eventually it makes sense.

I'd like to tell people that we must remember there's always hope, always hope. If you can look beyond someone's problems then there's hope, and Lee Duffy had problems. I just wish I could have met him when I was in my new life and helped him.

R.I.P Lee

"They said there could never be another Elvis Presley. They'll never be another Lee Duffy, not in our time"

Brenda Duffy 1993

Den Hunt – Friend

Den Hunt is now 52 years old and is from the Whinney Banks estate in Middlesbrough. Den told me he had a love/hate relationship with Lee. He also told me that from the day he met Lee, Lee took a bit of a shine to him saying "I'll even let you keep your jaw" when Den asked for his car back after Lee had borrowed it without asking to go to Redcar races.

Den said:

The first time I would ever hear the name Lee Duffy was in 1983 when I had my radio cassette stolen, it ended with me and my mate Phil Horrigan having to go get it back from the thief's house in North Ormesby who had it. We had planned to kick his front door in, but the lad's Dad had let us in the house and had apologised profusely on his son's behalf for nicking it. The son wasn't as amicable and as we were leaving with my radio cassette player in hand was shouting from his bedroom "I'm going to get Lee Duffy to batter both of you"! At the time Lee was a rising star in the town but I didn't have a clue who he was, that was the first time I ever heard his name that day in '83. Over the years Lee Duffy was a name you just couldn't avoid hearing in Middlesbrough.

It wasn't until he got out of jail in May 1990 that I would meet him properly though. That day I was in Brian Charrington Snr's car sales place on the Longlands. The reason I was in there was that I'd been working at Smilies (garage) but had them over for 24 grand. I used to get instant credit with Smilies and I was selling all the gear to Brain Charrington. Brian turned out to be an international drug dealer and it was in his place that I first met Lee Duffy.

Brian at the time had one of them powerful paint ball guns and Lee got Brian's gun and went outside and started shooting every cunt walking past the Longlands road. Anyway, somebody must have tipped the old bill off and the C.I.D turned up because they were after Lee, Lee had only just got out of the nick as well. The coppers were shouting "Are you gonna come quietly Duffy" and Lee shouted back "Am I fuck" As soon as Lee saw the cops he was off over the allotments towards North Ormesby and he was gone like a fucking whippet. Before Lee ran off we were having a good laugh shooting people.

I was knocking about with Dave Woodier at the time but from that day on I got really friendly with Lee. Many weekends I would go to the Ramsey's blues on Princess Road and Lee would be in every single weekend without fail. For people who don't know what a blues party is it's like one big house party. You'd have to pay a couple of quid to get in and within the price would be a little carton of curry & rice with it. It was very dark in there, I dare say you had to be brave to go in them places or know every cunt in there. These places would open after the nightclubs closed in the town. In the blues there would be rooms full of girls and always plenty of drugs. Reggae music was mainly the music of choice.

A lot of the time the music would be supplied by the Duff's best mate and DJ Lee Harrison. Lee would arrive at most places, a lot of the times, with the Sayers from Newcastle but many times just on his own. Even on his own Lee had a presence like Darth Vader entering his ship. When Lee walked in he'd always say, "Now then now then" and he'd normally be in his purple Fila boots size 10s as if to say I'm here don't worry!

When Lee turned up at the blues parties, half the time it would empty just like when he was in a nightclub. When Lee was at these parties he would make it clear he was the boy in there, I have to say I did see him hit people in there I have to admit that. I saw Lee get one lad up against the wall and because I told Lee the fella was sound, he only gave him a little slap because I could vouch for him, that's how he was. Although it was only a little slap you should have heard the noise it made when he did it and the poor lad left straight after.

Another thing I did see was genuine hard men in the town get on their bikes when Lee would turn up, Lee on the other hand wouldn't run from anyone. Lee's arch enemy in the town was Joe Livo, he always used to talk about wanting to fight with him.

Lee would carry a little Smith & Weston gun in his trousers or shorts like a cowboy. He shot that through ginger Maca's wall in Thornaby. It's well known in Middlesbrough that he fired it through the roof of a taxi and the Brambles Farm pub roof too. I had a replica and you really couldn't tell the difference, it looked that real. Anyway, Lee came around my Mam's one day and just for a laugh I pulled it out and pointed it at Lee and he dived over the privet in sheer panic, looking back I suppose it was all the attempts on his life which made him jumpy like that. I was laughing my head off but Lee got up off the floor shouting "You fucking stupid cunt". In the end I had to lend it to Lee because he hadn't seen the funny side to it. Lee asked where I got it from, I told him I'd paid £50 for it but because it looked that real Lee said he'd give me £200 for it. Anyway, Lee went over Stockton with it and taxed a lad £600 with my replica gun. Lee came back an hour later and give me £200 for the gun which I didn't even think I'd see.

Another night in Ramsey's blues kitchen, Lee got a gun out and shouted, "Ere Den, this isn't a fake" and pointed it at my head, Lee was with a lad from Sunderland who looked a right naughty cunt and Lee asked me and Dave Woodier to drive him back to Sunderland that night. I absolutely shit myself because when he'd pointed it at the bog door it blasted a whole right through the door. Lee didn't even know if anybody was in there and if there had been they would have been fucking dead, he just started laughing his head off. Dave Woodier was there with me and he witnessed that also. Believe it or not Lee had a side to him that was sound as fuck, he was just crazy, and he was well into his guns.

The only thing I could ever bad mouth Lee for was that I had a red XR3i and he took it off me. He did it in a very sneaky way as well although polite I suppose. What happened was a fella called Sean Day was taking his car back towards the old speedway on Stockton Road and

Lee asked me to follow him which I did. So, when I got there, Lee asked me if he could borrow my car for five minutes just to drive past somebody's house to see if they were there. Lee did what he had to do and when he came back, instead of getting out he waved at me and put his foot down. I thought you sneaky bastard! Now I wasn't sure what to do, it was Lee Duffy after all and he'd just nicked my car. I went to a phone box and phoned 999 and told them Lee Duffy had just stolen my car, the police said we'll get someone out to get a statement against him. That's when I said it didn't matter and that I'd get it back myself. You don't make police statements against the Duff! So, what I did was I went in search of Lee in my sister Christine's mini metro and after hours of looking I drove past Lee's Mams on Keir Hardie Crescent in South Bank late that night and I saw my car and I thought "YEESSS". I didn't wanna knock on his door because I didn't know what kind of mood he'd be in. I had the spare key, so I just opened the car and climbed in, but the alarm went off. There was only one fob for the alarm and who the fuck would have thought Lee Duffy would have had the alarm on, it was on Lee Duffy's front! He came bouncing out, all 6ft 4 of him and 17 stone in just a pair of shorts and his jaw was all over the place from the drugs he'd been on, he was well and truly off his boiler. That's when I asked for it back and Lee very generously let me keep my jaw intact. I just said, "listen Lee I need my car back for work in the morning". That car was my pride and joy at the time and I'd had it for five years. He looked at me and said, "Yeah no bother, was gonna bring it back later". I couldn't believe he gave me it back so peacefully I was convinced he was going to break my jaw for even asking for it. Anybody else

I'd ever heard of being in that situation with Lee got laid out, I think he had a little soft spot for me. When I got my car back I found a big hunters knife (which I still own today), a metal bar in the back of it and about 50 E's (Doves) on the floor which I picked up and ate. The only damage that was done to my car was he'd cracked my wing mirror, but I thought 'result' I was expecting it to be in a far worse state.

One of the times I did see Lee shit himself was when I was driving him home from leaving the blues. I was driving whilst off my napper when there was a man on a motor bike all dressed in black hovering around. Anyway, when we were about to drive off the bike pulled up at the side of us, bearing in mind this was about 6am in the morning. The bloke goes to put his hand inside his jacket and pull something out and Lee shouts "FUCKING DRIVE DEN" so I put my foot down and shot off. Lee was shouting "drive to the bobby shop" because that was, without doubt, somebody who was waiting to do him in. In them days I knew all the streets and back alleys of the town and we got away. There was only Lee who could back me up on that story and of course he's not here but that guy on the bike was waiting to do Lee in for sure 100%.

Lee used to love going in The Havana having a dance about. When Lee was in, the people who weren't supposed to be in would leave instantly. Lee would normally be hanging around the DJ box with his best mate Lee Harrison because he was the DJ in there.

The last time I ever saw Lee alive was outside the Afro-Caribbean Centre about a month before he died. He waved me over when I was in my car, but I didn't go see him, I wanted to run him over. At the time I was tripping my tits off, but I was also still pissed off with him for taking my car and with the way he had done it, there was no need for that. He sickened me when he done that to me.

That place the Afro-Caribbean Centre was of course just another blues party. It was a big place with an upstairs and you always paid over the odds for drinks. It was just the same as the Steam Packet when Terry Dicko had it and you had to know everybody, or it would be dangerous if you didn't.

For a lad who was a fitness fanatic, Lee loved his whizz, Es and coke. He loved getting off his face. Sometimes if you were lucky you'd catch Lee loved up on the E's.

One thing Lee used to always say to me is "Den I'm nice to nice people and bad to bad people". If he knew people were drug dealing he demanded what they had and if they didn't like it, they got it. Lee always told the people he took drugs off that if they didn't like it then "go tell the people who you sell them for to come and see me". Lee feared no cunt! I only ever saw Lee use his fists in a fight, just one punch and they were gone. Whatever he hit he broke. Lee actually knocked one of my friends out not long before he died, you know what it was for? It was for helping me look for my car that day when he nicked it. My mate said I wasn't bothered about him hitting me Den, I had £400 in my pocket I didn't want him to find. That was the reason I didn't go over when I saw him outside the Afro-Caribbean Centre because I thought, well if he's knocked my poor mate out, what's he gonna do to me? Lee taxed a few people of a few cars that I know of.

I wasn't there when Lee died but I was there not long after. I was at Gary Ando's in Whinney Banks but it spread like wildfire that Lee had been stabbed, you didn't need a mobile phone in them days.

I drove down about an hour after off my napper and I saw it all cordoned off. Back in them days if your eyes were popping out your head they couldn't do anything about it, there was no drug tests then like there is today so even if the police pulled you there was nothing they could do about it.

I found out about 6am in the morning Lee had died. I was numb with disbelief because it was just a waste of a life. Lee could have put his brawn to good use with a security company for example, he just didn't give a fuck about anything.

In the days of Lee's life, it was called the underworld. What happened in an average day of Lee's, people only read about in books these days. Things that happened in his time will never happen again purely because of today's technology. There's too many cameras in today's society for the things that went on then to still be going on now.

Lee was in my Mams one day and he was that scared of my Mam he didn't want to tell her he didn't like the sandwich she made him. My Mam used to do Pec sandwiches and she made him some, he didn't like it but he didn't want to upset her by telling her. I think he put it in his pocket in the end because he was scared of her.

Lee was good to good people like my Mam for instance. He was forever being the perfect gent with my Mam and having a cup of tea. Lee was a chameleon he could change to suit his surroundings. If he was with an elderly gentleman he would be polite, then again if he was with somebody nasty God help them.

One of the scams me and Lee used to do was go all over with dodgy £10 notes. We'd go all over spending like 20p in a newsagent. Lee used to say we couldn't go in any Asian owned shops because they were shit hot at sussing them. I don't know where Lee used to get them from, but they were fabulous for the time.

I'll never forget I went to call for him one day at the home he had in Eston with his girlfriend. Lee came to the door with just a towel wrapped around him and I looked down and couldn't help but notice his foot. Obviously, this was after he'd been shot. His foot looked like plastic. He had like a splattered foot, it wasn't nice to look at and was full of pink blotches. He'd had plastic surgery on it but it didn't bother him. I don't think Lee Duffy felt pain he was like the fucking Terminator.

When that daft cunt that poured petrol over Lee couldn't light it because he'd got the matches wet well Lee ended up really going to town on him and ended up getting done for assault on the assailant. I was told afterwards that Lee was singing Jim Morrison's Come on Baby Light My Fire.

When Lee died it was an end of an era in Middlesbrough. Love him or hate him he was a fucking legend. Nobody could ever do what he did in his lifetime. He did not give a fuck about anything and he's the closest Middlesbrough will ever have to the Krays but there was only one of him. He didn't need anybody else. He was the real deal and the only thing plastic about him was his foot.

Lee was the most streetwise person you'd ever meet in your life. I think being from arguably the roughest council estate in Middlesbrough made him like that.

Lee Duffy put all the little wannabes in Boro to shame. The people who've slagged him off since his death wouldn't have dreamt of saying it to his face. Lee would have went around any cunts house for a battle and he feared no one.

Lee wouldn't suffer fools gladly, I'd seen him smash pint glasses over people's heads because he didn't like them. He had eyes in the back of his head and he would respect the right people. He just wouldn't tolerate bullshitters.

Lee Duffy was like the sheriff in Middlesbrough and when he walked the streets he kept all the bad guys at bay.

"Hell is empty, and all the devils are here".

William Shakespeare

Barry Faulkner
Club Owner / Employer

Club owner Barry Faulkner's name is a very well known name on Teesside. Barry owns the very popular Empire nightclub in the heart of Middlesbrough which has been home to some of the biggest DJ'S in the world. It's one of them major nightclubs that people from all over Britain come to just for a night out in. Barry has had his fair share of other clubs in Middlesbrough over the years such as Blaises, Faulkner's Bar, Ossie's Bar, Kirklevington Country Club, Charlie Parkers and The Medicine Bar among many others.

As I grew up in Middlesbrough I'd been in a lot of Barry's places, so I knew what he was about. One of the things I wanted to put in this book before I started it was somebody exactly like Barry Faulkner. Barry and maybe the Spensley families have been the main club owners in the town over the last 30 years and right through the Duff's reign. Luckily the likable Brambles Farm man agreed to share his views with me in this book and I sat and listened.

Barry said:

I'm now 70 years of age and I was from the Cargo Fleet area of Middlesbrough. I grew up with nothing and I've lived in Middlesbrough all my life, so I suppose you could say my life's been a true rags to riches story.

Many years ago, before Lee Duffy there was a man around town named Jackie Parsons (the authors relation) and he was a proper hard case. He wasn't a bully like Lee Duffy was, Jackie Parsons was a proper fighting man like they were in those days of the 50s/60s. The difference between Boro legend Jackie Parsons and Lee Duffy was everyone liked Jackie Parsons in the town. Wherever Lee Duffy went he'd just cause mayhem and he was very racist with it was Lee. Lee despised 'Blacks' and 'Paki's' as he would put it. Whenever Lee came in my clubs, everybody in that room was rigid with fear and he'd clear the place just by his presence. Of course, you didn't get Lee Duffy in a public environment without him laying somebody out cold, most of them were sly punches that's how he broke so many people's jaw's. Lee Duffy himself actually really liked me, but to tell you the truth I didn't like him in my places because it was bad for business with people buggering off sharpish, also I always knew what it was leading too.

The first time I ever heard the name Lee Duffy was in about 1984. Lee will have been around 19 years old. Lee had lived in Middlesbrough all his life but as he was put away in prison in November 1983 for Robbery he didn't really visit the clubs until after his release and then Lee arrived in the town of Middlesbrough like a whirlwind from nowhere.

The first thing I heard of him was that he was this lunatic from Eston way and that he was a regular in Bowlers nightclub. I would hear that Lee was this young kid just punching people for fun and he was out almost every night of the week doing it.

Lee was like the pied piper and this little gang used to follow him around. Rumours nightclub used to be big on a Monday and every single week Duffy and his sidekick Ducko would be in there scrapping, they'd fight other people using extreme violence. Duffy and Ducko would never stop at just punching people no, they'd be kicking their heads in for a laugh.

What was big around that time in the Boro was football hooliganism, so Middlesbrough was just oozing with tangible violence in the air 24/7. Lee Duffy gets a lot of bad press for his violence but Ducko was just as bad as him.

Many years ago, I used to have another dangerous lunatic coming into my clubs named Terence Nivens, I used to pay Terence a few quid for looking after me and getting me and the stars a bit of space in my club when they came in. Well, one night Ducko came in the Empire and began causing bother, so Nivens and Ducko got stuck into each other. Ducko was just on his own but was a tornado of bother himself so can you imagine what they got up to when the Duff and Ducko teamed up, crazy times. Violence was just a way of life for Ducko and the Duff and they just bounced off each other.

Another crazy guy in Middlesbrough was Terry Dicko, now I like Terry but he's your worst nightmare when you're trying to run a club and he's on your case. I love Terry, but it only takes a second to upset him as well but he's a good guy although rather dangerous.

I used to get a lot of raw violence in my club Blaises, in fact I had riot cops running in at times it was that bad for fights with bottles flying about all over it was an horrific place at times. Normally when there was hell on in Blaises it seemed to get even worse week after week and that's why I took Lee Duffy on as security for the Blaises door in the first place, I was hoping it would stop some of the trouble, but it turned out to be a big mistake. Lee, don't get me wrong was always very polite to me. Lee worked on my door for a little bit with Dale Henderson-Thyne, but Lee was a twat. I'll tell you for why, Lee would be working and getting paid but at the same time he'd be letting people in the back door and charging them. Then when the customers were in Lee would be taxing them of all their drugs. Lee was just an unsavoury character he really was horrific in the things he was getting up to while working for me and that's why I say it wasn't one of my most clever moves.

When Lee came out of prison in the May of 1990 I think the police wanted him dead. I know that because I knew big Brian Leonard who was on the force and he hated Duffy, along with another few other coppers that I knew just from being in business, because I was always getting watched. After Lee's death a good few of them told me they were so glad Lee Duffy was off the streets and gone. Another top police name was Martin Shallows who I saw Lee threatening in Blaises one night.

The police told me out of all the bad lads in Middlesbrough Lee was the main one. He was the jewel in the crown the coppers wanted more than anyone else. The police said there were others in Middlesbrough who would burgle your house, but Duffy was never into anything like that ever.

Lee's total modus-operandi was extreme violence and plenty of it!

When I used to sit and talk to Lee he surprisingly gave you a decent conversation, it's just you had to be on your guard and careful with what you said to him. I never really felt comfortable stood next to Lee because he was always on his toes. He was extremely boisterous and would jump about. He was really just a bigger version of Terry Dicko if you know what I mean.

I could never have allowed Lee in places like the Empire with the DJ'S I used to have because he would have terrified them. I'm talking about your Pete Tong's, Paul Oakenfold's and Boy George's. I didn't mind Lee in Blaises but not the Empire. I always made sure I had lads on the door like Marty Mandeville with Lee in mind, someone who could have dealt with Duffy mob handed if you like. I know one to one nobody would have beaten the Duff, but I always made sure I had a good six men on in case he came around demanding to be in because he really was a lethal weapon. I had seen him batter lads but a lot of the ones I saw hit were young student kids in Blaises.

On a Thursday night there used to be like goth nights and they were the nights he would just batter people for fun. Even when Lee wasn't on the door he'd turn up and they'd be like two or three bodies laid in the foyer. I lost count of the times I would go up to these kids who were sat there crying holding their nose or mouth bleeding and I'd ask them who's hit you, if Lee Duffy was in the building the answer would be that big bloke over there with the hairstyle. Lee Duffy on the door for me was total carnage on legs.

Lee's Mother on the other hand, Brenda was the opposite, she was one of the loveliest people you could wish to meet, and I got on well with Brenda, I was sad to hear she died of cancer.

I heard about Lee's death literally an hour or so after. It was the early hours of Sunday morning and I was locking the Empire up. Honest to God the news spread like wildfire. When Lee Duffy died in Middlesbrough it was as if God had put a sentence in the sky above the place. The rift between Lee and Allo was always going to result in one or the others death. David Allison was another tough lad who used to fight for fun with the Boro hooligans, so he could really have a fight.

I wish Lee hadn't have died and that he'd had the opportunity to grow to an age when he'd have been a proper man and changed his ways I really do.

I can't describe Lee Duffy any other way to you if I'm being honest other than a picture of evil. He really was next to the devil because everything he did was bad. I hate bullying, but it was more than bullying what he did. Lee wanted to take over the whole town of Middlesbrough and he more or less did. Most clubbers in Teesside were terrified of him and the bodies were all over.

Around the time Lee came out for the last time, Cleveland police, headed by Superintendent Peter Fox, set up pub watch around 1990, really just because of Lee. It has gone to other towns now, but it was never going to work how it should have done when Lee Duffy entered the premises. What I mean is that the police would ring pubs saying for instance is Jimmy so and so in or is Lee Duffy in and when it came to Lee, many of the club staff would lie and say he wasn't in when he was, because they were that scared of him and didn't want him wrecking their pubs if he found out he'd been grassed up.

Lee Duffy was a corrupt human being, but the tragic thing is he hadn't lived a life yet. He was still a baby when he left us that's the tragic but most frightening thing because imagine how he would have ended up. The world was his oyster if he only stopped doing crazy things, he could have done anything.

I wish I could sit here and say more positive things to you for this book, but I'd be lying if I did. The things that stand out for me on Lee Duffy when I think back is the violence.

In the last year of his life he really became a loose cannon. You could never sit him down and say hang on a minute Lee don't you think you're becoming a bit too violent?! I knew Lee and he'd have just turned around and laughed at me. Whenever I said anything sensible to Lee he would go off it and tell me to fuck off. Now I've had big threats on my life over the years from people like Paul Sykes and Charlie Richardson, but I never ever had any threats from Lee Duffy. I never liked to be in Lee's company, but I never wanted to see him die like he did. If I told you anything else in this chapter on Lee Duffy I'd be lying, what I've told you is just the way he was I'm afraid.

"There's so many languages around today and so many people don't understand them, but everybody understands a punch in the mouth".

Dominic Negus

Richie Davison - Associate

Richie Davison is 50 years old and is from Hartlepool. He got to know Lee pretty well over the two years he cooked Lee steaks and Parmos as he worked as a chef in Bibby's which was in Redcar.

Richie said:

The first time I was aware of the Duffer was probably when I heard about him through my football circle of friends from Middlesbrough, that will have been around 1983.

When I used to go follow the Boro, I'd sit in the Holgate end and a lot of the talk was about a young man from Boro and stories were whispered on the terraces about what Lee used to get up to around town, it all sounded like tales of the underworld.

I wasn't what you would call a football hooligan, but if there was anything that went off, I'd usually end up backing my mates up and getting into silly punch ups and needless scuffles.

In the Middlesbrough FC hooligan department, Davey Allo was the top lad followed by Boola, Bambam, Paul Debrick, Clive Ramsey, Gram Seed and Cyril and Eddie Williams. The Boro used to have some really naughty people going to the matches on a Saturday at Ayresome Park. Game as a badger Clive Ramsey was involved in the Barnsley slashings but I never got involved in anything serious like that. Your Allo's were usually at the front line and he'd have a "square go" with the hardest away fans that would come. When it went off Allo was always in the thick of it. I just stayed on the periphery because I used to watch the football, whereas them lads just went for the fighting. I did see Lee very occasionally at Ayresome Park, but I don't think he had any great interest in football. The only games I would see Lee at were against the likes of Millwall, Chelsea and Leeds, these were the big games if you were looking for potential football violence. Middlesbrough had a huge problem with football violence all the way through the 1980s. It was an addiction to them lads I've just mentioned. Of course, their name was the Boro Frontline, but they'd also call themselves the Boro Beerbellys and Joeys. At times Middlesbrough hooligans would travel to places like Sheffield Utd, 300 mob handed and all smartly dressed. They'd also go pinching stuff in clothes shops, all the best designer sportswear like Lacoste, Burberry and Fred Perry gear. Big Gram Seed always had to stand out with the best clothes and more often than not he'd have them ripped off him by the end of the day and he'd have to go rob another lot. Middlesbrough was very limited in what you could get clothes wise so all the Boro boys would have to rob on away days.

I would get to know Lee very well for around two years out of the three that I worked at Bibby's restaurant in Redcar. Lee used to come in and he got on well with the manageress, a lady named Norma. He would always stand speaking to her a good while.

I found Lee Duffy to be a wonderful guy, just a down to earth normal guy who had a great sense of humour and was extremely humble. I would say he definitely had an aura about him.

Lee would usually come in dressed in boxing gear after he'd been to the gym. Although he was extremely friendly, he looked like one of them guys you don't mess with. For me, Lee's eyes gave him away. He had a look in them that was different to anyone's I've ever seen. I have to say even though he did look a bit mad, he was always a gentleman in the restaurant.

Lee had a cockiness in his walk, but he was so funny with it and he loved to have a craic. His hair was always immaculate even though he'd just been training at times and the times when he wasn't in his gym gear he always wore designer makes.

Bibby's was a big thing in the late 80s, particularly with the invention of the Parmo which was only really served in Middlesbrough then. Lee would often order huge steaks, but he also loved his Parmo's when it was a cheat day from his diet he used to say. Lee was a huge eater.

I moved away from Teesside at the back end of 1990 to Great Yarmouth. My old man used to send the gazettes down because I was missing home at first. Quite often the Gazette referred to alleged underworld incidents. Although it never named Lee Duffy outright there were reports in there of a man being shot twice and reports about bouncers getting assaulted left, right and centre, I knew it could only have been the Duff.

I'll never forget getting told by my Mam that the Duff had died. I was shocked like everybody in the world who knew of him, but in a strange sort of way I knew it was going to come and it was inevitable. The way he lived his life it was always only going to be a matter of time before he was taken out.

I only ever found Lee to be a gentleman when I was in his company, but the guy really did have a lust for violence. His lust was so great that really it was his release in life, like his way of relaxing by ironing people out.

Lee died a young lad, he left children and you can only feel sorry for them. They're also the victims who have been left with their lives shattered. He just went down the wrong path and paid the ultimate price in doing so, the price was having his life snuffed out even before he was in his prime.

I found him to be a nice lad I really did. We all were aware that he had a dark side to him but in the two years I cooked for him we never ever had any problems with him. He gave us all mutual respect because we were feeding him I suppose. He'd have a Parmo then come in the back and give us a pat on the back, chasing us around the kitchen sometimes to give us a hug, he was very tactile.

Those who had a bit of bottle normally hung around Lee wanting to be his best mate, although a large amount would just piss off sharpish as soon as they saw his large frame looming.

I must have cooked for Lee nearly a hundred times, but even if you only met the Duffer once you'd never forget that meeting with him.

"Duffy was hated on the streets and other dealers were hoping he would die. It was a race to get him because so many people wanted him. He was just an out and out thug".

*The woman who put the second contract on Lee's life
Maria Nasir*

Dean Lewtes - Fellow Lag

Dean Lewtes is 54 years old and comes from Salford in Manchester. Dean contacted me because he'd spent time with Lee in two prisons in the North West in the 80's.

Dean said:

In my youth I was running around with a little crew in Salford and got myself shot.

To cut a long story short I got nicked for being in possession of a Mach 10 and received 8 years for my troubles.

The first time I came across Lee Duffy was in Strangeways prison on A wing in the mid 80's well before the riots. He was a big strapping lad and forever training in the prison gym. He was a giant of a man with really good boxing skills. A lot of people in Strangeways were extremely frightened of Lee, I got on with him though. He would float about the jail and he was always on his own. The screws were up Lee's arse and even gave him bottles of booze in there.

Not only did I see Lee in Strangeways but when I got to Walton prison in Liverpool he was the gym orderly there. I saw him once pick a lad up, and this kid was a handy lad as well, but Lee picked him up over his head and threw him against the wall. The man's head was the shape of a rugby ball from the few digs Lee had also given him. He was a fucking handful and a complete lunatic. He would train all day every day in prison and in all the time I did with Lee, he was a fanatical trainer. He would get all this diet food from the canteen.

I admit when I first came across Lee I was a bit stand offish but as I got to know him I liked him very much. All the other prisoners were very weary of him and didn't know how to deal with him. He did give a few good hidings out in both prisons we were in together.

Lee knocked a person out in the gym in Walton over a bar for the weights. That was purely down to the fact that the kid had the bar before him and Lee went up to him and said "That's my fucking bar get off it" then let a punch go and the lad was out.

I would say Lee definitely had a screw loose mentally. Lee Duffy had a huge name in the prison like that guy Paul Sykes from Wakefield. Both guys were classed as Gods inside. I'd have put Lee Duffy up against Paul Sykes easily, both men's name stood for violence in a big way.

"He represents the end of an era in Middlesbrough without a doubt. There are people who since his death have tried to emulate Lee but have failed miserably. We've had problems with people coming from Newcastle to Middlesbrough and causing problems, but none of them have ever caused us problems like Lee Duffy did. I don't think they'll ever be a man of that stature and power in the Middlesbrough area again".

Det Sgt Ray Morton, 1993

Anth Walls – The Thankful

Anth Walls is now 38 years old and he grew up in Guisborough which is located just outside of Middlesbrough.

By his own admission Anth was brought up being moved from pillar to post during his childhood and in early adulthood he was getting into some heavy trouble which included getting shot and spending some time in prison.

Anth has now managed to steer himself away from his old life and now runs a successful business in his hometown of Guisborough. For Anth, Lee Duffy is a person who is very close to his heart and even to this day it is emotional for him to speak of Lee.

I met up with the 6ft 2 Anth in my favourite pub in Middlesbrough's town centre Isaac Wilsons, we sat down, and he began to tell me of his experience of Lee Duffy.

Even though Anth's tale is slightly different to most people's in this book because Anth was too young to be around in Lee's heyday, I still think it's pretty relevant and it also shows a side to the Duff that's never been documented before. Also, it explains how spiritually important Lee was to Anth even after his death all these years later. Anth managed to repay Lee for his help when he helped a close family member of Lee's out after Lee had passed.

Anth told me:

When I was growing up I would get into a lot of fights, in truth I think it was always down to me trying to impress my Dad and I know that sounds sad, but it was as if I was trying to get him to notice me.

The only time my old man would ever praise me was when I was knocking people out. I just got myself into fights to make my Dad want me or take an interest in me, which saddens me greatly when I look back now. My old fella walked out on my Mam when I was about three and I think I always had issues over it. My Dad had been to jail and had done a few naughty things in his life, so I was always looking for his approval, if I tried to follow in his footsteps and did what he had got up to then so be it.

Every school I went to I was forever getting into a lot of fights and wanting to be the top dog in the school. When I was at home, all I was seeing was violence and when I occasionally went to my Dad's it was the same there and the same with my older brother too. Things didn't get much better for me when my Mam got with a Scottish bloke called John who was an absolute psychotic nutcase. The kids on our estate called him "Mad McGill" and he was clearly schizophrenic. One time, due to his illness, he convinced himself that my sister was the devils child and he was looking for the 666 marks on her forehead because he was about to stab her. Another time he slit his own wrist and dropped his blood on my five year old sisters head. He was that wicked he killed both his dogs and buried them in the back garden. He was awful to me growing up and I suffered real problems with my nerves because of him. If I wasn't in at a certain time that he said, then he would smash the house up going berserk. He tortured me and my Mam for years and made our lives hell, that was until one day Lee Duffy came and saved us.

What happened was that after many years of my Mam and I taking beatings from him, my Mam finally got the strength to leave him and we moved away. So, one day when John was still trying to harass me and my Mam he must have done something that was quite extreme because a mate of my Mam's Alan said, "enough is enough now, I'm gonna go get him sorted once and for all and get Duffy involved". My Mam hadn't met Lee before but had heard all the stories of him turning cameras off in pubs and battering lads to avoid jail, so she knew what he was about. She was just so glad to be able to speak to somebody who may be able to stop this complete nightmare we were living in. At the time, this John was getting away with really bad things and had even attacked my Mam so brutally that he kicked a baby out of my Mams belly. John himself had been using the Duffy name, without him even knowing the Duff. So, Alan was true to his word and arranged for my Mam to go to the Duffy's family home. Lee sat back and listened and told my Mam he normally didn't get involved with doing something for nothing but at the time my Mam was skint, so Lee said on this occasion he would help because he didn't believe in men hitting women, he agreed to come and deal with John for free.

The Duff came down and knocked on the front door, John saw it was Lee and wouldn't open the front door, not only did he refuse to answer the front door, but he opened the back door, jumped over the fence and was never seen again for 20 years. From that day onwards, we never ever saw John again because of Lee's involvement.

I was must have been around 8 years of age when I first heard the name of Lee Duffy. A lot of my school friends used to talk of sightings of him walking around drinking a bottle of milk in the exact way people spoke of seeing Big Foot. Even being as young as 8, the kids in the playground would talk of this legend who was strutting his stuff with an iron fist. I would hear so many stories of Lee Duffy and when he came over to help me and my Mam he became my hero.

When I saw Lee the couple of times I did I was in awe but of course I was only a little kid, I was only 11 when he died. Even in my adult life I would use Lee as a strength when I was running about doing silly things, I used him as my inspiration because he was a one-man mafia and I wanted to be the next Lee Duffy.

Over the years I've learnt so much about Lee and I've even ended up with some of his stuff. It so happened that Lee's younger Sister was living in Guisborough for a while and she was having a few problems with a few people. Basically, she was being attacked and getting endless amounts of shit and she wanted it stopping so she came to see me and asked me to help her and her children out, I didn't know her but she sought my number out from people who told her I maybe somebody who could stop her problems, so I did, just like Lee helped my family out all them years ago in the early 90's I was only too happy to do this for her. After I made her problems go away she gave me a few of Lee's actual possessions as a thank you for helping her. I told her I didn't do it for any beneficial reasons but she knew Lee was a hero of mine and she gave me a big sheepskin jacket which had blood on it and a bandage with his blood in the pocket, a leather jacket, his mobile phone, his records and one was his favourite song the Whole of the Moon by Little Caesar and I have his little voodoo doll, his electric shaver and a few photos that not many will have seen before.

Lee has a special place in my heart forevermore for what he did for me and my Mam back in the day I was just a kid and I couldn't protect her and my sister.

Lee Duffy is a lesson to us all that we're only human and you can't go around just doing what you want, we're only flesh and blood. I know from the close people I've spoken to that if Lee hadn't had been killed that night in August '91, he wouldn't have lasted another six months because people were getting money together to have him done and of course he'd already been shot twice. Nobody's invincible, not even the Duffer!

In my early 20's it's no secret that I lead a life in my hometown of Guisborough that I'm not particularly proud of, of course nowhere near Lee's level but it ended up with me being shot. Still to this day I have the bullet lodged in my hip. It's a part of my life that belongs in my past, but it was all on the front covers of The Gazette back in 2003. I had been getting up to things maybe I shouldn't have, at the time I was young and daft thinking I was immortal, and I was set upon by maybe six or seven lads with knuckle dusters in the Black Swan in Guisborough. I was covered head to toe in blood and had part of my ear bitten off, but they couldn't put me down, I mean at the time I was around 21 stone, this infuriated them greatly. I even waved to them and said goodnight lads before I left the scene. Anyway, the next day I made a point of still getting myself out and about, so they'd hear all about it and I went in my local gym which was Body Zone in Guisborough. I should have been in hospital really, but I wouldn't stay in, I wanted to carry on as normal. When I was in the gym the next day I saw two of the several attackers from the night before. "Right you and you I want to fight both of you now" I said. Both made it clear they weren't interested and wanted to forget about it all, that was until the two had left the scene then I received a phone call saying that they now wanted to fight me, and I had to get myself up to the rugby club in thirty minutes time. Of course, I was just enraged, and I didn't think it through, I mean why wouldn't they want to fight me in the gym? The reason was that I was being lead into a trap because as soon as I arrived at the rugby club, a few guys in balaclavas ran over to my car, smashed my windows and shot me. Luckily enough I dived back at the last second and what had been aimed for my chest had luckily only hit me in the hip which of course saved my life.

The doctors who saved my life said that where I'd been hit was 1mm from an artery which would have been fatal, and I'd have bled to death in minutes. Surprisingly, being shot doesn't really hurt because of the adrenalin (although I wouldn't recommend it) I managed to drive myself to the hospital. The doctors decided that my gunshot wound was serious enough for me to be kept in a fortnight. I was also kept under armed guard to protect me from the attackers coming in and finishing the job of what really was a botched assassination attempt.

Looking back now as a 38 year old grown up and family man, I can't believe how naïve I was going to meet a couple of guys who wouldn't fight me 30 minutes before hand but now wanted to, especially as it was in a place where there was nobody about. If it happened now I'd laugh, have my tea and forget about it but of course I thought I was a jack the lad and ran about like Lee did thinking I was immortal, at the time my only thoughts were fuck this I want it over with I wanna go kill them, when in reality I'm extremely lucky I'm even sat talking to you about it 15 years on, with the gun they used it should have been game over for me.

As annoyed with myself as I am, even to this day about it, I must put it down to experience. I wouldn't go to meet anybody now and especially in Teesside. I've just been lucky enough to have a second chance in life. Of course, Lee had many attempts on his life and sooner or later your luck is gonna run out and in his case, it just did, being shot once was enough for me.

The people who did it never got done for it, purely because I told the police I didn't know who did, it. I'm not a grass. I'm glad they never went down for it because although this sounds bizarre, I didn't want to be the reason they went down on a ten stretch. If they want to fuck their own lives up that's up to them. Funnily enough I even speak to them these days, because of the way I was living my life back then I forced them into a position, if you corner a rat it's gonna go for your throat isn't it. They were scared, and they threw the dice that day, they came out lucky in the end.

These days I run my own business Paymatetwentyeight.co.uk, so I've well and truly turned my back on my old life.

Going back to my childhood hero though Lee, I think he was a product of the South Bank environment, but he took it way beyond the next level. He was never going to sit on his arse in South Bank taking shit in life like he did in his childhood. Lee was bullied for years at school by lads 10 years older and wasn't prepared to sit back and take it when he left school, so he started doing what he wanted by knocking people out left, right and centre and taking what he wanted. Lee just took it that far that Middlesbrough couldn't cope with him.

Of course, Lee helped me, my Mam and my sister out back in 1991 when our lives were a living hell. He didn't have to do that because he never gained a penny from it, but it shows a side to Lee that not many will know about. If it wasn't for Lee that hell would have continued for many years after that. It was only when my Mam got Lee on board did John fuck off and leave us alone and I'd like people to know this. Thank you Lee I'll always be eternally grateful for your help.

For many years I looked up to Lee's memory too much and wanted to be him, which of course got me into trouble and led to me getting a five year sentence myself. Ironically, I did time with one of the men from Newcastle who shot Lee.

I don't think they'll ever be another Lee Duffy but even if Lee was about now, society has changed so much back from what it was then. These days it's a 5-year sentence for even carrying a gun before a balls been kicked in court. Back in Lee's day Middlesbrough really was the wild wild west. It was cool to fight every day, these days it's not the in thing to do but back then to a young lad from South Bank climbing his way up the ladder it was the only thing that mattered. I'd love to see his life being made into a film one day.

I always swore that I'd kill John when I grew up because of what he did to us as a kid, when in actual fact I saw him only a few years ago on Guisborough High Street. He was no longer the scary sadistic step father he once was, he was now an older frailer guy but in truth I froze. I'm now 18 stone and I know I could have put him away as I promised myself I always would if I ever saw him again, but I never. I never said a word. I regressed back to that 10 year old boy again who used to pick his face until it scabbed because I was that nervous.

It was only Lee Duffy who ended mine and my families living hell with that man.

From me and my family, thank you from the bottom of our hearts. R.I.P Lee.

"He would not have wanted this man to go down. Even though I would like his head on a stick in my garden".

Brenda Duffy on David Allison's NOT GUILTY verdict, February 1993

Peter Wilson – Suffered a Broken Neck at the Hands of Lee

Those who have read the Steve Richards books that touch on the life of Lee Duffy will already be aware of Peter Wilson. Peter was on the receiving end of Lee's sheer brutality one night in March 1991 whilst Peter was working as a doorman.

I'd spoken to Peter and he told me that he'd been mentioned in the previous Lee Duffy books, but the information printed was a very inaccurate account of what happened that night.

I tracked Peter down via social media, he didn't know me from Adam. I messaged him to tell him I'd like to speak with him regarding that fateful night in the Wickers World pub, which is just under Albert Bridge in Middlesbrough, and I half expected him to tell me to fuck off! Thankfully though he sent me a message back saying, "yeah no problem", I have to say it took me by surprise.

Peter told me:

I'm 51 years old now and I'm working as a tree surgeon but for many years I used to work the doors as a bouncer.

I've been asked over the years why Lee Duffy attacked me that night in Wickers World and there was only one reason behind it, he was bully, he did it because he could, no other reason than that, I didn't even know him. He used to intimidate people is all I knew. There were many times when I was on the door at Wickers World that Lee would walk in and the bouncers would literally walk out of the building. They just didn't want to be anywhere near him, that was the usual vibe when Duffy was in the building.

I must admit, if I was downstairs and had seen Duffy come in, I'd probably have walked out as well. He used to put the living fear of shit into people so that if he told them to do something for him they would. He would just walk past someone in the bar and punch them for no reason.

He could walk into any pub in Boro at the time and half of that pub would empty within minutes, he was just a bully, that was his job if you like, that is just what he used to do. Go in, bully people, get everyone frightened of him and that's what he was like.

I was working this night and I remember thinking that it was rowdier than usual. The whole episode with me wasn't started by Lee, I'd had words with a friend of Lee's, a big guy called Joe Livo first. Lee was with Joe, Jamie Broderick and about four others who all looked like fighting men. As things got more heated with Joe, Lee Duffy stepped in and pulled my bow tie off my neck and threw it over the balcony. Then he shouted, "Nobody needs a bouncer when I'm in here". I wasn't the head doorman in Wickers World, Paul Debrick was, so I was unsure what to do in this situation. So, I figured the best thing to do was to seek further backup as it was as clear as a flare rocket being shot into the night sky that Duffy was about to kick off. I turned my back on Lee, like a dickhead, and he smashed me in the back of my neck with a can of Red

Stripe lager. He broke three vertebrae in my neck, totally shattered it. If I'd never have turned my back maybe Lee wouldn't have punched me but that's what happened, he sneak shotted me. I was a keen Kickboxer at the time, so I could look after myself, but I couldn't when I got hit from behind!

I had a full-time job and I was only doing the doors for a bit of extra cash I didn't even need to do it; besides I was very naïve at the time. I never thought about people punching you from behind. Lee did hit me hard, obviously he was a big lad. I don't know what happened after that because I was knocked out.

Apparently, I swallowed my tongue but luckily there was a nurse there and she flicked it back out. Paul Debrick was walking upstairs seconds later and hadn't seen what had went on, he thought I'd just been sparked out by some random, Paul picked me up and put me over his shoulder and carried me downstairs. I was told that when I came around I was walking around in circles not knowing where I was. As soon as Lee Duffy hit me he disappeared as fast as he could I was told later.

That night I'd been paired up to work with a lad called Micky Saddler upstairs in the bar, you always worked in two's normally. The head doorman, Paul Debrick, had grown up with Duffy, and from the impression I always got from talking to Paul they were close friends. Paul took me down the spiral staircase and apparently he sat me next to the front door. I gained consciousness then, I'd describe it like coming out of water, but you can hear things. I remember people were asking me if I was alright repeatedly after it happened, and I just said yes, obviously I wasn't aware of just how heavy the blow had been, I only heard it as I obviously didn't see it coming. My neck and shoulders were hurting a little but nothing to suggest I'd broken my neck.

Last orders had just been called when Lee had hit me, so when I was sat at the front people were leaving. As we'd finished it was my door partner, Micky Saddler, who suggested that he should take me to hospital. I got in Micky's car, he had a little Mini at the time and as soon as I sat in it I just slumped forward onto the dashboard. I also couldn't control my right arm, it was shaking uncontrollably.

As soon as I got to the hospital they put a neck brace on me for precautions just until they X-rayed me. It was very clear from the X-ray that I had broken my neck and the hospital staff had me rushed to Hartlepool hospital for an operation. Overall, I was in the hospital over a month. I had to have bolts screwed into my skull and a bit of bone from my hip grafted to the bones which had been broken in my neck. The surgeons couldn't believe I was still walking about!

I put my strong neck down to my boxing training, I think it helped strengthen it and the Doctors said that by rights I should have been paralysed. I had major surgery on the front of my neck and they put a metal plate in there somewhere. I had to wear a neck harness for months.

The police eventually came to take a statement from me, I told them I was hit in the back of the neck. The police mentioned Duffy and I told them, that as far as I was aware Lee Duffy was the culprit.

*Shortly after that Paul Debrick came to see me and said to me "Lee Duffy's offered you £2,500 to keep ya mouth shut Peter". I was told that the police had enough for it to go to court anyway, even if I hadn't testified. Then I was asked by Lee to stand up in court and say, "Lee Duffy wouldn't have done this to me, we get on". I told Paul Debrick to tell Lee to fuck off. Lee had broken my neck for nothing and at the time I didn't think I was ever going to get better. "Tell him to fuck off, I just want to get better" were my words I think. Paul Debrick just said fair enough and I think he could see he wasn't getting anywhere with me.

The very next day after Paul Debrick had been to see me, god knows how but Middlesbrough C.I.D came up and told me that they were aware that I'd been offered money by Lee Duffy to drop the charges. I never confirmed it or denied it because I didn't want to drop Paul Debrick in it. I asked them what they'd heard. The police told me they knew I'd been approached by someone (they never said Paul) to keep my mouth shut. I just didn't answer.

Lee Duffy, as far I'm aware was charged for what he did to me but died before it came to court. Lee Duffy would have been looking at around six years for what he did to me. Most bizarrely in his defence, Lee said that I had approached him, which I wouldn't have done as if I'd have had a problem with Lee I would have gone to see Paul Debrick and told him that his mate was getting a bit lairy and could he have a word with him and try and control him.

*On speaking with a close friend of Lee's he confirmed it was true that money was offered but Lee wasn't planning on handing any money over to Peter.

There was no way I'd have gone up to Lee Duffy on my own like that. Lee's version of events to the people of Middlesbrough was that I'd approached him being cocky, and it was only then did he punch me in the face.

Can I just say now, to clear it all up, that is a load of utter bullshit! Lee Duffy never ever made any attempt to apologise to me. I hated him for what he did to me without any reason in the world.

Lee was just an incredibly violent man who preyed upon people weaker than him. Of course, with him being 6ft 4 and 17stone in weight everybody was smaller than him, but he lived for belting people or taxing folk of whatever they had, there was just no need for it. He was very well known for just smacking random people for nothing or doing other similar acts of evil.

It was on the Sunday morning of August 25th around 8am that I received a knock on the door. A guy named Brooky knocked on my door and said, "He's dead" I said "Lee Duffy"? and he confirmed it. That moment we both jumped up and down on the front of my house and cuddled with joy. What you must know is Lee Duffy made Brooky's life a living hell also for months. Lee broke into his home, half killed his dog and he had the cheek to come back for money from poor Brooky.

I didn't know Lee Duffy that well but when I did see him around, I'd seen him belting people for no other reason than maybe he didn't like the wallpaper. Lee Duffy was all just about having the biggest and baddest reputation a man could have.

Regarding my injuries, it took a year out of my life to recover from them, I am just about as I was before it happened, but it has taken a lot of hard work and training to regain the strength I had in my neck. I even gained the confidence back to start working the doors again, and as you can imagine that was quite a big deal, it took a lot, but I did it and I started working the doors at Zanzibar in Stockton. I didn't let it put me off working the doors, I only gave that up a few years ago.

Being a bully served Lee's purpose in a way, he had to be that person to do the things he was doing, like taxing people. If he wasn't the way he was those people wouldn't have taken any notice of him, so to be successful at intimidating the people that he'd earn his money from he had to have a reputation.

In my opinion there was no mental illness, I know people that are ill, are on medication and behave bizarrely and irrationally sometimes but Lee didn't have that as an excuse I don't think, that didn't account for the way he was, I think he just chose to be that way as, like I said before, it served his purpose. He needed to be the top kiddie to uphold his reputation and to make sure that no one would be going to the police about him when he went and punched a random person. He was confident that no one would press charges against him because of who he was.

When my neck was broken the hospital gave me three choices. One of them was to put two steel spikes down each side of my neck and they told me that I'd not be able to turn my head properly and that my movement would restricted, the second choice was to leave a halo on for a long while and it would eventually knit together itself, but they couldn't tell me how strong my neck would be and it might have even just taken a little knock or fall and I'd have been back to square one and possibly paralysed with it. So, I went with the third choice which was the operation where they operated at the front of my neck, they moved my oesophagus to one side, which is dangerous on its own as you have two main arteries either side of your neck, then they took a bone out of my hip and fused it on to the two vertebras then put a metal plate in with four screws going into the vertebrae in my neck at the front then put it all back.

They told me that they had the best surgeon to do it, the first surgeon that was going to operate bottled out, he just didn't want the responsibility of doing it as it was so risky. The surgeon that I ended up with said to me that he hadn't lost anyone yet but that it was a really hairy operation to have, luckily everything went well.

These days my neck doesn't really bother me anymore, it did take a lot of physio to get it to anywhere like it had been before the attack, I even started a bit of boxing after it had happened, they recommend that I didn't do it but I needed to get back to where I was, but if I'm honest, I rarely think about it now, I'm living my life, I'm settled with a girlfriend and I don't look back.

Truthfully, I haven't even thought about Lee Duffy for years, its best forgotten, I've still got my life and I'm getting on with it, there's no use in looking back, it was a long time ago.

*Authors note – Earlier that day Lee had been in the Jovial Monk pub before going to Wickers World. Lee had had an altercation with, to quote my source "a no mark" and was rolling about the floor. Lee's friend Joe Livo ended up knocking the man out. I've been told that Lee was rather embarrassed by this and had been looking for an excuse to knock someone out for the rest of the night.

"He was trying to establish himself as the top criminal dealing drugs in Cleveland. He appeared to fear no-one. He was offered police protection after the two shootings, but he refused. He obviously thought he was invincible and could handle the situation himself. He was not well liked on the drugs scene. But he was streetwise and good with his fists. He was muscling in on deals in Middlesbrough and South Bank. He was more effective in Middlesbrough because no-one stood up to him. He built up a fantastic reputation, but it was one he did not deserve".

Detective Chief Inspector Brian Leonard.

Terry Downes – Associate

Terry Downes is from Grangetown, Middlesbrough and is now 48 years of age.

Terry was a former amateur boxer from the age of nine and went on to have thirty six bouts for the Grangetown and North Ormesby boxing clubs.

Terry by his own admission had been a bit of a lad and was very familiar around the Middlesbrough drug scene when Lee Duffy was around. I knew of Terry from around the Middlesbrough amateur boxing scene myself and I met up with him in Isaac Wilson's pub in Middlesbrough to interview him for this book. I went to meet him for a pint and to sign a couple of my other books as he told me he had bought a friend them and asked me if I would sign them. Of course, I thought it may be a good idea to bring the Duff up and have my Dictaphone ready by chance and when I asked if I could interview him he said yes.

As soon as I decided I was going to do 'The Whole of The Moon' book I kind of had Terry in the back of my mind of people that I wanted to speak to on Middlesbrough's most infamous son. Of course, Terry grew up in Grangetown as I've already said. If anyone's not familiar with the Teesside area, then that's the next area to Lee's manor of South Bank and it was equally just as rough.

Terry told me:

The first time that I heard of Lee Duffy was in 1985 when I was around 16 years old, the Duff will have been around 20 years old then.

The things I would hear were just about how much of a bad lad he was. I always found that the lads from the centre of Middlesbrough would always say bad things about him, but the lads who I used to knock about with from Eston/Grangetown/South Bank and who would know Lee personally always said he was an ok fella.

The stories that I heard predominately before I met Lee was just how much of a bully he was, also that Lee used to play a game that involved him and his mates placing bets on whether they would run up and knock out the next person to walk through the door in the pub. I heard from a few people Lee played this quite a bit.

When I was working the doors in Bennett's nightclub Anthony Hoe's crew always used to attack Lee. There was a massive rivalry between Lee and the Hoe family from Eston that would go on for years.

I'll never forget once there was a big riot outside of Bennetts. All Anthony Hoe's crew were there, and the police had been called. Now Lee didn't start this let me just say. The Hoe gang had been running up to Lee at the bar and kicking his crutches away, this was after he'd been shot in the knee. Lee did knock one of the doormen out that night, but he didn't start the riot, and neither was he looking for any trouble, it was the other gang that started on him.

Outside all hell was breaking loose and the coppers just couldn't put a stop to it. That was until Lee walked outside shouting "NOW THEN NOW THEN, OI OI" and stopped the riot in its tracks for the police. That fight only stopped on Lee's command, I was there and I saw it with my own eyes.

All the hard people of that time were definitely wary of Lee when he was about, and he was the No.1. Lee's name was the main name on everybody's lips in South Bank in them days, more so if he was out of prison. Lee was, to be quite honest, the most famous person in Boro at the time even the greengrocers knew the name Lee Duffy.

Lee had some funny ways about him, I'll never forget the day Tony Boyes shouted him over one day when I was in a bar in South Bank. Lee came over, but it was just after he'd been shot by a couple of men in the foot. He was being very polite and friendly towards me because I was a local lad, he wanted to talk about my amateur boxing career, so we chatted about boxing. To sit down and speak to Lee Duffy I found that he was very different to what I'd heard about him, he could talk very nicely to people. Lee was very alert, but I just put that down to him being on the wifter (coke). Lee told me that he wanted to join South Bank ABC, which had just been founded at the South Bank Cons Club. I said I'd speak to the coach of the club and let him know that he wanted to join. Anyway, when I told the coach of South Bank ABC that Lee was going to come around and train he said, "He's fucking not like", I said, "Well do you mind if you tell him that"? (Terry Laughs).

What I found out of this world was, while we were in deep conversation, he got up and started doing that Russian dance where you go down on a knee then back up. I'm watching Lee stood up dancing on a foot he'd just been shot through.

That day when I was chatting to Lee about starting training at the gym, he lifted his top up and showed me his rock solid six pack.

Sometimes I would see Lee in the Turkish baths in Eston and he loved walking around with nothing on showing his physique off. The guy was built like a mountain and he was seriously ripped.

People often thought Lee had a lot of money but that was never the case. I mean Lee could tax some drug dealer of their money and ecstasy tablets and be living it large, but the next day him and Boothy (Neil) would be cashing their giros in, they'd be completely skint.

In all my time of knowing Lee I wouldn't have said he was a bully, certainly not to me, to me he was the perfect friendly gentleman. He may have bullied the bullies I suppose, but not your everyday guy like me or somebody smaller than him, I never saw that side of him.

Lee loved going on little adventures and rides out, I know one day he pulled up in a car and picked up a few friends that I won't name. None of them had a clue what was happening but got in Lee's car and went along with it. Lee was driving but he didn't divulge what he had planned for the evening, but he drove to the roughest pub in Newcastle. As soon as Lee walked in he exploded into violence and battered a load of Geordie lads. Lee more or less kidnapped his mates without telling them that he was taking them to what basically was an orgy of sheer violence!

When Lee was out of prison he was seriously the talk of South Bank/Eston/Teesville/Grangetown all them areas. It was almost like the king was back, it was crazy, and it was a totally different atmosphere. When Lee was at large you could see a change in the other so called hardman around the local areas. There weren't many smack dealers in them areas like there is today, not when Lee Duffy was about.

If people saw him as a bully, then so be it that's their opinion but if you look how much smack was about in his day then again after his death I bet there is a substantial difference. Lee would have got wind of who the smack dealers were and battered them and closed their shop down well and truly! Lee wouldn't tolerate heroin dealers.

When I would see Lee around our areas I only ever saw him, at most wearing a vest and shorts, many times just the shorts! There was no dress code for him, wherever he decided to go. He would even go nightclubbing in the Madison nightclub in Middlesbrough in just his shorts I'm telling you. Never before, or since, have I seen anyone do that.

Lee was forever harassing the door staff on the Madison to the point where they had just had enough of him. So, the Madison started putting a few big men from Leeds on their door as none of the usual staff could deal with him, but nothing came of it.

That morning when Lee died it is a morning that I'll never forget. I woke up on that Sunday morning and as I was coming out of my Mam and Dads house in Grangetown, there was some kids on bikes as young as 9 years old singing "The Duff is dead" like a nursery rhyme, honestly. I didn't think it was true at first, so I ran around my mate's house and on the telly was this massive news of Lee's death. The news of his death was in the national papers it was everywhere and that day I never left my mates house as we were just watching it all for hours sat in disbelief. It wasn't like some guy off the estate had been killed, it was like some superstar had been killed, it was huge.

Everybody has their own take on Lee but that day I was so down and gutted he'd gone. He was just a bairn at 26, all day I was thinking over and over you poor young bastard. I was sat wondering how he became the way he was, there must have been a reason for the way he turned out and I was just really saddened by the whole events of that sunny day.

We've all done daft things in our past and in Lee's case he shouldn't have hit a lot of the people that he did, but he didn't deserve to die. I know a lot of people who Lee did hit personally but I'm not gonna name them and they were fucking bully's themselves.

I know after Lee had died the feeling from most people was one of relief, I personally didn't feel it because I liked Lee, but I know certain people were happy he'd gone.

Lee's funeral was massive it really was. People travelled from all over Britain to go. There's a certain few of Lee's friends who wouldn't go because they thought it was going to be a circus show because of the amount of people that would be there that had never even met him. I didn't go because I wasn't a close friend of Lee's, but I didn't have any bad feelings towards him. I just think funerals are a private thing and it wasn't for me to go like I was his best friend.

His funeral was by far the biggest Middlesbrough's ever seen before or since, you'd have thought it was the prime minister getting buried that day.

If I sum up Lee now at my age of 48, I can't help but think what a waste of a life, he really was just a young kid. Looking back at when he died, I was only 22 myself, I just looked upon him as a legend I must admit. I looked up to him and I honestly believe he just bullied the bullies from what I knew of Lee and he would have never bothered with the likes of me who wasn't in his league.

When I was young I worked the doors and obviously could look after myself through boxing, but that man was in a league of his own. From what I saw of him he feared no-one. The man was a total one-man band.

Over the years, when you've read a lot of the hardman books, you'd find that when it came to violence a lot of them always had back up from other hard bastards, well Lee's mates weren't even lads with reputations for fighting. Lee's friends were more known for organized crime really. Lee didn't need anyone, he knew he was capable of dealing with anything by himself.

You'll never get another Lee Duffy, he was a complete and utter one off.

"He knew he was living on borrowed time. Every minute of every day he knew there was a good chance of being attacked"

Brenda Duffy 1993

Michael - Your Average South Bank Kid

I wanted to gain many different points of view for this book. It's all very well putting in the people who knew Lee, but I was curious to find out just how big of an urban legend had the Duffer become to the next generation of South Bankers.

I met up with a lad called Michael who is 32 years old now and was only 5 when Lee Duffy passed away, just to get a feel for how Lee is seen today by those that have walked the streets that he had.

Michael told me:

I was born only a stone's throw away from Keir Hardie Crescent which is where the Duffy family home was. It is really bang in the heart of the South Bank estate. My primary and secondary school were both in South Bank, so I never had to go far, and I didn't really know anything else. I don't remember leaving the area of South Bank until I was 18 years of age when I went down south to join the Army and discovered there was life away from the place. It's an area which has seen better days, to put it kindly, but I had a marvellous childhood living there and I'm very proud of my roots.

The first time I was to hear the name Lee Duffy was when I was around 8 years of age and 3 years after Lee's death. Even though he'd been dead and buried for several years you just couldn't avoid hearing the Duffs name all over the place. Kids, teenagers and adults spoke of this man Lee

Duffy who I'd never even seen a picture of. I'd often been in my friend's houses playing on the computer when I'd hear my friend's parents talking of South Bank's most infamous son like he was still alive, it was crazy. My school friends even at 8 years of age used to talk of Lee Duffy like he was some sort of legend. Like I said I'd never seen a picture of what he looked like until many years later but as an inquisitive boy, I'd sit there listening in awe and in my tiny undeveloped mind I would picture this man 8 foot tall with super hero powers like no other man who'd ever walked this planet, honest to God that's how people used to describe Lee on our estate.

Even in the playground when we used to have play fights on the grass at school, instead of your Hulk Hogan's, Ultimate Warriors and Undertakers, kids would say "I'm Lee Duffy" I jest you not. They would pick Lee Duffy over their favourite wrestlers or superhero's, even though many were like me and didn't even have an idea of what he looked like! I don't imagine this happened outside of South Bank but that's what I recall when I think about hearing of him as a child.

It never really diminished. As I grew older I was more aware of hearing the stories from the parents who often sat enjoying the light nights, on their house fronts sat drinking in the Summer recounting stories of this Lee Duffy. I would overhear about how good a fighter Lee was, about the violence he could dish out at the drop of a hat. This was from adults and probably from people who should have known better but he was one of their own and of their era, to many of them it was like Lee had never gone away.

When I went down South to join the Army I did meet one bloke just on the off chance and he was one right big unit. The guy quite clearly had a broken nose and when he heard I was from Middlesbrough he told me Lee Duffy was responsible for the rearrangement of his facial features. I've also met people over the years in pubs that have almost bragged that one time they were put on their arses by Lee Duffy as if it's something to be proud of and a badge of honour.

As I said, I imagined Lee to be this huge monster of a man, but it didn't really hit home how big he must have been until I happened to see Lee's younger brother one time, it was in the park around 1996 and he was about the age Lee had been when he died. He had his top off and he was doing dips (psychical exercise) in Harcourt Road park and he looked a bit of a man mountain himself, I was looking at him imaging what his brother Lee was like. He came over and he was talking to us kids being very friendly and having a laugh with us all.

Thinking back, I never heard any bad stuff about Lee, I'm sure he did do bad, but he was a legend in his own right and certainly in South Bank.

There's a lot of people who have nothing in South Bank, but what they do have in abundance is loyalty and when you're from there you have a sense of belonging, Lee will always belong in South Bank.

There's famous people from South Bank like Wilf Mannion and Paul Daniels but the Duff is the most spoken of by far. Nobody comes close to his legend. There was nobody like him to the people of South Bank, the stories of how he used to revel in trouble with the law will keep going in that area for many more years yet and no doubt the next generation of kids will grow up being as curious as I was and want to learn about him. Hopefully the lesson they learn, like I did, was that that way of life doesn't pay off as Lee was still very much a young man when he died.

Over the years I've bumped into people who told me they had met Lee Duffy and how good friends they were with him, then when I've sat and thought about it they were maybe 9 years old at the time of his death so can't have possibly been a friend of his, but people still like to associate themselves with his name.

When you meet the real people of South bank who knew the Duff they've some fantastic and funny stories on him.

Lee's death did affect a lot of people in our area, I mean the real people who knew him. South Bank turned into a worse place after he died because he kept a lot of the "wrong uns" in line.

After Lee's death I've heard it from good authority that the area just went berserk and rife with drugs because they all came out of their hiding places. Lee used to keep a lot of the burglars at bay and when Lee went it all just turned to shit!

Lee was a celebrity in his own right and he kind of policed the area. South Bank used to be a thriving little place with regular markets. When Lee went crime escalated and with the arrival of Asda in the early 90's it killed off a lot of the little business'.

R.I.P the Duff... He will be remembered for many more years I'm sure.

"If you had a row with someone you'd want the likes of me and Lee Duffy there, but on the other hand if you're having a nice party with nice people, then you'd want people like me and the Duff hid under the stairs".

Dominic Negus

Dominic Negus - Ex Boxer/Doorman

I've added Dominic Negus to 'The Whole of The Moon' for two reasons. Although Dom never actually met Lee, it just proves a point and is an acknowledgment just on how well known Lee Duffy's name was, considering Dominic was based in Essex.

What you've got to remember was in the era of 1990/91, not everyone even had a landline so really Lee Duffy's reputation spread down south purely from being heard on the grapevine. Also, please allow me to put my top psychologist's hat on again and say that another point I wanted to put forward is that by Dom's own admission, as a kid he was kicked the shit out of on a daily basis. Dom was the little fat kid in glasses and for many years was badly bullied. Dom's nickname at school was "The Milky Bar Kid" for obvious reasons. Now maybe it's an uncanny coincidence but Dom grew up to become one of the most feared men/debt collectors in London when he hung up his professional boxing gloves which had seen him take on Olympic gold medallist Audley Harrison at Wembley Arena in July 2002. Dom told me after his boxing career was finished he turned to 'the dark side' and wanted respect from the people who'd bullied him for years. Almost the mirror image of how Lee Duffy felt when he had become bigger and stronger than he was in his school days.

Dominic said:

I'm 47 years old now and I was born within the sound of the Bow Bells so I'm as Cockney as they come. I was brought up in Woodford Green in Essex. A lot of people know me as Dom the ex-boxer, from 'Danny Dyer's Deadliest Men' or the 2005 'Britain's Underworld' programme but what a lot of people don't know is that I suffered being bullied as a boy. Most days at school I was kicked the shit out of like Lee Duffy and that stayed with me for a lot of years after. In fact, when I grew up I used to look forward to the school reunions to see all the old faces who used to bully me. I know there's people who were bullied worse than I was, but it still scared me I mean it's not nice having your money taken off you like I did at school.

I was the original tubby kid with glasses and I didn't want to leave the house. My idea of a good time as a kid was staying at home with my Dad watching the telly drinking lemonade hiding away.

As the years went on, I got older and I learnt to fight, and I realised what I was capable of, I then became something I didn't like. I got bullied and I found myself being a bully just like Lee Duffy did.

After I got into my late teens, like Lee I went out to prove a point and I wanted people to know they couldn't bully Dominic Negus the Milky Bar kid anymore. I started taking my boxing seriously because I just loved fighting but there were times I would look in the mirror and I could see how lost I'd become. I was driven by hatred for the people who bullied me, and I was totally separated and really quite lost from my real self and I found myself caught up in a world of violence. When you're in the world I was in or Lee Duffy was in, you couldn't sit there being all happy then put on a mask to get some money off someone, that didn't work you had to have this image like Lee had. These days it's nice when I meet people and they say, "Dom it's nice to see your demeanour has changed". When people tell me that it confirms that I had become somebody I really despised. I had to turn away from that when I realised it was the wrong way to live. How many times do you hear these stories of these paedophiles that were abused themselves, so they carry it on, it's the exact same behaviour pattern.

Somebody asked me a question once and it made me really think, they said "who would you rather be the bully or the bullied?!" It's a horrible circle because I got bullied so I went and bullied somebody else and then he'll go bully somebody else and so on... It's like the little fish get bigger and the circle gets bigger and before you know it the whole worlds fighting with each other. Now I know this probably shaped Lee Duffy's life and I understand more than most, how Lee was dead at 26 but I suppose I was at my worst between the ages of 26 and 32 and I was wreaking havoc everywhere I went, and I didn't give a fuck about what anyone thought of me.

I got a kick up the arse when I was attacked by three geezers with axes, getting nicked as well as my daughter being born which really changed me. I always say three angels came at once in three incidents. I got the angels carrying axes aiming for my head, then my Dad went (passed away) as well as my daughter Annabella being on the way. Amongst all of that I consider myself bloody lucky that I'm not doing 15 years in Pentonville prison, but Annabella was what really changed the way I was living, nothing else.

These days what makes me sick is all these horrific things you see on YouTube where you see maybe five girls kicking the shit out of some poor kid. Now when I watch something like that, if that was my daughter getting a kicking I'd go fucking mad but what would be even worse is if I found out my daughter was the one doing the bullying because I haven't brought her up to be like that because I'm aware of how it made me feel as a young kid.

Going back to when I started doing the door work in Epping Forest clubs in Essex around 1990/91 I was always hearing the name Lee Duffy down in London, he was that famous I can assure you. Viv Grahams name was also spoken of down South but not as much as Lee's, people from up North would come down to London and even use Lee's name in certain circles and they probably never even knew Lee.

Being on the door at the time Lee was about, it was far easier to bend the rules a little bit. What I mean was there was no S.I.A badges for door staff or CCTV about, I mean the only qualification you needed in them days is that you could fight! If you were slightly psychotic, then even better.

Back in the day when Lee was about doormen had to rule with an iron fist and it was like in them fucking Steven Seagal films full of blood and gore.

I know when I look back on my life I'm very lucky not to have suffered the same fate as Lee Duffy because I was out of control just like Lee. I don't want to speak ill of the dead but in all the circles I've spoken to even up North the word was that Lee was a fucking bully, but I can understand him and what he went through more than most, it's all very sad.

One of the things I'm very sorry for myself was how I reacted to a guy who badly bullied me. Now this time I saw him, and I told my mate to pull over, my mate knows what's about to happen and he's shouting "Ah leave it Dom" but I just couldn't, I couldn't leave it. To cut a long story short the geezer who was the bully was begging me saying listen I'm not like that anymore I've got kids now I've grown up, but I give him a clump because he treat me so bad. Now that's one of the major things I regret in life, I shouldn't have done that, but I didn't deal with what he did to me very well as a child.

The one thing I can also really relate to regarding Lee Duffy is being frowned upon by society. I just wanted to be a nice guy and give and receive love but when I was walking in the pubs and clubs in my trainers people were walking out like they did with Lee. Sometimes I would walk into bars and people's reaction to me would be "Aah leave off Dom not tonight" and immediately I'd be thinking "WHO YOU FUCKING TALKING TO" so as I said earlier, everything was a vicious circle.

I'm just glad it wasn't too late for me to change like it was for Lee.

"In 1991 we played at the Town Hall in Middlesbrough. After the gig I had a drink with Lee in our room then he took us to the Havana. Lee kept saying you earn your money one way, I earn my money my way. Lee knew one of the lads on our tour. Lee was on his crutches still recovering from being shot. I only met him the once, but he stayed in my mind. You don't forget a character like Lee Duffy. He was memorable because he was larger than life".

Peter Hooton, The Farm.

Lorna Lancaster – Friend & Protector

I think by now it has become clear in this book that before Lee was the bully, he himself was the bullied. The one person on this planet who knows this more than anyone was a lovely lady who used to live in South Bank called Lorna Lancaster. These days Lorna resides in Sheffield, but Terry Dicko helped me get in touch with Lorna right at the end of my research.

Lorna told me that she first set eyes on a 6 year old Lee when he was doing somersaults off a garage roof! The next time she saw him a group of older boys were attacking him, she broke it up and from that day on Lee looked to Lorna for protection.

Lorna said:

I'm from South Bank and I'm 59 years old now. The very first time I met Lee was when I was 13 and Lee was 6 years old. I was walking past an old garage in South Bank, Lee was on his own and jumping off the garage roof doing somersaults and landing on his feet. I shouted "you need to be careful little boy" but he just smiled at me and continued doing them repeatedly.

The day after that I would see him again but this time he wasn't on his own, there must have been about six older boys and they were all circling him and sticking the boot into him. All these lads were my age or older. I immediately ran over and dragged them all off Lee and told the lot of them that if they went near him again then they'd have me to deal with. At the time I was a Judo champion who fought for Great Britain for four years, and I was well into my boxing, so I could look after myself. From that moment on me and little Lee would become inseparable. There would be times that I would carry him all over South Bank on my back like a little baby monkey clinging to his mother for safety.

Most days I used to knock at the door of his family home at 24 Keir Hardie Crescent and his mother Brenda used to give me money to take him out for the day. Brenda always felt reassured when she knew little Lee was being looked after by me, she knew I would take care of him.

At that point in my life I was getting into a lot of fights myself, so I think I could relate to little Lee and we just had a real bond.

Quite often I would take Lee to Eston baths and he even came to judo with me, the young Lee would just sit and watch me, but he'd be practising himself rolling around on the sidelines while shouting words of encouragement at me.

There were times that I even got into fights over little Lee because he would tell me that when I wasn't there the older boys would be kicking him again. Before I went to sort them out I always said to Lee "are you telling me the truth"? He always was, I found that he never made stuff up. They may have still picked on him when I wasn't there but when they saw us together those bullies would cross over the road. Even when Lee was only six and seven years old he would tell me he wanted to be like me when he was older. He'd say, "I want to be a good fighter like you Lorna", I would just give him a cuddle. That little boy looked up to me so much at that time because I stopped him getting the beatings.

I'd like to make one thing very clear, little Lee's bullying was really bad from the other children in our area. Not only that, but his Dad Lawrie Snr was a serious drinker and it's fair to say he was very moody and extremely aggressive. I know at times Lee would walk around the streets of South Bank at times just to be out of the way of his old man. My dad was the same, so this was something else me and Lee had in common.

If you ask me, I think the bullying from his Dad and these kids jumping on him did scar him for the rest of his life. The stuff he went through as a kid well, as he got older he just wasn't prepared to take any more and that's why he was the way he was later in his life. I myself used to get bullied by my older brothers and it made me hardened and want to learn my craft in a fighting sense, little Lee did the same.

Lee was a target from the day I met him at six years old until he was around ten. I'll never forget one day when I stopped Lee getting one of his usual beatings I asked one of the lads why they were always picking on Lee, his answer was simply "we like kicking him and punching him because he doesn't give in, we can never get him crying". I told the lad it was terrible, and he ought to be ashamed of himself hitting a little boy much younger than him.

I moved away for many years, but as we got older I always stayed in touch with Lee and the Duffy family.

The very last time I ever saw Lee was when I went training with him, John Black and a few of his door staff in the Wellington ABC.

I learnt of Lee's death when I went down to my Sisters in Peterborough and there was a man there and I could hear him saying to my Sister "have you told her yet"? and my Sister said "no". I knew right away that something was up, she pulled me to one side and gave me the awful news that Lee had been killed. I just remember collapsing, then I went to find a church, I was just in a state of shock.

I sat and remembered him telling me as a little boy how he wanted to be a good fighter like me when he got older. I used to say he shouldn't think like that because "when you're known as a good fighter Lee people will come and shoot you or stab you because they can't fight with their fists", I tried to make it sound less appealing to him.

After Lee's death I used to go to see Brenda a lot and stay with her. For years she was terrified about Lee's brother going out in case he suffered the same fate as his older Brother. The night Brenda told me that I went down to the nightclub his brother was in to ask the bouncers to keep a close eye on him. At the time there was a rumour going around that someone was going to come in and try to kill him, so I just drove down to put Brenda's mind at rest. She'd had enough heartbreak.

As an adult I became a Christian and I used to speak with Brenda about Jesus and that Lee will now be in his hands. Many people won't know this but around three weeks before Lee died he went to see a priest to try to change. Brenda showed me the letter Lee was given by the priest that day. It read that Lee had a good heart, but he needed to change his direction in life. Lee really did have a serious conversation with the priest that day and he did want to change his life but of course we all know he was never given the chance.

I don't care who you are, everyone on this planet is from the glory of god and everybody deserves a second chance. That doesn't matter if you're a prostitute, drug addict or Lee Duffy.

If you ask me who Lee Duffy is to me, he'll forever be a little 6 year old boy who I used to carry on my shoulders and who I taught to swim in Eston baths. He was an incredibly strong swimmer and I'm sure he'd have been capable of swimming the channel. He would have made a fantastic lifeguard.

Lee struggled at the beginning of his life because he was a target for people, he became that target again at the end of his life.

He didn't just wake up one morning and decide to be evil like he's been portrayed over the years. He was a victim himself.

I still have Lee's flick knife and I have his passport. His younger sister gave me them both as I hadn't anything of

Lee's. She gave me the knife because she knew it would never be used.

R.I.P little Lee old friend X

The Day The End Came

The final hours of Lee Duffy's life that morning on August 25th 1991 have always been a little bit hazy to many people on Teesside. As with many tales of legendary figures throughout history, Chinese whispers are rife. I have spoken to some very reliable sources who were on the side-lines that fateful morning who agreed to speak with me. It is through their accounts that I have been able to piece together what really happened.

The scene of Lee's final dual with his one time friend, but by then nemesis, was outside the now recently demolished Afro-Caribbean Centre on Marton Road which is one of the longest roads in the town of Middlesbrough. Some people who aren't from the area might not know but there was a first altercation five minutes before the fatal one.

There was an illegal blues party going on in the Afro-Caribbean Centre and there was in the region of around 100 people inside, only one person saw the first fight between Lee Duffy and his former friend David Allison (Allo).

Allo was already in the building with his gang of friends such as Lee King, Richy Neil and Anthony Allan (Ano) among others. Lee had arrived with a couple of his "gangster friends" from Newcastle high on a cocktail of cocaine, ecstasy, cannabis and he'd been drinking black Russians and champagne.

During my research I found out that when the doctors examined Lee's body the high traces of ecstasy alone were at a ridiculously high level and that they were present in a high enough dose to have been fatal.

Mr Hammond who is a Forensic scientist said the tests on Lee's body afterwards showed a very high concentration of metabolised cocaine and traces of alcohol. Mr Hammond said the Ecstasy dose in Duffy's blood was two micrograms per millilitre. He said "This is an extremely high level of the drug. In some cases that concentration could be life threatening. I have personally never seen a concentration higher than this and only the ones I have heard of have been where people have taken overdoses some of whom have died and some survived". Mr Hammond said that high doses of Ecstasy could produce anxiety, paranoia, symptoms of psychosis together with mood swings and violent irritability. He said cocaine could have a similar effect including causing aggressive behaviour. The combination of the two drugs would double the effects.

It is widely known in Middlesbrough that the Duff and Allo had had several confrontations over the years. Only weeks before, Lee and Allo clashed in Blaises nightclub on the stairs which resulted in Allo falling on top of Lee and then it was broken up quite swiftly. The year before Lee and Allo had come to blows again outside the law courts. Lee had arrived in a friend's car and approached Allo saying "I've heard you're looking for me eh?" Lee then told his friend to watch Allo's friends in case they intervened and the outcome, I'm told, from that incident was that Lee got the better of his old rival in a devastating fashion and beat him easily. This altercation was allegedly watched by two police officers.

Rumour has it that the real beef that night in August was due to a drug deal which didn't end as it should have. There was a little matter of Lee being handed a big sum of E's and when it came to handing them back there was a few hundred missing, Lee swore blind that he hadn't had them.

As Lee arrived at the Afro-Caribbean Centre at 2.45am looking wide-eyed and telling everyone to "MOVE" and "GET OUT OF MY WAY". People who were there said the mood in the place changed from jollity to apprehension. He saw one of his closest friends Mark Hartley who he'd not seen for a few months talking to Allo. Lee was annoyed and was overheard saying to Mark "What are you talking to that rat for, he's a grass". Of course, words were exchanged between Allo and Lee, Allo saying to Lee "Do you want it"? and Lee's response was "YES I DO WANT IT" at that point Allo reached into his pocket to put on his knuckle duster that he allegedly always carried, as Lee saw Allo reach into his pocket it is said that Lee said to him "don't be getting the fucking knife out". Both men walked out of the centre and the door was closed behind them so nobody else could come out to intervene. Lee was bare-chested and moving around like a pugilist making boxer noises with his nose like a professional boxer, he was stood up straight and letting the punches go. Allo wasn't really in Lee's league in a stand-up fist fight and it showed in that first fight. From the people I've spoken to who were there that night It was obvious to all that Lee really did a number on David Allison once again.

Don't forget that only a few months before Lee had been shot twice, once in the knee and once in the foot so he had a bit of a limp and wasn't as nimble on his feet as he may have once been. Lee's left foot had a hole in it that big you could have fitted a fist in it. He still had the pellets in his foot (Lee's party piece was to take his shoe off and show off the wound in pubs.) Still Lee did a demolition job on his onetime friend and David Allison must have thought he was surrounded by the way Lee was letting go with some crisp sharp and lightning fast combinations and Allo was knocked to the ground several times.

David Allison is a man who you'd need to nail to the floor to stop him coming back for more. People have said he was the Boro Frontlines No.1 fighter and he wouldn't give up against Lee. He was like Michael Myers in them Halloween movies, even though you may have floored him several times, he would come back for more like a dog who didn't know better.

People inside had got wind of the commotion and had started to come out of the centre by this time and at some point, towards the end of that first fight Lee was stabbed in his back by, it is widely believed, an associate of Allo's called Lee King. The wound wasn't life threatening but it was enough to get Lee off Allo when he had been banging Allo's head off the floor. It is said Mark Hartley broke up the first fight.

Lee had been known a few times, when he had someone on the floor, to pull them towards his head and nut them, only to bang their head back to the floor than back to his head and so on. This was something he was very good at and as violent as it gets. I've seen the police photo of David Allison and his face was badly swollen from his last fight with Lee.

In all my years of walking past the Afro-Caribbean Centre, in my mind I always visualised it happening in the car park to the right as you leave the building, it didn't. The fight was as you walk out of the building to your left near a little alleyway which is still there today.

By now the fellow party goers had all come out to watch just what was really happening between the two heavyweights of Middlesbrough. The scene was barely lit as the only light was the moonlight. Lee by now was sat on a wall (which was also demolished) wiping the sweat down from his body with his T-shirt, shattered from the sheer violence which had just erupted. At that point Lee didn't have any idea he'd been stabbed in the back, and the fight had been over with for about six or seven minutes when, out of nowhere it seemed, Allo came barging through the crowd and with a huge right hand (and the knuckle duster) smashed Lee on the top of his head around the temple. Remember the first fight had finished and was over, this was never brought up in court at the time, but it was all done with is what I'm told by people who were there.

When Lee was in his coffin it was said that you could see the bruising on the exact point where that knuckleduster had hit him. I have no doubt that if that was the case, that blow to the head more than likely fractured his skull because it's said that Lee wasn't the same fighting wise as he had been after he was hit with it. Whereas in the previous fight Lee had bashed David Allison to a pulp, Lee was now struggling, and I'm told from a few people that were there that he was shouting to Mark Hartley to help him while Allison was biting his cheek. Lee shouting for help during a fight was unheard of; this just wasn't Lee Duffy usually. Lee by this point was delirious and his balance was completely gone. Lee picked a bottle up to try to defend himself, he must have thought it was a glass bottle, but it was just a little plastic pop bottle and of no use as a weapon, people could tell he just wasn't right. It was at that point that David Allison lunged forward with the 3 inch lock knife and caught Lee Duffy in his left armpit and severed a main artery. Lee immediately put his left arm across his chest and screamed "FUCKING HELL ALLO YOU'VE KILLED ME, GET ME TO HOSPITAL OR I'M DEAD".

It must have been a truly horrific sight to watch, people that were there that night described the scene and said that the blood was just coming out like someone had put a tap on. They said they'd never seen anything like it and that metallic smell of blood was in the air. By now Lee had struggled to his feet and was desperately attempting to run down Marton Road zigzagging from one side to the other.

Lee Duffy was no longer the powerful awesome runner he once was. I was told Lee used to run to Rumours and back on a night out, he was just a natural when it came to running but his blood loss was so great that he couldn't run away with any great conviction. After a short distance Lee was frantically screaming for help and shouting that he was dying, all the while he was fading fast as the life was pouring out of him and making a smacking sound as it hit the pavement. David Allison began to run at Lee again and the autopsy report said that Lee was stabbed in his hip and his legs also, but of course the damage was already done, it was only a matter of time and as Lee ran past Steel City gym he got to the top of Fife Street still on Marton Road before collapsing in a heap and shouting he was dying. Witnesses told me that Lee's close friend Mark Hartley had run over to help and comfort Lee whilst screaming out to bystanders to get help for his friend, the bystanders stood watching, some of them shamefully with joy but all were completely stunned at what they were viewing. It was a very sobering sight.

Heartbreakingly, other witnesses have told me that Lee's lifelong friend and his only comforter that night Mark Hartley stayed with Lee right up until the end, he was overheard talking to Lee, telling him to stay with him. Not one but two taxis stopped but drove off when they saw who it was (God forgive you if that was you) but after around 20 minutes a taxi did come over and stop and agree to help. A man named "Peo" agreed to finally help Lee's friend lift him in the car. It was known that Peo didn't really like Lee and had even been shoved out of the way by Lee earlier, but he helped him none the less. Lifting Lee's, by now unconscious body, into the car was another thing. Not only because he was around 17 and a half stone by that point in his life, but also because of the amount of blood and sweat that covered Lee's large frame he was difficult to get a grip of.

In the taxi the men did what they could to try and stem the bleeding, but it was to no avail, nothing could have stopped the ferocity of his blood loss. Lee literally had minutes to live.

The taxi sped to the old Middlesbrough General hospital as fast as it was possible only for Lee's last gasp of air to leave his body as he entered the hospital gates. Doctors and nurses desperately battled to save Lee's life with everything that they had at their disposal, but it was all too late, he'd already gone. Lee was pronounced dead at 3:55am after being stabbed at approximately 3:20am. This does tie in with Cleveland police getting a call at 3:22am by someone reporting what they thought was a road injury on Marton Road.

When I've spoken with some of the many people who were there and witnessed Lee's last moments on this planet, my whole body went cold and the hairs on my neck and arms stood up. Of course, with me growing up in Middlesbrough I'd heard the stories before but not in such detail from people that were present in the early hours of that morning. Nobody deserves to die like that, no one. When Lee's body was put into the taxi to take him to hospital I'm told the watching crowd erupted in joy and started dancing, many of them saying that they hoped he was dead.

At the very moment Lee had been fatally stabbed the most shocking thing about it was that Lee knew how serious it was and that he was almost certainly staring death in the face. The only comfort to be brought by his passing like that was that he was not alone, he died in his friend's arms whilst he was speaking to him and they say your hearing is the last thing to leave you before you pass.

I can't imagine how horrific that night must have been for Mark it's devastating to lose a friend in any circumstances but in that way, it just doesn't bare thinking about. Not only did Mark just watch his best friend die in his arms but the police arrested him on a murder charge. Of course, the old bill didn't really think for a moment he had killed Lee, they'd had too much police intelligence on Lee to know who his good friends were, no this was done to keep Mark in custody and they put him in a cell.

Normally what happens is the police take your clothes off you and put you in a white boiler suit, but I was told that Mark was stuck in a cold dark cell on his own, in his own clothes absolutely saturated in his best friend's blood. Possibly that was a plan of theirs to break him, so he revealed all, maybe even as an act of torture. I was told by a close friend of Mark's that allegedly, Mark had been wearing a ring that night and that when he got it back many months later it was still covered in blood as a grim reminder.

Approximately ten hours later after Lee's death, David Allison handed himself in at the old Middlesbrough police station. In an attempt to find out what had really gone on in the early hours of that morning, they placed Allo in the next door cell to Mark I'm told, in hope that they would overhear every detail of Lee's death.

I just can't imagine what he went through early that Sunday morning. I personally think that it was this event that made Mark pull away from that sort of life, and from what I know, he is very much a family man and a successful business man today.

Normally when someone's cut they bleed red, and old blood will look very dark almost black but the next day the blood that Lee had lost in the street was as bright as if it had happened that very moment, I can only put that down to the fact that the blood that surrounds the heart is at its purist as it's then that it has the most oxygen in it. The blow that David Allison struck Lee with hit one of the main arteries to the heart, Lee had no chance of surviving that, not even if he was stabbed on hospital grounds, so the experts have said.

That early morning in the summer of '91, sent shockwaves through Teesside. Never in the history of Teesside has something so big happened, like the event of Lee Duffy's killing.

Myself, as I said earlier, will never forget that bizarre feeling the whole of Middlesbrough had over it for that sunny Sunday. A lot of the people connected to that night have been touched by what I can only call a curse. Lee King was murdered in January 2000 at only 32 years of age, just over 8 years later. He was gunned down by two shots and found in a garden on the Parkend estate clutching a couple of balaclavas and a knife. Nobody was ever convicted of his murder. Richy Neil tragically lost his own life suddenly aged 38 years old and Anthony Allan (Ano) was found dead in the Parkend pub aged only 42 in

2010. David Allison has also not been far from tragedy himself but I'll leave it at that.

If Lee Paul Duffy had ever done any wrong to people in life, then he was paid back a million times over in death.

I can't emphasise enough how much of a sad ending that young man got. I'm sure some people will be reading this saying 'oh well you reap what you sow', and 'you live by the sword you die by the sword', but as a Christian and a human being I think It's a horrific awful shame that that man had to die like that. The suddenness of it, the cowardly crowd smiling and revelling in this, once strong giant's demise. That to me is as bad as it gets. The only comforting thing to Lee's family is that he wasn't alone, and his body would have gone into shock as he slipped into unconsciousness before the very end.

A lot of people in Middlesbrough over the years have had their views. Some saying it was murder not self-defence, some say he got what he deserved, and it was pure social justice. Personally, knowing how much I have changed in the 12 years since I was 26, I think it's a shame that he didn't live long enough to get the opportunity to change paths, maybe he wouldn't have dreamt of having it any other way, but we'll never know.

What I do know is there was a lot of people who refused to make statements about what they really saw, no matter how much Lee's brother and his poor mother Brenda begged them.

David Allison was tried for the manslaughter of Lee in the February of 1993, 18 months after Lee passed, and he received a Not Guilty on the grounds of self-defence and David Allison and his friends celebrated. After the trial David Allison's only comment to the media was "I'm alright, I'm not sad about it anyway".

On another day in another court room it may have all been different. Brenda Duffy said the reason for the jury's decision was because they had brought up too much of Lee's past. For year's her and Lee's girlfriend campaigned for a retrial, but it always fell on deaf ears. Lee's girlfriend even went to the late Redcar MP Mo Mowlam to bring the case up in the Houses of Parliament but because of Lee's lengthy criminal past she refused!

Well Lee was a human being, he must have had the same rights as other people surely?!

The whole of Teesside knows the outcome and the rest is history, who am I to disagree. For me it's just a crying shame a young Son, Brother, Dad and Boyfriend lost his life. One thing's for sure, Lee Duffy and David Allison's names will be forever tied in Teesside. People know him as the man who killed Lee Duffy, but did he do any different to what anyone else would have done if they were fighting for their life? I'll let you decide.

I don't think the town of Middlesbrough will ever see such a titanic criminal trial again.

If Allo had swung a hundred times he couldn't have hit the same spot again. Lee knew as soon as he was stabbed his life was about to end. His luck had run out once and for all. The most feared thug on Teesside had danced with the devil in the pale of the moonlight once too often.

For all that's been said over the last quarter of a century in Teesside I believe David Allison has been affected by the events of that morning. As I've said, Lee was just a young lad well so was David Allison, in fact he was a year younger than Lee. Yes, he'd been a bit of a fighter at the football matches, but I don't believe in David Allison's wildest dreams did he ever think that that day out drinking on that gloriously sunny day would end in the death of his former friend.

As I've said at the start of the book, the word empathy is such a vital word when looking at the full picture. On that fateful night outside the West Afro & Caribbean centre Lee's family were not the only ones to experience tragedy as it has touched many of those that were involved.

Can I just say that may God forgive anyone who celebrated Lee's passing, I wonder how many people realised they were celebrating just a young kid dying and not the forces of supreme evil as he was portrayed. Many of those people that celebrated have had the chance to age and realise their mistakes, sadly Lee never had the opportunity.

It's because of stories just like these that I am not fazed by getting older and I am grateful for every day.

Do not regret growing older. It is a privilege denied to many.

Authors note: I have spoken to many people that were close quarter witnesses of that night. It wouldn't have been right had I not asked Mark Hartley if he wanted to put his side of that night's events across. Understandably though Mark declined to be interviewed for this book, but he did nominate the charity that will benefit from the paperback sales of this book.

The Last Months of Lee's Life

December 27th, 1990 – shot in the left kneecap outside a blues party on Princess Road, Middlesbrough. Lee did a back flip over a car or he would have been injured much worse than what he was. Lee was taken to hospital but refused police protection. Lee signed himself out of hospital after 4 days.

January 31st, 1991 - Shot in the left foot inside a blues party on Harrington Road which left a gory mess. The gun was aimed at Lee's torso, but he wrestled the gun down to his foot. This was by far the worst out of both shootings. Lee had over 70 pellets removed from his foot and skin was taken from his hip for a skin graft.

March 26th, 1991 – Lee attacks bouncer Peter Wilson in Wickers World which leaves Wilson with a broken neck and a month long stay in hospital.

April 1991 – Lee was remanded in Durham prison for GBH on Wickers World bouncer Peter Wilson. It was alleged Lee had offered Wilson £2,500 through a 3rd party to drop the charges. Because of these allegations Lee was charged with perverting the course of justice. A further charge was also added for an attack on Islam Gull who he also threatened to kill. Lee was put into solitary confinement for his own safety due to 18 men wanting to kill him. It's was also the same prison that his attackers from his 2nd shooting were being held on remand.

April 28th, 1991 – Lee had petrol poured over him, but the perpetrator got the matches wet this was in The Commercial pub in South Bank. Lee went on to punch his attacker senseless and break his jaw. Rather astonishingly Lee was charged with GBH for the attack on David Tapping. Lee never stood in the dock, he died before it came to trial.

August 11th, 1991 – Duffy was attacked by a group of men that were armed with baseball bats. As gruesome as it sounds, Lee managed to escape rather unharmed.

August 25th, 1991 – Lee's luck finally ran out and he was stabbed to death outside the West Afro Caribbean Centre by his former friend David Allison on Marton Road. Lee died in Mark Hartley's arms in the back of a taxi as he entered Middlesbrough General Hospital's grounds.

September 9th, 1991 – Lee's funeral service was held in St Peter's church in South Bank, the same church that he had been christened in. At his funeral they played his favourite song 'The Whole of The Moon' by Little Caesar one last time. Lee was laid to rest in Eston cemetery just up the road from his childhood home.

The Full Moon – A Summing Up

So, you've read the many different views from the good people of Teesside on their most notorious son! Newcastle had Viv Graham, Wakefield had Paul Sykes, Glasgow had Arthur Thompson, London had Ronnie & Reggie Kray and Middlesbrough had Lee Duffy. Boro will never have such an infamous lawbreaker ever again.

Has your opinion changed about him from what it was before you read 'The Whole of The Moon', and if so is it for better or worse?

In my humble opinion I think the upbringing Lee had and the mental scars he carried around with him were like a ball and chain throughout his adult life. Is it surprising Lee turned out how he did when you think of the way Lawrie Snr brought a young Lee and his siblings up? Lawrie Snr was known for having a sadistic streak in general, and he had some very strict ways about him I've been told.

I did this book to dig deep into the life of Lee Duffy and go beneath what people expected to hear about him to really find out what made him the way he was. I wanted to get across the point that he was just such a young man when he lost his life, a vital statistic that many people forget when they comment and judge Lee's life. I've wanted to put across a fair assessment that is from the heart and totally non-bias, but I couldn't escape the fact that Lee, however young and immature he was, was at times a ridiculously wicked and overly violent man.

Although not the trained boxer the media have portrayed him to be over the last 27 years, there's no doubt he was blessed with the power of the punch, in both hands!

One of the things I find rather astonishing when it comes to Lee Duffy is there's just nothing out there that was solely about him. We've all seen the video clips of Viv Graham or the captured CCTV of him attacking people in nightclubs but there's nothing whatsoever on the Duffer, unless you count the YouTube video of the old Havana tapes where Lee's DJ friend Lee Harrison is playing and after 11 seconds you can hear Lee's immortal catchphrase of "NOW THEN NOW THEN". This must be very sad for Lee's children who really weren't old enough to remember much about their Father.

Whilst touching on Lee's children briefly I had the pleasure of meeting Lee's only biological son during the research for this book. This South Bank born lad didn't learn that Lee was his real Dad until he was 12 years of age. Lee was never ever aware he even had a Son as the boy's Mother had kept it from him, she had her reasons and obviously thought it was for the best with the way Lee was living his life, although Lee's mother Brenda saw the young lad one day when he was around 3 years of age and said to his Mother, "That's our Lee's Son that, he's the spitting image of him". Having seen the baby photos and having met the lad I have to 100% agree with Brenda Duffy.

My own experience with Lee's lad was quite surreal. I'd arranged to meet him for a chat regarding this book as a possible chapter in Hogan's pub next door to Darlington train station. Whilst I was waiting I'd text him to tell him I'd get the drinks in and I sat messing around on my phone. Anyway, before I knew it I had this huge solid 6ft plus frame of muscle stood over me asking "Are you Jamie"? He completely blocked the whole sunlight out and my first thoughts on him was, god he is a big lad, he even had his hair combed back like his Father used to wear his. In fact, for about the first 30 seconds of speaking with him I was overawed with just how much he looked like his Father. I told him this and he just laughed and said he was used to it. He told me that when he first saw Lee's friend the DJ Lee Harrison that Lee started crying, also Neil Booth walked off shaking his head and couldn't talk with him and when I showed Lee's Uncle Rod a photo of him he said he had heard all the bullshit before but on looking at him said "I don't need a DNA test to tell me that that is our Lee's Son". Apparently, even Lee's girlfriend found it difficult to speak with him because he looked so much like his old man. As I've said I was possibly going to include him in this book, but he said he wasn't ready yet and I've fully respected his decision. It can't be easy when everybody glances at you like they've seen a ghost or even for that matter growing up knowing you'll never meet the Dad you look so much like.

As I've already said in the introduction there was a lot of names I'd have liked to have added to this book but for one reason or another I couldn't, but it wasn't for the want of trying. Many times, I had some fabulous interviews lined up only for them to be sabotaged by people saying, "Oh don't talk to him" and I've had to dust myself off and move on to other folks.

I'd like to think that when people read this book they'll realise I never ever had any sneaky manipulative motives. I haven't ripped Lee to bits or pulled people down as maybe the other books have when they've featured the Duffer. I wrote this as a bit of a straightener if you like, I was tired of reading the same one-dimensional accounts of his life. As I've seen on the Lee Duffy – The Whole of The Moon social media page several times, regardless of whether you loved Lee or despised Lee, he's a big part of Middlesbrough's history and the fact is that he happened.

While some of the stories you've read in this book are heart-warming and some very comical, I imagine that others have left you thinking that he was wicked and evil. This book, I hope has given you an insight into a three-dimensional version of Lee's life.

The one thing that stood out for me, and I said this to Lee's Uncle Rod, who completely agreed with me, was that Lee was just so selfish. What I mean was when he was running about taxing these drug dealers, beating people up or getting shot, he really should have been thinking of the people that loved him, his Mother, Siblings, Girlfriend, friends and most of all his children. He allegedly said that he knew he was going to die young, so why didn't he make a change to stop behaving like he was before he ended up dead, which was obviously the eventual outcome. He may have gained huge notoriety but to be dead before he even reached the prime of his life is no pay off. To never see his children grow up, he never got the chance to get married or see the grandchildren he has now. It saddens me that he never really reached maturity.

There's plenty of us that have done stupid things in our lives and I have to say, that when I was 26 I was still a little selfish but by gods good grace I've been around long enough now to grow up properly, marry and have children. Like I said before, Lee himself knew it was going to come and he had enough warnings to wake up and smell the coffee, but of course he was too cool and in his own words "I don't give a fuck" to even give it a second thought.

One of Lee's close friends told me that Lee lived in a world of power, sex, drugs and music. Even the money didn't really mean that much to him because he lived for the day. I think that really sums Lee Duffy up to a tee, from 1985 to 1991 in Middlesbrough everyone in his world was going to answer to him.

Lee's life was lived at one hundred miles per hour every single day he was on this planet. He burnt the candle at both ends and looking back with hindsight, even if he'd never died that awful morning in August 1991 he would have done well to see his 30th birthday. Lee quite often used to tell his friend Brian Cockerill that he (Brian) had too much bottle and he was never going to see 30, sadly it was a case of pot kettle black.

The one thing that really fascinated me whilst doing this book was reading several letters that Lee had sent from Prison. That was the first time I got a real insight into his mind and it gave him a voice for the first time. I couldn't help noticing how fantastically beautiful his handwriting was and how he covered every inch of the prison paper. I've seen authors and journalists with handwriting nowhere near the standard Lee had. Yes, I'd seen in the Stephen Richards books, copies of his prison letters, but to see his letters first hand blew me away at how neat and perfect his handwriting was. That's really something else considering he hardly ever went to school and left with only one GCSE in woodwork.

If you type in the Google search engine, there's very few things that really come up about Lee. I'd like to think that this has put across a balanced view of how he was thought of by people that were close to him, not just hearsay and rumour but from their mouths. He really was like no other human being I've ever researched, for reasons which I'm sure by now you'll have decided.

For many people in this life we can go through existing. Some of us will live to the ripe old age of 93 and never put a mark on this life. For good or bad, Lee Paul Duffy certainly put his mark on the town of Middlesbrough alright.

It's safe to say that from 1965 to 1991 Lee didn't give a shit about anything, he was fearless and ultimately that was his downfall.

Maybe rather selfishly he knew he wasn't going to be here for long, so he lived life at full pelt whilst on this planet and had a ball while he could.

I don't think they'll ever be anyone quite like Lee Duffy ever again. Not in today's society and certainly not in our lifetime.

Middlesbrough was Lee Duffy's stage and the play was badly cast.

R.I.P Lee Paul Duffy... I saw the crescent, you saw the whole of the moon.

"I'll be back."

Lee Duffy

'The Whole of the Moon' by The Waterboys

I pictured a rainbow
You held it in your hands
I had flashes
But you saw the plan
I wandered out in the world for years
While you just stayed in your room
I saw the crescent
You saw the whole of the moon
The whole of the moon

Hmm, you were there in the turnstiles, with the wind at your heels
You stretched for the stars and you know how it feels to reach too high
Too far
Too soon
You saw the whole of the moon
I was grounded
While you filled the skies
I was dumbfounded by truth
You cut through lies
I saw the rain dirty valley
You saw Brigadoon
I saw the crescent
You saw the whole of the moon

I spoke about wings
You just flew
I wondered, I guessed and I tried
You just knew
I sighed
But you swooned, I saw the crescent
You saw the whole of the moon

The whole of the moon

With a torch in your pocket and the wind at your heels
You climbed on the ladder and you know how it feels to get too high
Too far
Too soon
You saw the whole of the moon
The whole of the moon, hey yeah!

Unicorns and cannonballs, palaces and piers
Trumpets, towers and tenements
Wide oceans full of tears
Flags, rags ferryboats
Scimitars and scarves
Every precious dream and vision
Underneath the stars, yes, you climbed on the ladder
With the wind in your sails
You came like a comet
Blazing your trail too high
Too far
Too soon
You saw the whole of the moon

Songwriters: Michael Scott. The Whole of the Moon lyrics ©
Warner/Chappell Music, Inc

Coming soon from Warcry Press

Terry Dicko
'Laughter, Madness And Mayhem'
by Jamie Boyle

Terry Dicko has been the crazy man of Teesside, known as the "Mad Axeman" for years, there's a side to Terry that not many people will know of until now.

Terry for the first time will be going into detail about his crazy life in 'Laughter Madness And Mayhem'.

They'll be lots of fun and laughter along the way.

Also written by Jamie Boyle

Sykes:
Unfinished Agony
ISBN: 978-0-9955312-4-6

This book is my journey to find out what happened to Paul Sykes between the years after his 1990 cult classic documentary Paul Sykes at Large aired on the First Tuesday programme and his eventual tragic demise in 2007.

Further Agony
'One More Round with Sykes'
by Jamie Boyle
ISBN: 978-0-9955312-6-0

The sequel to the Amazon best seller 'Unfinished Agony' The 3rd and final book on the wild man of Wakefield.

Tales of Pugilism
by Jamie Boyle
ISBN: 978-1-912543-03-8

A unique look into the lives of some of the key players in and around the boxing world. Including: John Pearce, Kevin Mitchell, Peter Richardson, Davey Robinson (Repton ABC), Matthew Burke, Andrew Buchanan, Richie Horsley, Alex Morrison, Colin Hart, Joe Maphosa, John Spensley etc.